# You Don't Always Need a Lawyer

# You Don't Always Need a Lawyer

## How to Resolve Your Legal Disputes Without Costly Litigation

Craig Kubey
and the Editors of Consumer Reports Books

Consumer Reports Books
A Division of Consumers Union • Yonkers, New York

For Alan Kubey

Copyright © 1991 by Craig Kubey
Published by Consumers Union of United States, Inc., Yonkers, New York 10703.

Library of Congress Cataloging-in-Publication Data
Kubey, Craig.
    You don't always need a lawyer: how to resolve your legal disputes
without costly litigation / Craig Kubey and the editors of Consumer
Reports Books.
        p.   cm.
    Includes bibliographical references and index.
    ISBN 0-89043-437-9. — ISBN 0-89043-288-0 (pbk.)
    1. Dispute resolution (Law)— United States—Popular works.
I. Consumer Reports Books.   II. Title.
KF9084.K83   1991
347.73'9—dc20
[347.3079]                                                    90-20713
                                                             CIP
                                                             Rev.

Designed by Karin Batten
First printing, April 1991
Manufactured in the United States of America

Permissions appear on page x.

*You Don't Always Need a Lawyer* is a Consumer Reports Book published by Consumers
Union, the nonprofit organization that publishes *Consumer Reports*, the monthly
magazine of test reports, product Ratings, and buying guidance. Established in 1936,
Consumers Union is chartered under the Not-for-Profit Corporation Law of the State of
New York.

The purposes of Consumers Union, as stated in its charter, are to provide consumers
with information on all matters relating to the expenditure of the family income, and to
initiate and to cooperate with individual and group efforts seeking to create and maintain
decent living standards.

Consumers Union derives its income solely from the sale of *Consumer Reports* and
other publications. In addition, expenses of occasional public service efforts may be met,
in part, by nonrestrictive, noncommercial contributions, grants, and fees. Consumers
Union accepts no advertising or product samples and is not beholden in any way to any
commercial interest. Its Ratings and reports are solely for the use of the readers of its
publications. Neither the Ratings, nor the reports, nor any Consumers Union publications, including this book, may be used in advertising or for any commercial purpose.
Consumers Union will take all steps open to it to prevent such use of its materials, its
name, or the name of *Consumer Reports*.

# Contents

# Acknowledgments

This book could not have been written without the help of nine people and institutions, listed alphabetically:

The American Bar Association Standing Committee on Dispute Resolution, in Washington, D.C., including its director, Larry Ray; its chairman, Frank Sander; and its staff, including Ray Graveley and Margaret Walsh.

Robert Barrett of the William and Flora Hewlett Foundation (as well as his always helpful assistant, Dorothy Heisterberg) in Menlo Park, California. If I weren't going alphabetically, Bob would have to come first. Bob gave me more help than any other person. He referred me to many of the leaders in the dispute resolution field. He also diligently reviewed both the proposal that preceded this book and the manuscript itself.

The Center for Auto Safety in Washington, D.C., including its executive director Clarence Ditlow, Evan Johnson (now with the Montgomery County, Maryland, Office of Consumer Affairs), and Laura Polacheck. Clarence reviewed part of the proposal; Evan and Laura collected and sent the most authoritative materials available on "lemon laws" and the arbitration of disputes between consumers and car manufacturers. Evan reviewed the chapter on arbitration.

Thomas Christian, director of the Community Dispute Resolution Centers Program of the State of New York in Albany. Tom referred me to many others, sent useful materials, and reviewed both the proposal and the manuscript.

Consumer Reports Books, which not only agreed to serve the public interest by publishing the first comprehensive dispute resolution book for the layperson, but also displayed unusual enthusiasm and patience as the project went through the typical ups and downs of research and writing. I want to thank Chris Kuppig, executive editor Sarah Uman, her assistant Neil Wells, and my editors, Steve Ross and Peter Bejger, as well as the CRB staff in general and Consumers Union executive director Rhoda Karpatkin.

Author Dan Gutman suggested I call Consumer Reports Books about the possibility of doing a book with them. Without Dan's suggestion, chances are this book would not exist in any form.

The National Center for State Courts in Williamsburg, Virginia. Susan Keilitz revised and rushed me the extensive list of ADR centers (developed under a grant from the State Justice Institute) that appears in this book. Kenneth Pankey, Jr., Teresa Risi, and Todd Stickle sent important information.

The National Institute for Dispute Resolution in Washington, D.C. NIDR president Madeleine Crohn carefully reviewed the proposal for the publisher, and her comments helped direct this project. She also discussed the book with me and sent me valuable material. Later, she reviewed the manuscript. Michael Lewis and Patrick Fn'Piere at NIDR were also very helpful.

Entertainment litigator Robert Thau of the Beverly Hills law firm of Rosenfeld, Meyer & Susman. Although I am an attorney and have represented myself in most of my disputes, Bob has been my principal lawyer, representing me in one lawsuit and advising me in several other important matters. In his incisive advice and skilled representation, Bob has taught me what almost no lawyer learns in law school: the realities of adversarial law practice in the United States. He, too, reviewed the manuscript. I also want to thank Bob's secretary, Katherine Lane, for her help and her sense of humor.

I must also express my gratitude to the Advocacy Institute of Washington, D.C. (especially Helen Lichtenstein and Mike Pertschuk); the American Arbitration Association (especially Michael Hoellering, Richard Lerner, and Frank Zotto); the American Bar Association in Chicago (especially Barbara May, Alec Schwartz, and Lynn Sterman); Dean Florian Bartosic of the School of Law of the University of California, Davis; Gail Bingham of the Conservation Foundation; San Francisco arbitrator Norman Brand (who reviewed the arbitration chapter); the California Department of Consumer Affairs statewide mediation program (especially Alberto Balingit and Mary-Alice Coleman); Joe Carlson; San Francisco litigator Christopher Cobey (who provided advice on a wide variety of subjects); Steven Cole of the national office of the Better Business Bureaus; the Community Board Program (especially Rita Adrian, James Halligan, and Gail Kaplan); LeRoy Cordova of the State Bar of California; Bob Dalton; John Day, manager of Consumer Relations at General Motors; Sacramento, California, automobile warranty litigator Roger Dickinson; the dispute resolution firm Endispute (especially Pat Dyer and William Hartgering); Richard Falk; the Federal Trade Commission's Division of Marketing Practices (especially Gary Laden, Sarah Reznek, and Nancy Sachs); Professor Floyd Feeney of the School of Law of the University of California, Davis; Michael Gillie of United States Arbitration Services; Mark Green; the Institute for Civil Justice at the RAND Corporation (especially James Kakalik and E. Allan Lind); the private court system Judicate (especially Mike Carney and Alan Epstein); the private court system Judicial Arbitration and Mediation Services (especially Ilene Katz, Diane Levinson, and Toni Mc-Carver); Barbara Kaufmann of the Call for Action service of San Francisco radio station KCBS; Oakland mediator Carolyn Kendrick; Ken Kubey; Professor Robert Kubey of the Department of Communication at Rutgers University; Maki Kuper; William Lincoln of National Center Associates; Sacramento prosecutor Albert Locher; David Lohman; Marcy Lohman; Tim McKernan of Arbitration Forums; Catherine Meschievitz of the Institute for Legal Studies at the University of Wisconsin; class action litigator Beverly Moore; Professor Laura Nader of the Department of Anthropology at the University of California, Berkeley (who reviewed the manuscript); Ralph Nader; Nolo Press (especially Mary Randolph and Ralph Warner); Sacramento personal injury litigator Allan Owen; Jim Shultz of the West Coast Office of Consumers Union; Mark Silbergeld of the Washington, D.C., office of Consumers Union; Professor Susan Silbey of the Department of Sociology at Wellesley College; Nan Simpson of the Public Citizen Litigation Group; the Society for Professionals in Dispute Resolution (especially Joyce Blackwell, Leslie Butler, Laurie Church, Mark Kahn, Allison King, and George Nicolau); John Sproul; Gloria Swindell of the District of Columbia's Department of Consumer and Regulatory Affairs; Berkeley mediator Brad Warren; and Nancy Yeend of Alternative Dispute Resolution Associates.

This book is sold with the understanding that the author and publisher are not rendering legal or professional advice or other services to any reader. Every effort has been made to ensure the accuracy and timeliness of the information in this book. However, the resolution of legal issues often depends on specific facts and on varying state laws, which may have changed since the preparation of this book. For advice on a specific legal problem, readers should consult a qualified attorney.

# Introduction

You bought a beautiful new car six months ago, but it has never run right. The dealership has tried five times to fix it but hasn't succeeded. You're sick of taking the car in, sick of taking time off from work to drop off and pick up the car, sick of the expense of renting a car while yours is in the shop. You want another new car instead. The service manager at the dealership says your car is in better shape than when you brought it in for repairs. He points out that even though the car isn't perfect, it certainly will get you from point A to point B. The manager says he's already done more than a customer should expect him to do—after all, he's tried five times to repair the car and hasn't charged you. Nevertheless, he is willing to try one more time. When you tell him you want a new car, he says, "You've got to be kidding."

You've been married for a long time, but your relationship with your spouse has gotten worse and worse. Your spouse doesn't understand you. Your spouse doesn't try to meet your needs. Quite frankly, you don't understand your spouse as much as you used to, and you're not as interested in your spouse's needs as you once were. You want a divorce. But what about the kids? What about the house? You firmly believe the kids would be better off with you. And since you should have the kids, you'll need the house, too. Your spouse doesn't agree with you about the house or the kids or much else. In fact, your spouse doesn't think the relationship is so hopeless that divorce is the only answer.

You've gone into business for yourself. You were thrilled to reach an oral agreement with a large corporation to do a lot of work for them. As a result of your deal, you've turned down other lucrative work, you've bought equipment, you've started the job, and you've put a lot of hours into it. Then you get a call from the company saying that the executive you've been dealing with has left the firm and your services won't be required after all. "But we have a deal," you say. You get a call from the corporation's lawyer. "What deal?" the lawyer says. "There is no contract that I've seen, and as far as we're concerned, you've been working 'on spec.' In other words, if we needed your work and liked your work, we would pay you; if not, we wouldn't."

You had surgery a month ago. The postoperative pain has been much worse than your doctor told you to expect. Instead of missing two days of work, as your doctor predicted, you missed three weeks. The condition the surgery was supposed to correct is only slightly better if at all. Now, to top it off, you've just read that the type of surgery you had was extremely common until last year, when a study showed it was not very effective and that an alternate, less invasive, less expensive procedure, one that can be done in a doctor's office, dramatically helps the great majority of patients. You call your doctor's office and talk with his receptionist. She says the doctor is with a patient and will call you back. And she asks why you're calling. You say you've been having a lot of problems since the surgery and are wondering whether the other procedure might have been a better idea. The doctor doesn't call you back. You call three more times. The doctor never returns your calls.

You have lived in your home for ten years. Its location on a quiet street has enabled you to sleep with the windows open. This leaves you feeling refreshed in the morning. But in September a group of college students moved in next door. They play their stereo loud as late as one in the morning even on weeknights, with the bass rumbling through your walls and the music fully audible through your bedroom window. They also arrive in their driveway — about 20 feet from your bedroom window — at all hours of the night, usually with their car stereos blaring. Their home stereo frequently has kept you from sleeping, and their car stereos have awakened you on many occasions. You have asked them several times not to play their home stereo so loud and so late and to turn off their car stereo before turning into the driveway. Each time they comply for a few days or even a week, then revert to their disturbing habits. You have lost a lot of sleep, and now you have lost your patience.

You are in your car, waiting at an intersection, when you are rear-ended. You suffer neck pain for more than a year. Your medical bills, most of which are for extensive physical therapy, exceed $10,000. And you will require further treatment. A lawyer friend explains that the total settlement in personal-injury cases usually is three or four times the medical expenses, with the difference between the "medicals" and the total being for "pain and suffering." So even without further medical expenses, your case is worth $30,000 to $40,000. You send the other driver's insurance adjuster a 15-page letter with 37 pages of medical bills and doctor's statements. You ask for $50,000. The insurance company offers you $5,000 and says that according to the doctor they had review your records, you never should have had so much physical therapy. Physical therapy, the doctor says, is just for symptomatic relief.

In all these cases, you have a *difference:* a disparity between what you want and what you have. In all these cases, you have a *conflict:* a difference brought to the attention of the other party with the other party explicitly or implicitly denying your claim or request. If you choose to pursue the cases, you will in each instance have a *dispute:* an active conflict that apparently will not end until it is resolved by the parties or by others.

Let's say that each of these cases is important enough to you that you don't want to walk away. But maybe you *should* walk away. After all, isn't it true that you have only two choices—either hire a lawyer or give up? And you know what many lawyers are like. Costly in every way. Money, time, effort, annoyance, your own subservience. Many lawyers charge $100 to $250 an hour. A lawsuit of even moderate complexity can take $50,000 in legal fees and expenses.

In a big city, that lawsuit can take five years to come to trial, by which time it may be too late for justice to be served. And even if you win at trial, the loser might appeal the decision, taking years more. Your lawyer won't do all the work; you will have to collect documents, sit through a long deposition in which the other side's lawyer may try to pressure or trick you into making a damaging statement, and carefully watch your lawyer to be sure he or she understands the case and does what's in your best interest even if it conflicts with his or her own. And, though stereotypes never apply to every member of a class of people, you know that when you enter a lawyer's office you may well face humiliation. Although you pay the lawyer, the lawyer may not act as if he or she is in your employ. To the contrary, the lawyer may tell *you* what to do; the lawyer may insist on running the case.

But giving up isn't attractive either. Somebody has taken advantage of you. Somebody is not taking you seriously. Somebody owes you money that you badly need. As a matter of principle, as a matter of economics, as matter of self-respect, you need to resolve the dispute.

But do you really have only two choices? *The main message of this book is NO!* No, you are not limited to hiring a lawyer or doing nothing. More than at any time in American history, *you have many choices.* Many of these choices are new. Some are new because they have existed for only a few years. Others are new because they are recent adaptations of existing means. Others are new because they have recently become available in areas of the country that did not previously offer them.

In most but not all cases, these new choices fall into the area called *alternative dispute resolution* (ADR). ADR means different things to different people, but generally it means alternatives to full-scale litigation. (It therefore may include small claims court, which is litigation on a very brief, inexpensive, and informal scale.) This book describes many commonly used types of ADR (including small claims court) that will likely be useful to those who now or in the future may want to resolve a dispute, or potential dispute, in which they would act as individual citizens, not as members of a company, institution, or other group.

ADR is perhaps the hottest topic in the legal profession. In 1989, the main theme of the American Bar Association's annual convention was devoted to ADR. The ABA recently elevated its committee on dispute resolution from a special committee to a standing committee. Many lawyers promote ADR and use ADR, though some oppose it.

More important, ADR is becoming better known among the general public and more available to nonlawyers than ever before. In 1979, there were only three state-subsidized or state-coordinated ADR programs in the United States. Now, every state offers them. New York State alone has ADR centers in every one of its 62 counties. Each year, these centers provide mediation, conciliation, and arbitration for some 60,000 parties and furnish other services to some 100,000 more. California is not far behind: its state government now oversees county-funded centers in 18 of the state's counties, including 10 of the 14 most populous. Texas hosts some 300 public and private ADR programs. Other leading states include Arizona, Colorado, Florida, Georgia, Hawaii, Illinois, Iowa, Maine, Massachusetts, Michigan, Minnesota, New Jersey, New Mexico, North Carolina, Ohio, Oregon, Pennsylvania, and Virginia. The District of Columbia is also a leader.

This book provides the addresses of ADR centers that can help you resolve a dispute. But one of the most attractive attributes of ADR is that *you can do it yourself.* Yes, you may get a fairer resolution or engage in a more comfortable process if you get help from an ADR center; but, provided the other party agrees, you can, by yourself, negotiate a settlement or you can, by yourself, find an appropriate local person to mediate or arbitrate your dispute. Even without an ADR center, you can sue in small claims court. Even without an ADR center, you can band with other citizens who have similar complaints and go after the wrongdoer.

That is not to say that ADR is an uncomplicated field. On the contrary, the field is so complex that a book on every aspect of the subject would tax the patience of all but those who work in the area. This book is for the individual citizen who wants to find out what he or she needs to know to resolve an active or imminent dispute, and to do so without having to master the field.

Still, because you may encounter the complexities in the field, you should know about some of them. And at the same time, you should know that they should not get in your way. What you need to know is not complicated. You need to know that ADR exists as an alternative to either using a lawyer or giving up; you need to know the differences between the key types of ADR; you need to know some places where you can get help to resolve your case through ADR; and you need to know how to succeed in ADR. This book will help you in all of this. If you encounter some of the more complex aspects of the field, don't let them discourage you. Find out what is pertinent to your case and ignore the rest, *with one exception,* which is highlighted below.

Even the very phrase "alternative dispute resolution" is a source of controversy. Here are some of the many areas in which ADR professionals — mediators, arbitrators, researchers, professors, lawyers, ADR organization executives — disagree:

- What processes qualify as ADR types?
- Should the alternatives to full-scale (not small claims) litigation be called "alternative dispute resolution" or just "dispute resolution"? "Alternative dispute resolution" implies that the norm is full-scale litigation, when in fact it is negotiation, formal or otherwise, that resolves most disputes. (This book, though taking note of this point, will nevertheless use the term "alternative dispute resolution" because many people understand it to mean alternatives to full-scale litigation and would be confused by the term "dispute resolution.")
- Does ADR protect the small person against the big person (or firm) or vice versa?
- What qualifications should a neutral (a third party such as a mediator or arbitrator) be required to have?

- Should neutrals be required to have any qualifications at all? (Some unpaid, untrained neutrals have proved to be very skilled.)
- Who should determine qualifications: ADR professionals, ADR professionals and ADR volunteers, state bar associations, state governments, or the federal government?
- Who is an ADR professional: someone paid for his or her work in ADR, or simply someone paid or unpaid who observes certain professional standards?

Beyond these areas of disagreement, there are conflicts between groups with a professional or other strong interest in ADR. Conflicts sometimes pit lawyers against nonlawyers, paid ADR workers against volunteers, and ADR organizations against would-be government regulators.

Understanding ADR is made especially difficult by the many differences among ADR programs from state to state. In some states, state-run systems dominate; in others, private for-profit or nonprofit systems are more active. Court-annexed arbitration is widespread in some states, while in others it hasn't been tried yet. In several states, the limit in small claims court is $1,000; in parts of Tennessee it is $15,000.

Before 1980, little had been written on ADR. Since then, many books and hundreds of articles have been published. These both illuminate and obscure the field. By and large, they are written *by* ADR experts *for* ADR experts; they often deal with very narrow subjects that are of little importance to the typical citizen with a dispute. Not surprisingly, these publications about dispute resolution cause their own disputes — about facts, opinions, and methodology.

*Don't be discouraged by the complexity of the field.* ADR can and in most cases will be a fairly simple experience. Nevertheless, there is a *critical exception* to the general rule that you can ignore most of the controversies and complexities of ADR. You must not ignore the conflict over whether ADR has been promoted too strongly as an alternative to litigation. While ADR can indeed be a powerful tool for the weak against the strong, even for the average citizen against a gigantic corporation, it can also help the rich steal from the poor. For this and other reasons, some people known for their dedication to public service are more opponents than proponents of ADR. They see many advantages in litigation (lawsuits) that typically do not exist in ADR. They point out that ADR typically does not leave a public record of decisions. This record, especially where the decisions have been affirmed on appeal, helps establish legal precedent, which in turn helps future victims of similar wrongful actions to prevail in their own disputes. Further, the record can create a standard for legal and responsible behavior and discourage potential wrongdoers from violating that standard. In addition, the record can call public attention to a problem; an aware public can protect itself, particularly from dangerous products.

Critics of ADR fear that, for example, without litigation a thousand citizens in a hundred cities will individually enter arbitration with a particular auto manufacturer to resolve disputes about the company's unsafe brakes, that each will get some sort of resolution, but that there will be no recorded and reported court cases to form legal precedent or to call attention to the potentially fatal defect.

Therefore, assuming you care about your fellow citizens and your society, it is necessary, when considering which form of dispute resolution to use, for you to think about the potential impact beyond your own interests. If your dispute could have an important impact on other people, and if you can afford the money, time, and other costs of litigation, you have an ethical duty to consider it.

Partly for this reason, and also because litigation is sometimes the best route even if only one's own interests are considered, this book not only explains your choices in alternative dispute resolution but also explains why in at least some cases litigation is the best course.

It is not enough to choose the right kind of dispute resolution. It is also important to resolve the dispute in a way that ends your problem or compensates you for your injury or economic loss. Therefore, this book presents advice on how to succeed in dispute resolution—including both ADR and litigation.

After reading this book, you will no longer be restricted to a choice between getting a lawyer and getting nothing. You will learn that although litigation makes sense in some cases, in most cases there are alternatives that are much faster, much cheaper, and much more comfortable while still offering strong prospects for providing the justice you deserve.

# Alternatives to Lawsuits

# 1

# Arbitration

Arbitration is the hearing of and decision on a dispute submitted by two or more parties to an arbitrator or panel of three or more arbitrators. The hearing and decision-making process are almost always simpler and more informal than those of litigation, often dramatically so. In most arbitrations, the parties are expected to appear at the hearing. There they may present written and oral arguments as well as documents and other evidence.

Most arbitrators will consider arguments based not just on the law but on fairness, morality, or traditional industry practice, though some—especially those required to do so by the program or contract under which they are operating—will take into account only those arguments based strictly on the law. In most arbitrations, parties may bring witnesses and may question witnesses presented by the other side.

Parties may be represented by lawyers. Discovery (the prehearing collecting of oral and written evidence) is generally not permitted, although in some types of arbitration (such as that between a policy-holder and an insurance company regarding an auto accident) it is more the norm than the exception.

It can take anywhere from a matter of days to several weeks or months for the disputing parties to agree to submit the case to arbitration (this assumes they are not *required* to arbitrate the case by court order or by an arbitration clause in a contract) and to select an arbitrator or to have one selected for them. Once the parties take care of these steps (which *can* take only hours), the hearing generally occurs within two weeks to two months. The hearing usually takes from one to a few hours, sometimes one day, and hardly ever more than a few days. After presiding over the hearing, and before reaching a decision, the arbitrator may take additional time to consider written arguments or materials.

Usually within a week or two of the hearing, almost always within a month, and sometimes *at* the hearing, the arbitrator will issue a decision, called an "award." The decision will generally be in writing and may offer at least a brief explanation of its basis.

The decision may be binding on the parties, or it may be nonbinding. Both parties must abide by a binding decision and cannot appeal it, unless one of them can demonstrate that something very unusual has happened, such as patently unethical conduct by the arbitrator. Typically, if the parties have entered arbitration voluntarily, the decision is binding; generally, if they have been ordered into it by a court, the decision is nonbinding.

In some arbitrations, the decision is binding on only one party. This is typical of the arbitration systems offered by car manufacturers: the decision is binding on the automaker but not on the consumer.

Binding or not, arbitration usually means the end of the road for a dispute. Once they have received a decision from a neutral third party, the great majority of disputants will go no further. Regardless of whether they have won an adequate award, the fact that the parties stop here implies that they have gained *some* important satisfaction from the arbitration process. Perhaps they are satisfied only that they have held the other party accountable for his or her actions. Perhaps they are satisfied with the fact that—given that the arbitrator can make a decision based only on the evidence available—they have done as well as they can, and cannot do better even by resorting to litigation. Perhaps one side or both are exhausted by the dispute and ready, as long as the award is not too unjust, to call it quits.

This is an important point. Even if you don't win or don't win enough, it's very valuable to get the dispute *over with*.

A recent Rand Corporation study of court-ordered arbitration in Pittsburgh showed that 73 percent of litigants referred to arbitration were "very satisfied" (44 percent) or "somewhat satisfied" (29 percent) with the process. Eleven percent were "somewhat dissatisfied" and 17 percent were "very dissatisfied." (Because fractional numbers were rounded, these do not add up to 100 percent.)

## COURT-ANNEXED ARBITRATION

If the parties have been ordered into nonbinding arbitration, it is usually because they are part of a relatively new phenomenon called "court-annexed arbitration," also known as "court-ordered arbitration." In response to the backlogs in the judicial system, many state and federal courts now require all or a portion of their lawsuits seeking more than small claims courts can award and less than a certain amount in damages (typically $10,000 to $20,000, but as much as $50,000) to go to arbitration. In these cases, the court selects the arbitrator. Obviously, one way to get your case into arbitration is to file suit in a court that refers cases to arbitration, provided, of course, that the damages you seek are within the court's limits for referral.

If either party to a court-annexed arbitration is unhappy with the arbitrator's decision, he or she can appeal the decision to the court. The court will schedule a trial of the case, called a *trial de novo,* meaning the dispute will be tried as a new case, without consideration of the arbitration hearing or award.

Courts often try to discourage appeals of court-annexed arbitrations. They do so by imposing on those who appeal a fee that is often equal to the cost of the arbitration. In addition, more burdensome fees are sometimes charged to parties who appeal the arbitration decision but who at trial do not do much better (for instance, at least 10 percent better) than they did in the arbitration.

Court-annexed arbitration sometimes occurs in a setting called "med-arb," pronounced "meed-arb." Here the process begins as a mediation — an attempt to get the parties to agree, without a decision being imposed on them. In some cities, the mediation part of med-arb is very brief. If no settlement is reached, the process becomes an arbitration.

## ARBITRATION ORGANIZATIONS

In cases where you and the person with whom you are in dispute select the arbitrator, you have a wide choice. You can choose an experienced arbitrator or simply someone in whom you both have faith: a member of the clergy, a teacher, or—yes, it's possible—a lawyer. If this person is going to arbitrate the dispute, however, and not simply mediate it, it will be necessary to set down some ground rules, ideally in writing, before going ahead. These will involve what kinds of evidence the arbitrator will consider and how it will be presented (e.g., in writing, orally, subject to cross-examination), the length and scope of the hearing, whether the award will include an explanation, and, most important, whether the arbitrator's decision will be binding on the parties. Because this is much like inventing a process for just one case, the vast majority of all those who use arbitration choose to use arbitration organizations, which have their own well-established rules.

By far the best-known arbitration organization is the nonprofit American Arbitration Association (AAA), headquartered in New York and with offices in all major cities and some smaller ones. Also well known is the nonprofit Arbitration Forums of Tarrytown, New York, which has at least one office in every state and is available for arbitration of all types of conflicts but mostly handles disputes between insurance companies. A third big national organization is the for-profit United States Arbitration Services of Seattle, Washington. It, too, operates franchises in most major U.S. cities as well as in some smaller ones.

Each year, AAA handles some 11,000 "commercial" arbitrations (including insurance claims, construction contracts, homeowner warranties, and automobile "lemon law" disputes) and some 18,000 labor disputes. As of this writing, its fee for the smallest commercial dispute is $300; for a dispute involving $100,000 the fee is $1,750.

In the great majority of cases, AAA's arbitrators are lawyers or people with expertise in the industry involved in the dispute or both. AAA arbitrators receive no compensation for cases involving only one day of hearing; for longer hearings, AAA pays the arbitrators and the parties pay AAA.

The agreement you sign when you go into arbitration will spell out the charges, if any, that you will be expected to pay. If the hearing goes beyond a certain number of days, there may be an extra fee. (AAA usually assesses such a charge; in a recent case it charged $450 for the second day of hearing plus an additional $450 for the arbitrator's review of the evidence and writing of the award. Each $450 fee was to be shared by the parties. If the hearing does not go into a second day, no fee beyond the filing fee is charged for the review and the writing.)

This is a possible pitfall for the person who has chosen arbitration in part because of limited financial resources. Naturally, you have little control over whether the hearing will go so long that an additional charge will be assessed. Particularly by making its case in undue detail, your adversary may make the hearing go into an unnecessary second or third day, dramatically running up the fee that will be charged. Before you sign an agreement to arbitration, try to ensure that you will not be charged for delays that are caused solely by the other party. If you cannot be nearly certain that you can afford the fees of a particular arbitration organization, see if a more inexpensive organization is available.

In addition to AAA and other nonprofit services, for-profit arbitration services also exist. The advantage of groups like AAA is that if all goes right, they are inexpensive. But that may also be their disadvantage: because most of these organizations pay arbitrators nothing for a one-day hearing and do not pay them a great deal even for successive days, AAA-type arbitrators are under a certain amount of pressure to complete a case faster than careful consideration might require. For-profit arbitration groups have the luxury of spending as much time as needed on their cases. On the other hand, some for-profit groups have a motive for spending *more* than enough time: the more time they take, the more money they make (others have a set fee). Therefore, whether you deal with a nonprofit group or a for-profit one or with an independent arbitrator, do your best to get a written agreement between the disputing parties and the arbitration service or arbitrator that the hearing and other services will not take more than a specified amount of time and will not cost more than a specified amount of money.

## SPECIALIZED ARBITRATION SYSTEMS

Some industries, on their own or as part of the settlement of lawsuits brought by the Federal Trade Commission (FTC) or others, have established arbitration systems to deal with consumer disputes. Among these are stockbrokerages, manufacturers of major household appliances, moving companies, funeral homes, and some furniture makers. In addition, some 17,000 local businesses in a great variety of fields have arranged for the Better Business Bureaus (BBB) to arbitrate their conflicts with consumers.

Almost any arbitration system may be better than none at all, especially when an aggrieved consumer cannot afford litigation. But any system run by or for industry is suspect. Legal scholars and securities regulators have harshly criticized the stockbrokerage system, run by the Securities Industry Association. They say convincingly that the system is biased against investors in general and small investors in particular, and that it is inadequate to deal with disputes involving possible violations of securities law.

As measured by the number of consumers involved and the dollar amounts at stake in each case, by far the most important arbitration programs established by any one industry are those founded by the automobile manufacturers. All domestic and foreign automakers with dealerships in the United States have established or joined an arbitration program that deals with consumer disputes.

Although they are called "arbitration" programs, these are generally combination mediation-arbitration processes. First they try to mediate—to encourage the consumer and the company to reach an agreement. Then, if the parties cannot agree, the programs provide arbitration in which the decision is binding on the company but not on the consumer, who is free to move to the courts if he or she prefers. In most programs—including those of Ford and Chrysler—cases are considered by a panel usually consisting of both industry and consumer members. In BBB programs—used by General Motors and others— usually a single arbitrator considers the case. Some programs do not permit the consumer to appear at the hearings they hold; the consumer is required to present his or her case entirely in writing.

Auto industry arbitration programs usually claim to be limited to those disputes that arise over defects in and repairs on cars new enough to be under warranty. Nevertheless, the same programs sometimes agree to decide repair issues involving older cars.

"Lemon laws" have been enacted in 48 states and the District of Columbia. The only states lacking them are Arkansas and South Dakota. These laws generally require the manufacturer to provide a replacement or a refund for a new car that has a defect that substantially impairs the consumer's use of the car and that cannot be fixed. In order to take advantage of the "lemon laws," the consumer generally must bring the car to a dealer for repair when the car is less than 12 months old and has gone fewer than 12,000 miles, although some states have limits of 24 months and 24,000 miles. If the repair effort is not effective, the consumer must fairly promptly bring the car back. A car is generally deemed to be incapable of being repaired if it has a defect that has not been repaired despite four trips to the dealer or that has caused a car to be out of service for a total of 30 days even though the dealer has had a full opportunity to fix it. Nevertheless, manufacturers almost without exception try to deny a new car even to a consumer whose defective automobile meets the criteria. Worse, arbitration programs generally side with the manufacturer on the issue of replacement and refund.

*In many states, consumers can find arbitration programs that are fairer than those provided by the automakers.* In particular, government agencies in Connecticut, the District of Columbia, Florida, Georgia, Hawaii, Maine, Massachusetts, New Jersey, New York, Texas, Vermont, and Washington operate statewide arbitration programs that are better forums for the unhappy car owner. Whether your car is new enough to be covered by a lemon law, or older than that but still under warranty, seek the best program you can find in your state.

The most controversial of the programs has been the one mandated by the settlement of an FTC lawsuit against General Motors regarding defects in the company's THM-200 transmissions. The consent order that settled the suit mandated that GM would, until November 1991, submit to binding arbitration on any failure or alleged failure of any engine or transmission. The program is operated by the Better Business Bureaus under contract with GM. The Center for Auto Safety and the National Association of Attorneys General have severely criticized this vast program for too often making decisions unfair to the consumer and too often permitting unjustified delays before rendering a decision. Still, in April 1989, the center reported that GM had bought back some 25,000 lemons at an average price of $8,157.

Consumers wanting to know more about almost anything regarding disputes about car defects and car repairs—from common defects to the strengths and weaknesses of specific arbitration programs to the names of local attorneys who specialize in representing consumers against car manufacturers and dealerships—should contact the Center for Auto Safety at 2001 S Street, N.W., Suite 410; Washington, DC 20009; (202) 328-7700.

For lists of agencies that provide arbitration services, including courts that provide court-annexed arbitration, see Appendix A.

## ARBITRATION VERSUS LITIGATION

### Advantages

When contrasted to litigation, arbitration is almost always cheaper, faster, less formal, and less technical. A person with a reasonably just claim usually gets *something* (money or another desired result). If you seek privacy or just want to avoid publicity (not exactly the same thing), arbitration is much less likely to gain anyone's attention, and it may be possible for the parties to agree to a confidential arbitration.

### Disadvantages

The outcome of arbitration is harder to predict than that of litigation (the arbitrator is usually not strictly bound by statutes and previous cases). A person with a strong claim may get half a loaf instead of the full damages a successful lawsuit would bring (some arbitrators and other ADR practitioners are derided as "splitters" rather than "deciders"). If your car is a lemon, the arbitration program will probably not permit you to recover money for defects in optional equipment or tires or for renting a car. If you want publicity (to pressure the other side into conceding, to embarrass the wrongdoer, or to warn other people who may be able to avoid damage or who may be able to take action themselves), litigation is much more likely to do the job. Although arbitrations can usually be publicized through press releases or other efforts, lawsuits are by nature public and may naturally attract media attention. If you want a binding precedent that will help other people with problems like yours, litigation is the only way to go.

## HOW TO SUCCEED

Within dispute resolution in general and ADR in particular, "success" is not a simple concept. When one is in a dispute, one usually (at least at first) thinks that success is the same as winning. You win; the other person loses; you therefore succeed. But the truth is not so simple.

What if you win $10,000 and the other party loses that $10,000, but your legal fees are $50,000? Have you won? That's the cost-benefit complication of the concept of success.

What if the arbitrator makes a brilliant decision that puts you *and* your adversary in a better situation than you were in at the beginning of the dispute: the arbitrator gives you things that you need and the other party doesn't want and gives the other party things that you couldn't care less about but the other party desperately needs? You have succeeded, perhaps you have won, but you haven't won within the simplistic framework that where one party wins, the other party loses.

Such win-win results are more commonly seen in areas such as mediation. In arbitration, particularly an arbitration in which the third party is really doing his or her job—making a decision, not splitting the difference—usually one party does win in the traditional sense, with the other party losing.

In an arbitration, how do you make yourself the winner? Most of what you need to know is applicable to almost anyone in almost any dispute, regardless of type of dispute resolution. Concepts that apply widely can be found in Chapter 14. But there are some strategies that apply specifically to arbitration. For example, if you are designing your own rules, be very careful. For ideas, review the rules of one or more arbitration organizations. If you are not creating your own rules, become very familiar with any rules provided by the entity involved in your arbitration, whether it is a court, the American Arbitration Association, or an independent arbitrator. (AAA has a full booklet of rules on each broad area of conflict, such as commercial disputes.) If the party handling your arbitration doesn't provide its rules on its own, ask for a copy. Remember that in most cases you and the other party can agree to change the rules. Ask for whatever other publications the arbitrator or arbitration service has available. You may get something beyond what is usually sent, and beyond what your adversary receives, and what you get may help you.

Your next concern is picking the right arbitrator. In arbitrations, the most common course is for parties to consider a list of arbitrators. Either the arbitration service will provide a list, or you or the other party will suggest a list to the other side. A list typically has about five names on it.

In making a selection, the key word is *bias.* Everyone has biases, whether they admit to them or not, and whether they try to suppress them or not. So you can expect to have a choice between arbitrators who are biased—at least slightly and maybe a lot—against you or against the type of outcome you seek in the case and arbitrators who are biased in your favor. Obviously, you will prefer an arbitrator who is biased *for* you to an arbitrator who is biased *against* you.

So whether you receive the list or make up the list, find out everything you can about each arbitrator. If everything else is equal, you should look for people like you in sex, race, ethnic group, nationality, religion, age, and social status. Avoid people who you have reason to believe may be biased against people with your characteristics. If you have met a prospective arbitrator and gotten along, that's a plus. On the other hand, if you are close friends or relatives, that's going too far. Whether or not anybody finds out, it's just plain unfair. If anyone does find out, it could cause a postponement or the invalidation of the arbitration, not to mention embarrassment or worse for you.

Perhaps the most important bias to look for is bias in cases similar to yours. If you were injured in an auto accident and are in an arbitration against an insurance company, look for an arbitrator who seems more sympathetic to victims than to insurance companies. Even better, try to find out what a prospective arbitrator has done in cases like yours. You may find to your surprise that an insurance defense lawyer who does some arbitrations is known for being fair or more than fair to auto accident claimants. Maybe he or she doesn't like his or her own clients; maybe he or she bends over backward to avoid the appearance of prejudice.

How do you find out about prospective arbitrators? Many arbitrators are lawyers. For very basic information on lawyers, look them up in the *Martindale-Hubbell Law Directory.* All law libraries have this publication, as do some general libraries. Some librarians will read you a minute or two from *Martindale* over the phone.

This annual directory has several volumes, each on several states. Each volume is broken down into two sections. One lists, by state and then by city, nearly every lawyer alive, including nonpracticing ones. It gives each lawyer's name, year of birth, a number representing the college attended, and a number representing the law school attended. (Look in the front of the volume for the list of schools represented by the numbers.)

In some cases, *Martindale* gives a lawyer a rating based on confidential recommendations from lawyers and judges. "Legal ability ratings" are "a" (very high), "b" ("from high to very high"), and "c" ("from fair to high"). The only "general recommendations rating"—on "faithful adherence to ethical standards; professional reliability and diligence; and other relevant factors"—is a "v," for "very high." Most lawyers agree that *Martindale's* ratings correlate with reality, but not too highly.

The second section of each *Martindale* volume gives biographical information, usually a paragraph or more. This includes items such as law school distinctions, professional memberships and offices, law courses taught, and publications. In some cases it also lists "representative clients" of a lawyer or law firm. Because one must pay a high fee to obtain a biographical listing, most lawyers are not listed here.

Nevertheless, if a prospective arbitrator is listed in *Martindale's* biographical section, pay special attention to any information you find there. You can learn a great deal, especially if the lawyer or firm lists "representative clients." If you're an environmental activist and the "representative clients" are major corporate polluters, think seriously about rejecting the arbitrator's name.

For more information about arbitrators, ask people in the arbitrator's own industry, especially people who will not be reluctant to criticize the arbitrator. Ask not just about bias, but about skill and about experience in cases similar to yours. Ask lawyers about lawyers, accountants about accountants, full-time arbitrators about full-time (and part-time) arbitrators. If you are about to hire a professional arbitrator, ask for references and call these references. Tell the person you're calling that you will keep his or her advice confidential, and honor your promise.

If you can't find out anything about a prospective arbitrator, cross him or her off the list—if a list is provided to you—and do not add him or her to a list you propose. An unknown arbitrator may be just as bad as one who is known to be incompetent or known to be biased against people with characteristics such as yours.

In making your case orally and, if you choose to do so, in writing, explain applicable law as you understand it (it might be a good idea to pay a lawyer for an hour's advice on the law that applies to your case). Emphasize the facts of the case. Unlike a judge in a court case, the arbitrator will probably permit you to focus heavily on fairness and on traditional practices, such as what people in the profession or industry involved usually do in cases such as yours. For instance, let's say you buy a dress and don't put it on until six weeks after the purchase, at which time you find that the hem is badly stitched. But the store refuses to take back the dress. Check with similar stores in your area—if you find that the typical practice is to take back any new and defective merchandise even several months after the sale, bring this up in the arbitration.

The arbitration process is less formal than a trial but much more formal than most everyday negotiating. Unless advised otherwise by someone familiar with the particular arbitration service or arbitrator, dress in business clothes. Behave politely. Speak correctly.

Because of the formality of the typical arbitration, do not presume that the arbitrator will believe you simply because you're a nice person. Being a nice person helps, but it is not enough for building the most convincing case. Provide documentation, present witnesses.

If the case involves technicalities that cannot be convincingly explained through documents, or that may simply be more effectively explained by an expert, consider getting an expert to testify on your behalf. You will probably have to pay such an expert—a doctor, an accountant, an engineer, a geologist—but it may well be worth it.

If you need a witness or expert witness who is not willing to testify, try to find someone of equal persuasiveness who wants to help. Failing that, check the arbitration rules to see if you or the arbitrator can *subpoena* the witness to appear: force the witness to show up whether the witness wants to or not. (Expert witnesses who did not witness a relevant event cannot be subpoenaed.) Remember, however, that a witness who is coerced to testify may try to find a way to hurt your case, while a sympathetic witness may try to find a way to help you.

Although at first glance ADR in general and arbitration in particular seem like a great way to avoid lawyers, reality is not so simple. First of all, the arbitrator may well *be* a lawyer. Then, the other side may be represented by a lawyer. And you may want to hire a lawyer.

There are several ways in which a lawyer can help you. As noted, you may ask a lawyer to spend an hour or so advising you on the law pertaining to your case. A lawyer can also give you an idea of questions the other side may ask and how the arbitrator could be expected to react to certain evidence and certain arguments you may present. Finally, if you can afford one, you may want to hire a lawyer to represent you in the arbitration. This may be the right move if your case is complicated: many lawyers are good at analyzing a complex set of facts and then making a clear, well-organized presentation. It may also be the correct choice if the other side will present many witnesses who must be cross-examined. Hiring a lawyer is probably the right move if your case depends less on the facts of the dispute, on fairness, and on traditional practice than it does on the law itself. Hiring a lawyer is also probably advisable if the arbitrator will run a formal hearing in which rules of evidence and other legal formalities will be observed.

# 2

# Mediation

Mediation is the New York City of third-party alternative dispute resolution: ADR involving someone other than the disputing parties. Just as New York is by far the biggest city in a big country, mediation is by far the largest area of the large field of third-party ADR as measured by any standard—number of cases, practitioners, or agencies offering it. It's also like New York in other ways: it's amazingly diverse, a combination of the very old and the very new, and, to the outsider (and sometimes the insider), highly unpredictable.

Mediation is far more varied than many people think. What one person thinks of as mediation is not what someone else thinks. What some people call "mediation" is what this book describes as "conciliation." Some might refer to a program as a mediation project, when in fact it provides not straight mediation but "med-arb," a combination of mediation and arbitration.

Therefore, if you think mediation is for you, it is important—probably more important than in any other ADR field—to find out exactly what you're getting into.

As defined here, *mediation* is a process in which a third party (the mediator), or team or panel of third parties, attempts to help two (or more) parties resolve their dispute by meeting with them and helping them to agree upon a settlement. *Conciliation* as defined here and discussed later in this chapter is a process in which a third party (the conciliator) does approximately what a mediator does but without meeting with the parties.

Mediation can be better or worse than negotiation. Negotiation can be over in a flash, and both parties can be satisfied. But it can also cause an insecure relationship to turn into a war. Because negotiation is simpler and more available (any two people can do it anytime they want), it is usually the first step to resolving a dispute. And because mediation is the next most informal, next quickest dispute resolution alternative, it is often the next step when negotiation has failed.

The main reason mediation can be better than negotiation is that the mediator, especially a skilled mediator, can turn the parties into much more effective negotiators. In particular, the very *presence* of a mediator will tend to cool off the parties and encourage reasonable initiatives and responses: what a person will say when no one is looking is one thing; what a person will say when there's a witness is something else again. And a mediator is not just any witness: he or she is usually someone seen by the parties—properly or not—as something of an authority figure. This cools the parties further.

At the beginning of the mediation, a good mediator explains certain ground rules, which serve to calm the parties even more. Some mediators ask the parties to help develop the rules. The mediator may ask the parties to address the mediator, not each other. He or she may also ask them not to interrupt, not to call each other names, not to yell.

As the mediation gets under way, the mediator tries to understand both sides of the dispute. He or she does so by hearing out each party without much interruption from the other party. Then, while trying to avoid heated argument, the mediator gives each side an opportunity to contradict what the other party has said. The mediator may then suggest ways to settle the case.

From time to time in most mediations, usually at the mediator's initiative and usually with the permission of both parties, the mediator holds a "caucus" with one party. In a caucus, the mediator meets separately with one party, leaving the other party alone. The person meeting with the mediator can speak confidentially here. In particular, the party and the mediator can discuss a possible settlement or possible elements of a settlement, and the party can do so without fear of the opposition's finding out how far the party will go. Partly to provide a sense of fair play, a mediator who caucuses with one party will almost always caucus with the other as well.

Mediation sessions generally take 30 to 60 minutes. In major labor disputes, however, these sessions may go around the clock on some days and take a total of several months; even in everyday conflicts there may be several mediation sessions, each lasting several hours. Both parties attend. The parties usually are not represented by lawyers and ordinarily do not bring witnesses, though they may bring documents and other evidence. The mediator does not usually review any documents outside the meeting.

Mediations do not always work. Some cases are inappropriate for mediation—for example, cases where one party seeks a binding legal precedent. Even cases that are right for mediation may result in an unbreakable impasse, owing to a firm unwillingness or inability of the parties to move toward a settlement (which is not necessarily the same as a compromise) or because of a lack of skill on the part of the mediator.

But mediation often is the best move. In both money and time, it generally is far less costly than many alternatives, including litigation and arbitration. It is especially appropriate if the two parties need to get along after the dispute resolution process. This tends to be true of spouses, parents and children, relatives, neighbors, employers and employees, coworkers, and others.

If the parties reach a settlement, it sometimes is formalized in a settlement document drafted by the parties or, with the parties' involvement and approval, by the mediator.

Mediation is offered by a great variety of people and services. Among them are government agencies such as district attorneys' offices and, in states led by New York and California, local mediation centers subsidized or coordinated by the state. Such centers are available in all 62 New York counties and in 18 of the 58 counties in California (including 10 of the most populous 14). Whether you live in New York or California or another state, call the offices of your county government to find out if there is such a center in your county. You can also check in the Yellow Pages under "Mediation" and "Dispute Resolution."

Many private, nonprofit services also offer mediation, from local agencies to national ones including the Better Business Bureaus (headquartered in Arlington, Virginia), and the American Arbitration Association (with headquarters in New York City). Among national and regional private, for-profit firms providing mediation are Dispute Resolution, Inc. (headquartered in Hartford), Endispute (Chicago), Judicate (Philadelphia), Judicial Arbitration and Mediation Services (Orange, California, near Los Angeles), and Resolve Dispute Management (Chicago). Also offering mediation are some of the many consumer complaint phone lines run by radio and TV stations. (Usually, such lines provide conciliation.) In addition, there are many for-profit mediation agencies and mediators (see Appendix A).

Consumers generally find mediation highly satisfactory. A sampling of 1,399 complainants and respondents in the New York state-assisted county mediation programs found that 74 percent were "completely satisfied" (40 percent) or "satisfied" (34 percent) with the process, while 19 percent were "somewhat satisfied" and only 3 percent were "dissatisfied" and 4 percent "completely dissatisfied."

Because most mediators use caucuses, let's take a look at a mediation that includes them:

Let's say there are two neighbors, Danielle Dogowner and Sammy Sleep. Ms. Dogowner is a computer engineer who works during regular business hours. Her dog—a Doberman—lives outdoors 24 hours a day. Not only does this dog bark loudly, he barks all the time.

Mr. Sleep is the night editor at a newspaper. He works from 8:00 P.M. to 4:00 A.M. He gets home at 4:30, watches TV, then goes to sleep around 6:00 A.M. If things work out, he sleeps until around 1:00 P.M. But things don't work out.

Because Ms. Dogowner's dog barks all the time, he by definition barks between 6:00 A.M. and 1:00 P.M. So Mr. Sleep doesn't. He turns into Mr. Tired. Then he turns into Mr. Angry.

One day around 8:00 A.M., after trying for two hours to get to sleep but being unable to do so because of the barking, Mr. Sleep phones Ms. Dogowner. The conversation goes like this:

Hello?

Ms. Dogowner?

Yes.

This is Sammy Sleep next door.

Hi.

I need to talk to you about your dog.

Yeah, well, listen, I can't talk right now. My car pool will be here any minute.

Well that's a damn shame, but I've got a bigger problem than that. For two months, ever since you got that stupid dog of yours, I haven't been able to sleep worth a damn.

I don't see where that's my problem.

What do you mean, it's not your problem?

You're the one who's too sensitive to a little noise.

No, you're the little broad who's too insensitive to anybody but herself.

Broad?

Yeah, broad. Anybody who wakes up her neighbors all the time is a broad.

I'm not a broad and it's not my problem and my car pool is honking right now.

Oh yeah? Well, I'll make it your problem. I'm going to sue you for
all you're worth.
(Click.)

The above conversation gives you a sense of the kind of dispute that
can be mediated; it also provides at least a dozen examples of how not to
talk with a party with whom you have a potential dispute.

What Mr. Sleep and Ms. Dogowner have done is conduct a negotiation: a conversation about the interests of the parties in which one or both
parties try to resolve a conflict between them. They have not done a good
job. Perhaps they will calm down and talk it out more effectively,
perhaps not. Let's say Mr. Sleep sends Ms. Dogowner a typed, certified
letter threatening a lawsuit. Let's say Ms. Dogowner has heard of a good
mediation program and has prevailed upon Mr. Sleep to go with her to a
mediator. Let's call the mediator Marjorie Mediator. Further, let's say
that in discussing the ground rules she suggests that caucuses be allowed;
both parties agree.

Ms. Mediator hears all about Ms. Dogowner's dog barking and all
about Mr. Sleep not getting any rest. And she hears more. Mr. Sleep says
he sleeps soundly once he gets to sleep but that he can't get to sleep
because of "that damn barking." He thinks Ms. Dogowner should keep
her dog indoors whenever Mr. Sleep is at home, a period that can extend
from 4:30 A.M. until 7:30 P.M. Ms. Dogowner says she can't keep the dog
inside because when the dog is in the house, he tends to tear things up
and knock things down. She says Mr. Sleep should wear earplugs, but
Mr. Sleep says he can't sleep with them because he finds them
uncomfortable.

Then Ms. Mediator asks Mr. Sleep if he will give her permission to
caucus with Ms. Dogowner. Mr. Sleep says, "Sure."

Ms. Mediator tells Mr. Sleep they'll be back in five or ten minutes.
She and Ms. Dogowner move to another room. Ms. Mediator wants to
caucus because she has an idea. As is often the case, the mediator sees the
forest when the angry parties see just the trees.

The caucus goes like this:

Ms. Dogowner, do you feel there's anything you can do to accommodate Mr. Sleep's needs?
No, I think we're at a standstill because my dog needs to be out all
day and my dog by nature barks. I don't see why Mr. Sleep doesn't
just move.
Move?
To Argentina.

Let me ask you a question. What do you do after you get up in the morning?

Well, I get up around five-thirty, work out for a half hour with an aerobics show on TV, then go for a jog for maybe another half hour, then take a shower, dress, have breakfast, and, if there's time, read the paper.

What would you think about taking the dog with you on your run, so Mr. Sleep could get to sleep?

Why should I do that for him?

It would be neighborly. Also, he's talking about taking you to court.

I see your point. Maybe I could do that. Let me think about it.

Fine. Do I have your permission to bring this up with Mr. Sleep?

OK, but only when all three of us are together.

Agreed.

Ms. Mediator and Ms. Dogowner return to the room where the mediation began. Now Ms. Mediator asks Ms. Dogowner if it's all right with her if there's a caucus with Mr. Sleep. "OK," says Ms. Dogowner. "We'll be back within ten minutes," says Ms. Mediator.

So now it's Mr. Sleep's turn to be in a caucus. This one goes like this:

Mr. Sleep, where do you think we stand?

I don't know. It doesn't look good to me. That dog should be indoors. Preferably, indoors at the dog pound.

Well, what's the main problem here?

To tell the truth, the dog doesn't bother me that much when I'm just at home and watching TV or whatever. Sometimes I don't even hear him over the TV, and even if I do hear him, it's not that big a deal if I'm not trying to sleep.

Didn't you say you sleep soundly once you get to sleep?

Right.

Isn't the dog still barking then?

I suppose he is, but once I'm asleep, I'm *asleep*.

Do you see any possible solution?

Not really, because that dog barks all the time. It takes me at least twenty minutes to fall asleep, and he never stops barking for more than two or three minutes.

What if when you went to bed at six in the morning you knew the dog would not bark for half an hour?

That would be perfect! But it's impossible, because old Ms. Dogowner demands that the stupid dog be outdoors a million hours a day.

But if somehow the dog didn't bark from six till six-thirty, you'd be in good shape?

I would show up for work well rested for the first time in two months.

Do you have any problem with me bringing up that point with Ms. Dogowner?

None whatsoever.

OK, let's go back.

Now Ms. Mediator and Mr. Sleep return to the mediation room, where Ms. Dogowner awaits them. This conversation follows:

Ms. Dogowner, Mr. Sleep, I have an idea. It seems to me that you're closer together on these issues than we may have first thought. Mr. Sleep's biggest concern is getting some sleep, and he says that if he is just able to get to sleep, he can sleep straight through, even if the dog is barking. It takes him about twenty minutes or less to get to sleep. Ms. Dogowner needs to leave her dog outdoors most of the day, but, just when Mr. Sleep goes to bed—at about six in the morning—she goes out jogging. And she says she might be able to take the dog with her on her jog, and the jog takes half an hour. Do you see any basis for settling this problem?

If they are reasonably intelligent, and if they've been calmed by the presence, demeanor, and rules of the mediator and by having gotten their say, Ms. Dogowner and Mr. Sleep will likely agree that Ms. Dogowner will take the dog out from 6:00 to 6:30 each morning and Mr. Sleep will drop his demand that the dog be indoors most of the day. Nobody will lose anything important, and litigation will be avoided.

## CONCILIATION

Conciliation is very similar to mediation, except for the fact that the third party, called the conciliator, does not deal with both parties at the same time. He or she contacts them separately, usually by phone but sometimes by mail and occasionally in person.

Many dispute resolution agencies provide a combination conciliation-mediation service, in which the dispute is first handled through conciliation and then, if still unresolved, proceeds to a face-to-face mediation.

The effort of the conciliator can vary greatly but generally consists of one or two short phone calls per party. The parties are not normally represented by lawyers, nor do witnesses participate in conversations with the conciliator. The parties generally do not provide documents or other tangible evidence, but if facts are in dispute and documents such as receipts are available, the conciliator may ask for them.

Although less common than mediation, conciliation is widespread and is offered by both public and private agencies. Often the very agencies that offer mediation also offer conciliation, including in particular district attorneys' offices and radio, TV, and newspaper consumer-complaint lines. Citizens may also arrange for their own conciliator. Conciliation services in most cases do not charge a fee.

Like mediators, conciliators have widely varying amounts of formal training and experience.

## "MED-ARB"

"Med-arb," the combination of mediation and arbitration, is one of the newest types of ADR. It is most commonly found in programs in which courts refer litigants to ADR, with trial still available if this process fails.

There is nothing hard to understand about "med-arb." You try mediation first; if that doesn't work, you go to arbitration. Usually the parties can decide whether or not they want to proceed to arbitration. If one party doesn't want to, the dispute goes no further, even though it isn't settled.

If there is an arbitration, it is often handled by the same person who handled the mediation. This saves time but discourages some people from being totally frank with the third party: these people legitimately fear that if the mediator turns into an arbitrator, he or she may hold some of a party's frank statements against that party. If you're going to a "med-arb," find out at the beginning if your mediator will be your arbitrator, and check to see which elements of the mediation session—including in particular caucus statements—the arbitrator will be permitted to consider. Nevertheless, even if the arbitrator is expected not to take caucus conversations into account, remember that he or she, being human, might still be influenced by them.

Then find out if you can keep the mediator from becoming the arbitrator, either by terminating the process or demanding a different arbitrator. If so, and if the process begins to turn from mediation to arbitration and you don't want the same person arbitrating, courteously demand that this not occur.

## FEES, TRAINING, AND EXPERIENCE

The great majority of mediation services—including those providing conciliation and med-arb—charge no fee. While any future government regulation would result in more standardization, mediation services currently vary widely in procedures, time per session, and, especially, the training and experience of the mediators. Some have no formal training whatsoever. This doesn't necessarily mean they're incompetent, but a consumer should be wary of an untrained mediator, particularly if the mediator also lacks experience and if the dispute involves complicated facts, law, and/or personalities.

Most mediators have taken courses ranging from 90 minutes to 8 hours to 40 hours or more. The programs coordinated by state agencies in New York and California require 25 hours of formal training plus 10 hours of apprenticeship.

There is not yet any reliable certification program for mediators. You may run across someone with a certificate attesting to the fact that he or she has taken a course, but that doesn't mean the course was well taught or that the student was paying attention. You may even find someone with a framed document saying he or she has been certified after passing an examination. Unfortunately, the only such examination and certification program of which the author is aware allows would-be mediators to take a test in their own homes, to work with open books and with the help of other students, and to take the test over and over until they pass.

For cases requiring a well-trained neutral who can spend more than a short time on the dispute, the parties may want to hire a private, professional mediator, often at a cost of $30 to $150 per hour. (Some mediators set fees by the day or by the case.)

## MEDIATION (AND CONCILIATION AND MED-ARB) VERSUS LITIGATION

### Advantages

Mediation is usually free and is almost always far less expensive and far less formal than litigation. Meetings and decisions can be obtained in a short time (often less than two weeks). A person with a reasonably just claim usually gets something (money or another desired result). The process ordinarily is private and not publicized. (Of course, this is an advantage only in some cases.) The process is sufficiently conciliatory that it can be used by parties who hope to get along socially or professionally after the process is over. *(Di-*

*vorce—including custody, child support, and visitation—is the classic example.)*

Probably the greatest advantage of mediation versus litigation (and versus arbitration) is that you don't have to get stuck with a result you don't want. A mediation does not have to result in settlement. If, despite the efforts of the mediator and the other party and yourself, no one comes up with a settlement plan that you find acceptable (particularly once you consider your other alternatives, which range from doing nothing to going to court), express your thanks but say you don't see any way the mediation is going to work out, and walk away.

### Disadvantages

The outcome of mediation is harder to predict than that of litigation because the parties are not bound by statutes and previous cases. Since the goal is a settlement acceptable to both sides, the party with a strong case is likely to get far less than might be available through a lawsuit. Mediation is not appropriate for parties who out of a sense of righteous revenge or for other reasons not only want justice but want the other party to lose, to be punished, to pay a price, to be held publicly accountable. It is not the right option if for strategic advantage or other purposes you want publicity. Mediation provides no precedent for subsequent cases involving similar disputes. Mediation can lead to unfair results when there is a large disparity in power between the two parties: a mediation between an employer and an employee, for example, may end in an agreement unfairly favorable to the boss.

### HOW TO SUCCEED

From the preceding chapter on arbitration, you will remember that succeeding and winning are not the same. You should look for the best result realistically available to you, not necessarily for a result that simply gives you a better deal than your adversary.

That much said, there is a lot you can do to improve your chances of success. Your first opportunity comes before the mediation begins, in finding the right mediator. Remember the points made in the arbitration chapter about bias: that the "neutral" will be at least slightly biased, and the choice between a neutral biased for you and one biased against you is an easy one. So find out all you can about prospective mediators.

Speaking for Mediation, a mediator group that operates a speakers' bureau in the San Francisco Bay Area, has published a helpful pamphlet (see Appendix D). From that pamphlet comes the following key list:

### How to Choose a Mediator

You should prepare a list of specific questions about your special needs in making a choice. These questions may include:

1. What training and experience have you had?
2. What is your area of expertise?
3. Do you have a bias or preference about — — — ?
4. How would you describe your style of mediation?
5. Do you work alone or on a team with another mediator?
6. If I have an attorney, may I involve the attorney in the process and if so, how?
7. How frequent and long are the sessions?
8. Will you accommodate the parties' needs in scheduling sessions?
9. Are the sessions confidential?
10. Are children or other concerned parties brought in?
11. Do you ever meet separately with individual participants?
12. Do you deal with underlying conflicts?
13. Do you deal with feelings?
14. What is/is not included in the service?
15. Who will draft the agreement?
16. What is the fee and how is it handled?

The page with the list concludes, "There are no 'right' answers to these questions because each situation is different. After hearing the mediator's responses, ask yourself if your needs will be met and whether you would feel comfortable working with that person."

Good advice.

Particularly if your dispute is with a business, give special consideration to the consumer-complaint lines operated by many radio and TV stations and newspapers. These services rarely get involved in disputes involving more than a few thousand dollars; more often, the conflicts are about amounts totaling $100 or less. So if you have a $50,000 breach-of-contract case, look elsewhere. But if a repair shop didn't fix your TV, if a catering service that handled your daughter's wedding charged you for wine it never poured, if a mail-order company hasn't sent the merchandise, if a restaurant got a spot on your best coat and the coat can't be cleaned, you're in the right place.

Radio, TV, and newspaper complaint lines offer two great advantages to consumers: they provide free advice—often very solid, very sophisticated advice based on the training and experience of their directors and volunteers—and they offer conciliation that may speak softly but carries the big implicit stick of possible widespread, bad publicity. When a consumer complains about a company or individual and one of the consumer-complaint line volunteers contacts the party in an effort to obtain a fair settlement, the party knows that if the case isn't settled fairly it just might make it on the air or into print. So the company or individual is very likely to settle the case.

If you are going to use a mediation program or a private mediator, be prepared for the relative informality of a mediation. Business clothes may be too much: if possible, ask the mediation service or mediator what people usually wear. Be respectful of the mediator and the other party, but be yourself: your goal should be to work out a realistic settlement, not to intimidate or impress anybody.

Bring documentation. Although your goal is not to persuade the mediator, you may persuade the other side of a particular fact or that you can *prove* a particular fact if the case doesn't get resolved in mediation and must proceed to arbitration or litigation.

Because the goal is settlement rather than beating the other person into the ground, think hard about the other person's point of view and in particular about what is of *value* to the other party: you may want something that is easy for the other party to give up (these items are not limited to money; they may include services, refraining from doing something, changing the hours of an activity, making an apology, or avoiding contact with you or with someone else).

Follow any reasonable rules suggested by the mediator; these might include not talking to your adversary, not swearing, and not yelling. Avoid inflammatory remarks. In the joint sessions, don't be so frank that you give an advantage to the other party. (You can be more candid in the caucuses.) In particular, don't offer to give too much or to take too little.

If you feel a need to talk with the mediator outside the presence of the other side, and the mediator does not call for a caucus, ask for one yourself. In a caucus, you can tell the mediator what is the most you are willing to give or the least you are willing to take, but the mediator should not, without your permission, tell the other side; more likely, the mediator will use such information from you and such information from the other side to find some common ground.

If your mediation is to end in a written agreement and if the agreement is complicated or deals with legal issues, you may want to get advice from a lawyer.

# 3

---

# Neighborhood Panels and Neighborhood Disputes

The front pages of newspapers are filled with the stories of disputes between countries, disputes between giant corporations, and disputes involving major celebrities. Every day, however, thousands of disputes are boiling that make neither page one nor page 88 but are terribly important to the parties involved. Many of these are the supposedly small disputes between neighbors or otherwise involving a neighborhood. Disputes about damage caused by pets, noise caused by stereos, reduction in property value caused by a nearby building's cracking paint and weed-infested front yard. Disputes about harassment, parking, property lines. Disputes between family members, between workers and bosses, between landlords and tenants, between consumers and merchants.

These disputes, sometimes far more than the multimillion-dollar lawsuits that make the news, can be the central focus of the parties involved. If your neighbor's dog has been leaving small brown gifts in the yard where your kids play, and you have phoned the neighbor to ask him to do something about the problem and nothing has happened, you may legitimately be very concerned about the diseases that can be transmitted by pets to people. And, legitimately or not, you may be very upset that your neighbor doesn't seem to respect you and doesn't seem to think you can do anything to protect your interests.

If your neighbor plays loud rock music every night until 2:00 A.M. and you're sleepy at the office as a result, this is no trivial matter to you. If you need to sell your condominium for $100,000 in order to move into a house, but your real estate agent says that though your property should be worth that much, it is currently worth only $75,000 because the buildings and yards on your block aren't maintained as well as those down the street, your very quality of life depends on getting your neighbors to take action.

For these and other neighborhood problems, neighborhood panels present one of the most effective forms of dispute resolution. These panels are groups of volunteers who provide mediation and, less commonly, conciliation for disputes arising in their own communities and, in some cases, in their very neighborhoods.

While new in the sense that until recently few if any formal programs offered neighborhood panels throughout large metropolitan areas, these panels are in another sense very old. In previous centuries, when dispute resolution systems were not as formal as they often are today, citizens regularly went to neighbors or a nearby authority figure, such as a member of the clergy, for help in resolving their dispute. Even today, in supposedly more primitive cultures, this system still prevails in local disputes involving minor civil and criminal offenses (although sometimes the process is more one of informal arbitration than informal mediation).

Neighborhood panels therefore present disputing parties with an alternative that is newly available but is, when contrasted to most other forms of dispute resolution, so comfortable and natural that it has existed in other forms for hundreds of years. Another advantage of neighborhood panels over most dispute resolution mechanisms is that the third parties are not people unfamiliar with the neighborhood involved or who have no direct stake in the outcome, but rather panels of people who may know exactly what street you're talking about and may personally benefit if the dispute is resolved in a manner satisfactory to both parties.

In addition to providing panels of community members who furnish mediation or conciliation services, neighborhood panel programs differ from other ADR forms in another important way: they tend to handle not only disputes that occur in the neighborhood but the *kinds* of disputes that arise between neighbors. These tend not to be consumer-manufacturer or employee-employer conflicts, but rather neighbor-neighbor problems involving dog and cat noise and damage, noise from stereos and parties, maintenance of property in an unsightly manner, parking in driveways, children, vandalism, threats, harassment, and fights. Less commonly, they involve disputes often handled by more formal dispute resolution mechanisms, such as those involving landlords and tenants and those concerning consumers and merchants.

Although many neighborhood panels have been organized with little or no outside help, many have been heavily influenced by the Community Board Program in San Francisco. Founded in 1976, this nonprofit program trains volunteers to serve on panels and refers disputants to panels. It provides training in San Francisco, New York, and Washington, D.C. The program also offers courses and publishes manuals to help experienced mediators train others. It has "divided" San Francisco into 24 neighborhoods, and it provides neighborhood panels made up of three to five members of each of these sections of the city. If it is impossible for a panel from the involved neighborhood to mediate the dispute (perhaps the panel members all work during the day but the disputants are available only for a daytime hearing), the program brings in a panel of people from a nearby neighborhood.

The program tries to make up a panel that closely matches the age, race, ethnic group, sex, and economic status of the parties. The panel holds informal hearings in the very neighborhood in which the dispute has arisen. The Community Board Program is the model for similar programs in cities in many other states and at least one Canadian province.

Although it began as a program to assist people in traditional neighborhoods, the Community Board Program has expanded to help resolve disputes in a less traditional neighborhood: the "neighborhood" of the school. Now, the Community Board Program trains volunteers—teachers, administrators, students, and parents—to mediate school-related disputes involving people such as themselves. It also trains people in dispute resolution in general and specifically in the resolution of disputes arising in the workplace.

The members of some neighborhood panels established with the help of the Community Board Program have received 26 hours of training; some have taken advanced mediation courses. Before a panel holds a hearing attended by the parties, Community Board staff interview the parties and others with an interest in the conflict and report back to the panel. The panels try to conduct their interviews within one week of being asked to help resolve a dispute. The goal—usually met—is to resolve the dispute within three to four weeks. Sometimes the dispute is resolved without a hearing even being necessary.

In the San Francisco program, hearings usually take two to two and a half hours. In most cases there is just one hearing, though sometimes there are two and occasionally three. Lawyers are prohibited from appearing to represent or even to advise parties. Neighborhood members who are interested in the dispute—relatives or close neighbors of the disputants—are asked to attend the hearing. Witnesses, often including these neighborhood members, sometimes provide information. Parties sometimes present documents. There is no fee.

The hearing has four phases:

In *phase one,* the parties talk to the panel and the panel asks questions. According to Rita Adrian, director of the San Francisco Community Board neighborhood-panel program, the panel not only listens to facts but also attempts to "support and validate" each party as he or she presents his or her side of the dispute. At the end of this first stage, the panel summarizes what it has understood from the parties and checks this understanding with them.

In *phase two,* the parties turn their chairs to face one another and talk with each other. The panel will often ask one of the parties to talk with the other about an issue raised in phase one. The panel asks the parties to be frank but not insulting. In this phase, the parties may come up with a solution to part or all of the dispute.

In *phase three,* the panel asks the parties to "acknowledge what they have learned": what they know that they did not know before they came to the hearing.

In *phase four,* the parties and panels focus on solutions. The panel goes point by point through the dispute, asking each party what he or she believes might be a fair solution to each issue. Assuming all goes well, the dispute is resolved, the solutions are written down as an agreement, the parties sign the agreement, and the panel members sign as well. The panel provides the parties with copies.

## PREVENTING DISPUTES WITH YOUR NEIGHBORS

Unnecessary disputes are much more likely between strangers, or near-strangers, than between friends. So—especially if you've had disputes with neighbors before and therefore may well have disputes with these or other neighbors in the future—make your neighbors your friends.

Because of everyone's proximity—and, therefore, everyone's ability to affect each other's lives—in a neighborhood, your neighbors rank high among the people you know who may one day become your adversaries in a dispute. This makes it worth your while to introduce yourself to new neighbors when they move onto your block and to warm up your relations with neighbors you have already met.

There are many natural ways to do this. When someone is new to the neighborhood, walk over and introduce yourself, welcome her to the neighborhood, tell her she's picked a good place to live (this presumes you're fortunate enough to like your area), offer the use of your phone if hers hasn't been installed yet, say you'd be glad to pick up her newspaper when she's out of town.

Similarly, find a way to strike up a conversation with a neighbor you don't know very well. Say something complimentary or helpful, or raise a subject you think may interest the neighbor. Say his new car looks great, mention that the day for garbage pickup has changed, ask what he thinks about how the local pro football team is doing. Avoid politics and religion, unless you know you'll agree—at least until you know each other better. The easiest topic, and not all that boring in most parts of the country, is the old standby, the weather.

In welcoming a new neighbor or strengthening a relationship with an old one, don't turn into a chattering busybody. Just a short conversation, maybe as brief as 10 seconds, every once in a while. The payoff can be phenomenal. Not only is it usually pleasant to have a friendly talk, but by turning a relationship between strangers into a relationship between people who are friendly (if not necessarily friends), you have dramatically changed the likely course and outcome of any problem that may arise in the future.

That's "problem," not dispute, because the main point is to avoid a dispute in the first place. If your neighbor's sprinkler system always overwaters her lawn and because of the water's high mineral content leaves white spots on your car that are very hard to remove, you have a problem. Would you rather bring this problem up with a neighbor you welcomed to the block, or one you've never met? And if you do bring up the problem, who's more likely to turn down the sprinkler a little and not tell you off for meddling in his or her life: the neighbor with whom you've developed a friendly relationship, or the neighbor who doesn't even know your name?

Not only does establishing good relationships with your neighbors avoid conflicts, it also helps to quickly and amicably resolve the few that crop up even between people who know each other and usually get along well. Still, conflicts can arise between the best of friends and the most loving of spouses, so they can certainly occur between neighbors. You or the neighbor may bring a problem to the attention of the other and, despite the goodwill between you, find that no ready solution exists that both parties find acceptable. If one party or the other insists on taking the conflict elsewhere for resolution, your conflict has turned into a dispute.

A dispute between neighbors can be handled through a brief negotiation or mediation (perhaps best handled by a neighborhood panel) that leaves the disputants friends or even better friends, or it can escalate into name-calling, litigation, vandalism, fights, and worse. If you've already established a friendly relationship, there's a good chance that in the unlikely event a dispute arises, you can resolve it in a friendly, fair, and fast manner.

Finally, if you have the time and inclination to work to have an effective neighborhood dispute resolution program available in your area, contact the Community Board Program for information about how to set up a neighborhood panel and where to go for training: The Community Board Program, Inc.; 149 Ninth Street; San Francisco, CA 94103; (415) 552-1250.

## NEIGHBORHOOD PANELS VERSUS LITIGATION

Many of the advantages and disadvantages of neighborhood panels as contrasted to litigation stem from the fact that these panels practice mediation and conciliation. Other differences arise from the fact that these are panels made up of members of the *community*.

### Advantages

In litigation (or arbitration), it may be difficult or impossible to get enough evidence admitted for the person(s) deciding the case to fully understand the neighborhood (or school) in which the dispute has arisen. Without understanding the area—what the buildings look like, how close they are to one another, the changes the neighborhood has experienced over the last few decades, and the particular tensions in the area—the third party may be handicapped in his or her attempt to help resolve the dispute. But members of a neighborhood panel, assuming the ideal case where they are also members of the community in which the disputing parties live, will know the neighborhood before the dispute resolution process even begins.

Because neighborhood panels specialize in neighborhood disputes, they may well have more experience than a judge with the kinds of disputes that often break out between neighbors and with the kinds of solutions that have worked in the past in similar conflicts. In addition, because of their specialization and because they live in the community, panel members may well have more *respect* for the kind of neighborhood dispute that a judge may too quickly write off as "trivial" and unworthy of his or her serious consideration. After all, if you've just handled a $500 million antitrust case between two giant corporations, a dispute over someone parking in someone else's driveway may seem like a joke. But between neighbors, dog problems and stereo problems and car problems can be just as vexing as an attempt to monopolize an industry can be to a corporate executive.

According to Rita Adrian of the Community Board Program, the San Francisco neighborhood-panel program works because its very *process*, not just its resolutions, makes the parties feel better. She says they feel they have had the opportunity to have their say and to confront the other party. This enables them, she says, to "feel empowered." Adrian also says that the program usually results in very voluntary agreements that are "much more likely to be carried out" than many agreements coming through more traditional means—that is, when a person in authority imposes a solution.

### Disadvantages

See "Mediation Versus Litigation" in Chapter 2.

## HOW TO SUCCEED

Don't forget: success and winning are not exactly the same thing. This is never truer than in disputes between neighbors. If you beat your neighbor into the ground in a lawsuit or an arbitration, you may win the battle but lose the relationship. Do you want to win damages of $100 or $500 but for the next 10 years either avoid your neighbor or risk a shouting match or a fight? Do you want to live next door to somebody who for revenge may refuse to do you the smallest favor no matter how badly you need it, or may harass you and your family at every opportunity?

Neighbors are in a position to ruin your opportunity to enjoy your home in peace; likewise, they are in a position to save your life or property, as when they see smoke coming from your living room or, when you're on vacation, spot somebody lurking in your bedroom.

So, if you have a dispute with your neighbor, do you really want to defeat him or her? More likely, you want to work out a resolution that is truly acceptable to both sides. It is not enough for each of you to *say* you can agree to the resolution; you should both be able to *live* with it.

This book generally counsels that you should look for a dispute resolution result you can live with *comfortably.* This is the ideal resolution in every kind of dispute, and so you should seek it when resolving a dispute with a neighbor. Still, the neighbor-neighbor relationship is so important that a resolution you can live with (even if not comfortably) may be better than escalating the dispute to arbitration or litigation, if escalation seems the only way to get the resolution you really want.

In all disputes, it is important to look at the specifics of the case: the people, their personalities, the facts, the law, the amount at stake. In all disputes, but particularly in those with neighbors, you must also consider how the dispute, its means of resolution, and its result may affect your life in general: your life outside of the dispute, your life after the dispute. You may find that it is better to make a somewhat uncomfortable compromise with a neighbor than to engage the neighbor in an arbitration or litigation that may be both highly adversarial and highly expensive. For example, if your neighbor's stereo annoys you every time you hear it, it may be smarter to accept a compromise under which he keeps the stereo down except for Saturday nights than to insist that even Saturday nights are out. To get everything you want, you may have to pay the price anyone pays for a hostile arbitration or lawsuit—an unpleasant proceeding and one that may cost thousands of dollars—plus the special price of trying to avoid your neighbor day after day, year after year.

In almost all disputes with your neighbors, mediation should be your first resort. And if there's a good neighborhood-panel program operating in your neighborhood, you should first look to that program for mediation.

You may already know about such a program. If you don't know whether there is one, check with local people: neighbors, the clergy, merchants, the police department, the offices of the city council member(s) who represent your area, and dispute resolution professionals— such as mediators, arbitrators, lawyers, and judges—who live or work in your city. If none of this works, you still may want to contact the Community Board Program (its address and phone number are found earlier in this chapter). It may know of a panel operating in a nearby community that would be willing to hear your dispute and that, even without intimate knowledge of your neighborhood, might still present the best alternative for mediating a dispute between neighbors.

# 4

# Negotiating a Settlement

Negotiating a settlement can be seen as a form of alternative dispute resolution or as a way to avoid a dispute in the first place. Since ADR focuses on alternatives to litigation, negotiation certainly qualifies.

A negotiation can be simple and informal, and it can take only a few seconds: "Look, why don't I pay you $100 and we'll forget about the damage to your car?" "You got it."

A negotiation can also be complex and formal and take months or years. In the negotiations to end the Vietnam War, the representatives in Paris took weeks just to decide what shape the negotiating table would be.

Negotiation holds the potential for nipping a dispute in the bud. Before involving any third party, such as a mediator or arbitrator or judge. Before spending a single penny. Before spending much time. For this reason and because any conversation between disputants by nature almost always is some sort of negotiation, it usually precedes any other type of dispute resolution. Because negotiation often completely resolves disputes and because disputes often do not seem worth the trouble of other types of dispute resolution, negotiation usually is the end of a short road.

There are two main schools of thought on negotiation. One is *position-based negotiation*. The other is *interest-based negotiation*.

## POSITION-BASED NEGOTIATION

Position-based negotiation is the more traditional style of negotiation. It is the one you are most likely to encounter and the one you will often be all but *forced* to practice. This is because it's far harder to change the style of a traditional negotiator than it is to win a negotiation.

Position-based negotiation focuses on positions taken by the parties instead of on their underlying interests. A party may have an interest in economic security or in getting retribution. Although these are very different interests, his or her *position* may be the same. A position usually is a money demand. Starting a negotiation by saying you are willing to settle the case for $100,000 is taking a position. So is demanding that a nonpaying tenant vacate an apartment or that a neighbor stop having loud parties on weeknights.

The lack of candor inherent in taking positions rather than disclosing interests leads to negotiations that often involve hardball tactics. These include lying, deception, and stonewalling (refusing to move toward settlement). They also include attempting to conduct a war of attrition (refusing to concede much, based on the theory that the other side will cave in because it can't afford the time or money—such as attorney's fees—to continue negotiating or cannot afford to wait for any money it will receive in settlement from the delaying party).

In position-based negotiation, the outcome often depends on factors having little or nothing to do with fairness or with the underlying interests of the parties. As prominent negotiator Herb Cohen and others have pointed out, among these factors are power, time, and information.

There are many other kinds of power, but a party with greater *bargaining* power may win against the party who on the basis of fairness alone should prevail. An example of a party with greater bargaining power is a buyer who is in a negotiation with the supplier of a product that is easy to find. Although the supplier may be depending on the buyer to keep his or her business afloat, the buyer may easily be able to find another supplier.

A party who has more time may win. And a party who knows the other's deadline may be victorious, regardless of the merits. This is because experienced negotiators know that concessions often do not come until a deadline is imminent, and may not come until after a deadline has passed.

A party who has more information may win. Of particular value is information about the other side. Information can be verbal or nonverbal. Nonverbal information can be anything, from the way a person dresses to a person's posture or facial expression. You can learn a lot about the other side during a negotiation, but you can also learn a lot *before* the negotiation. That doesn't mean you should look at every relationship as one between two people who will one day be in a dispute. It means that if you find yourself in a dispute, you should think back on everything you have learned about the other party. More than likely, he or she was much more frank with you before the dispute began than once it is underway, so old information may be more valuable than recent information.

In position-based negotiating, perhaps the most important factor to determine is to what extent the other side will be willing to change his or her position. If you're dealing in dollars and you have a good idea of how much the other side is willing to settle for, you have a great advantage.

As Cohen points out, one way to tell is to watch the progression of offers. If you have made a claim and the other side's settlement offer goes from $30,000 to $45,000 to $55,000, the other side is all but drawing a red arrow to a willingness to settle for something in the neighborhood of $60,000 to $65,000.

Another factor is attorney's fees and expenses. Let's say you have convincingly told the other side that if a dispute between the two of you cannot be settled, you will have to file suit. Let's assume the other party uses a prestigious corporate law firm, and your attorney friends tell you that such a firm would likely bill a minimum of $50,000 to defend a suit such as yours. Further, let's suppose you know your adversary cares more about money than principle. So even if the other side thinks your claim is invalid, he or she may not be willing to pay more than $50,000 to settle it. (This assumes the other side believes you are making your claim in good faith: people and institutions rarely pay much to settle a claim that they see as a "nuisance claim"—that is, one filed by someone wanting no more than to be paid to go away.)

## INTEREST-BASED NEGOTIATION

Popularized by theorists such as Roger Fisher, William Ury, and William Lincoln, interest-based negotiation has become increasingly common in recent years. This type of negotiation encourages the negotiators to disclose almost everything (of relevance) to the other side, so that each side knows as much as possible about the other's needs and therefore has every opportunity to figure out a way to satisfy the other party.

The interests you disclose may include your need for income, for financial security, for career progress, for societal status, to feel you have been treated fairly, or to clear your name.

In an interest-based negotiation, you may learn that there is something you have that is of little value to you but of great value to the other side and that, by providing that item, you can satisfy the other side at very low cost to yourself. Similarly, through exchanging information about interests, you may find that the other party could give you something of tremendous importance to you at little or no cost to it.

There is an old story about two sisters angrily arguing over who should get an orange. As position-based negotiators, they argue and argue strenuously, each insisting she is the one who should get it. Later they learn that one sister wanted the orange only for its rind, which she needed in order to make marmalade, while the other wanted the orange only for its pulp. If these negotiators had practiced interest-based negotiation, their negotiation, which became so protracted and belligerent, could have been finished amicably in a matter of seconds.

Let's suppose you were financially harmed by another party when the other party breached a lucrative contract with you, or when the other party caused you an injury that made you lose months of employment income. If you were a position-based negotiator, you would likely demand a certain amount of money from the other side. But if you were an interest-based negotiator, you might make clear something that may seem to be only a nuance but may make all the difference in moving the case toward settlement: that you need money, but not necessarily as a settlement payment from the other side. This approach would open up additional possibilities for resolving the disagreement: the other side could hire you for a job; the other side could recommend you for employment; or the other side could give you an idea of how to make money.

What if your main problem is that the other party has humiliated you? Perhaps the other side said it wanted you to do some work and you did the work. You put in long hours and did a good job. But then the other side said it hadn't needed the work after all, didn't know you had gone ahead, and can't and won't pay you. You've wasted some time, but the worst thing is that you feel used, that the other side thinks your time and effort were worthless. As a position-based negotiator, you are likely to be limited to asking for money. As an interest-based negotiator, however, you may disclose that the other side wounded your sense of self-esteem. The other side might apologize or might make clear that there was a terrible misunderstanding and that he or she meant no disrespect. Certain words can be worth a great deal more than money, and the words you hear may bring you a peace of mind that is priceless.

Interest-based negotiation works. Nearly as important, it's dramatically more pleasant, more relaxed, and (usually) more ethical than traditional position-based negotiation.

## NEGOTIATION VERSUS LITIGATION AND OTHER FORMS OF DISPUTE RESOLUTION

### Advantages

Negotiation can instantly resolve a dispute, saving money, time, and emotional distress. It can avert the involvement of third parties (including both neutrals, such as mediators and arbitrators, and representatives, such as attorneys), who may be incompetent or unethical, who may move the dispute in a direction neither party wants, and who may hear information that one or both parties want to keep private.

Negotiation permits the parties to talk and listen directly to each other. This can promote unusual frankness, respect, and compassion.

If negotiation fails, you can always try something else. But if you start with another type of dispute resolution—which almost inevitably will be more costly in money, time, and annoyance—you will never have tried what might well have been the most efficient means of resolving your dispute.

### Disadvantages

A lawyer and the court system itself (or other dispute resolution mechanism involving a neutral) can help prevent one party from taking advantage of another. This is particularly important when there is a disparity in power between the two parties. A lawyer and a court are therefore especially likely to be valuable if you have a dispute with a boss, particularly one who has consistently acted in bad faith or has consistently taken advantage of his or her power over you, or with a spouse, if that spouse has for years dominated the relationship.

Litigation or another third-party dispute resolution process also offers advantages if the other party is the more effective negotiator. Because negotiation usually occurs between two parties with no one else present, it lends itself to unconscionable but effective tactics that few people would try if anyone were looking.

A third-party neutral, such as a mediator or arbitrator, can avoid the counterproductive heat that can arise when disputing parties deal directly with each other. A neutral, out of objectivity or skill or both, can encourage or impose settlement terms that might not have occurred to the parties themselves.

In addition, it is important to note that one adversary will generally be reluctant to accept a settlement plan suggested by his or her opponent, especially if there is strong animosity between the two. The same plan promoted by a mediator or other neutral will often be far more acceptable.

In a negotiation, each party usually gives in somewhat, so settlement is not for those willing to take risks, potentially high risks, in order to win every cent or to humiliate the adversary.

A negotiation is also inappropriate for a party seeking a legal precedent or wanting to publicize an issue or the wrongdoing of the other party.

All things considered, negotiation probably makes sense, at least as a first step—with other mechanisms available if it fails—if (1) you believe you can negotiate about as well as the other party given your relative power, your relative negotiating skill, and the subject matter of the dispute; and if (2) you believe that you and the other party can control yourselves well enough that because of angry accusations or other factors you will not leave an unsuccessful negotiation much angrier and much farther apart than you were when you entered it. Of course, you can also turn to negotiation even after another form of dispute resolution has begun.

## HOW TO SUCCEED

It's best to know how to use both interest-based and position-based negotiation. Then, as the dispute requires, you can apply one or the other or—as is more effective in most negotiations—a combination of the two.

The interest-based community pushes frankness a little too far. Indeed, you should be completely honest, but frankness and honesty are not the same thing. You should not make disclosures to the other side that the other side can exploit to its great advantage. If the other party's only strong fear is that you may sue him or her, but you know you can't afford litigation, don't let the other party know this. If the main reason the other side wants to settle a consumer dispute with you is so you'll remain a good customer but you know you're moving to North Dakota next month, don't disclose this fact either.

Perhaps the greatest weakness of interest-based negotiation is that a sophisticated and ruthless position-based negotiator can take advantage of an interest-based negotiator who is too inexperienced to recognize position-based negotiation and to recognize the effective but deceptive techniques often used by its practitioners.

To avoid becoming a victim, it's important to know how the other side operates. Reading a book on position-based negotiation is a good place to start. A negotiation course could also help.

Almost any negotiator, even an interest-based one, expects some movement during the negotiation. So don't give your last-resort position at the beginning of the negotiation. For example, if the smallest amount of money you will take for your injury is $20,000, and you say at the outset that you want $20,000, almost any negotiator will expect you to come down considerably, to $15,000 or $10,000. Except in extraordinary circumstances, you *must* start higher than where you are willing to end. This is the essence of position-based negotiating: you say $50,000, the other party says she can pay you nothing. You say $40,000, she says $10,000. You say $35,000, she says $15,000. You say $32,000, she says $18,000. You say $30,000, she says $20,000 now and $4,000 in a year. You say yes (or no). Experienced negotiators know that it is usually possible to do much better than one's last-resort position.

In seeking more than you're willing to accept, don't feel you are limited to dollar amounts. In particular, consider making requests or demands for other things: property, an action you want the other side to take, an action you want the other side to stop. These need not be things that are important to you: if you (credibly) ask for things you don't need, you may be able to concede them to the other side and give the other side a sense of having gained something and a sense that you have moved a lot in its direction even though you have not given in much at all on what's most important to you.

Drawing on interest-based negotiation strategy, consider proposing concessions that you can make that cost you little but that help the other party a lot. Similarly, consider requesting things that the other party can easily give up but that mean a great deal to you.

There is one other reason to ask for more than you expect to get: you may just get what you ask for. Just as it is important not to overestimate what the other side will give you, it's important not to underestimate it either. Because the other side may know less about the case than you do, or even because the other side may know *more* than you do (perhaps it knows of a recent legal case you haven't heard of, or perhaps it has business plans that would be ruined if anyone got wind of your dispute), it may be willing to settle for more than you have expected. Or the other side may be very careless with its money (particularly if the other side is embodied by an insurance adjuster or other person who is deciding whether to give up someone else's money) or may have a deadline—even one unknown to you—that makes it more important to settle quickly than settle cheaply. So if you will take no less than $10,000 and think the case is worth $15,000 but you offer to settle for $20,000, you might just have that offer accepted.

If you want to make your first position your final position, make abundantly clear that your offer is your final offer and that you cannot and will not budge from it. Some prominent and highly successful negotiators use this tactic. If you use it, make your offer as credible as possible by backing it up with reasons for arriving at it. Whether making an initial offer or a final one, give strong reasons for arriving at the precise figure you are promoting. Especially convincing are numbers from objective sources: the *Kelley Blue Book* for used car prices, the Consumer Price Index for inflation rates. Also convincing are numbers from expert sources (doctors about the cost of surgery, appraisers and merchants about the value of property). If you are trying to prove your income, your most convincing source will be your own tax return.

Don't get so wrapped up in the negotiation, and its goal of settlement, that you agree to a settlement in which you give too much or receive too little. Before beginning a negotiation, calmly and deliberately set a bottom line. But be realistic. If, for instance, you are a claimant, don't set a bottom line that is too high. A bottom line is too high if settling for a lower amount would be a better outcome than continuing the dispute. In establishing your bottom line, consider all costs—including legal fees and expenses, time, vexation—of proceeding with the dispute.

Finally, before you engage in a high-stakes negotiation, practice in settings where it's okay to make mistakes. Consider taking a course in negotiation that involves role-playing exercises. You can also practice a lot on your own. Get together with a friend or relative, set up a fact pattern (your own case, another real set of facts, or something you make up), and play the role of a negotiator for one side. If you have time, try the same fact pattern but negotiate for the *other* side.

For practice, try both position- and interest-based negotiation techniques—not only in minor purchases and the like, but in one or two cases where you've been dissatisfied with a product or service, ideally cases that have turned from differences into disputes. You are especially likely to be successful when dealing with a company that provides a service almost identical to that provided by other firms: the company knows that if it doesn't satisfy you, you can easily go elsewhere. Many examples exist, particularly in the travel industry.

Practice, practice, practice. Soon you will be ready—and more confident—when there is an opportunity to negotiate the end of a dispute.

# 5

## How to Get the Other Side into ADR

Getting the other side into third-party ADR may be the highest hurdle you face. Presumably you have already tried negotiation and not been able to reach a settlement. You aren't getting along well with the other party, so why should he or she go along with your suggestion? Furthermore, the other side may never have heard of the ADR alternative you are suggesting or may be suspicious of it because he or she has never tried it or because you are suggesting it.

Ideally—assuming you want ADR—your dispute is covered by a contract, product warranty, or other document that requires this form of dispute resolution. If so, to initiate ADR, follow the rules in the document or get advice from any ADR organization that is specified. If not, it's still not too late to start ADR.

Review the ADR programs that are available in your area. If you are comfortable doing so, suggest one to the other side. But what if you feel you cannot bring this up with the other party, or what if the other party does not immediately agree to submit the dispute to mediation, arbitration, or some other form of alternative dispute resolution and instead wants to spend a few years and a small fortune on litigation?

Mediators and arbitrators, as well as organizations providing mediation and arbitration, commonly offer to contact the other party to suggest mediation or arbitration. So consider finding a mediator or arbitrator or service that makes sense to you and may make sense to the other party and asking that person or service to contact the other side. Remember, nothing prohibits you from asking a person who knows or may have influence over both sides—such as a friend or a member of the clergy—to suggest to the other party that the dispute be resolved outside the courts.

On the other hand, perhaps the problem is that your initial suggestion to the other party was not persuasive enough. If so, you should try to point out more effectively the advantages of ADR and the disadvantages of litigation. Nevertheless, in recommending ADR, you may face what some attorneys consider a major potential pitfall: that your suggestion will be seen as "a sign of weakness."

To avoid having your suggestion taken as a sign of weakness, it's important to imply in your approach, whether in conversation or by letter, that your case is strong and that you can afford to litigate. Don't overdo it, or the other side may think that you "doth protest too much": that your emphasis on your supposed ability to litigate into the next century shows that you will faint at the sight of a courthouse.

Here's a letter, or part of a letter, you might write, assuming it accurately describes your situation. This letter might be an initial effort to encourage ADR or might be sent after a more informal effort, such as a brief mention in a conversation, has failed.

Dear Mr. Respondent:

I regret that we have been unable to resolve our dispute. At first, I assumed that litigation was inevitable.

Recently, however, it has been suggested to me that this dispute might be resolved more rapidly if we were to refer it to mediation, with arbitration to be used in the event mediation is not successful.

I have reservations about this, as you may yourself. Nevertheless, if you believe an alternative to litigation may be appropriate, I would be pleased to hear from you by phone or letter.

If I do not hear from you within 15 days of today's date, I will assume that we will have no alternative but the courts.

Thank you for your consideration.

Sincerely,

Note that the letter does not mention what is perhaps the biggest selling point of ADR: its generally low cost. This is because mentioning it may signal to the other side that you can't afford litigation or that you believe litigation isn't worth the cost. This, of course, is a terrific way to encourage the other side (if he or she is a potential defendant) to wait forever, figuring that you can't force him or her into ADR and that you won't file suit. It is also a terrific way to encourage the other party (if he or she is a potential plaintiff) to sprint to the courthouse and file a lawsuit against you.

If you feel secure that the other party knows you have the money and the will to undertake litigation in this case, your letter might be more effective if the words "and inexpensively" were added to the second paragraph, so that it said:

> Recently, however, it has been suggested to me that this dispute might be resolved more rapidly and inexpensively if we were to refer it to mediation, with arbitration to be used in the event mediation is not successful.

If you are comfortable in dealing with the other side, or if a conversation turns in some detail to the advantages and disadvantages of ADR, you might point out that although litigation most likely would result in a decision that is acceptable to one side or neither side, mediation or a similar ADR alternative is designed to result in a voluntary settlement that is acceptable to both sides.

If you can get the other side to agree to arbitration, the American Arbitration Association (AAA) has a clause just for you:

> We, the undersigned parties, hereby agree to submit to arbitration under the Commercial Arbitration rules of the American Arbitration Association the following controversy: [cite briefly]. We further agree that the above controversy be submitted to (one) (three) arbitrator(s) selected from the panels of arbitrators of the American Arbitration Association. We further agree that we will faithfully observe this agreement and the rules, and that we will abide by and perform any award rendered by the arbitrator(s), and that a judgment of the court having jurisdiction may be entered on the award.

Here is a non-AAA clause you can use if you prefer mediation:

> We, the undersigned parties, hereby agree to submit to mediation the following controversy: [cite briefly]. The controversy shall be mediated by [write name of mediator or write "a mediator provided or suggested by (give name of organization, such as the American Arbitration Association)"] under [give rules, such as "the Commercial Mediation Rules of the American Arbitration Association," the rules of another organization, or "rules to be determined by the mediator"]. If, 60 days after the appointment of a mediator, either

party demands to terminate mediation and demands arbitration, the controversy shall be settled by arbitration in accordance with the Commercial Arbitration Rules of the American Arbitration Association, and judgment on the award entered by the arbitrator(s) may be entered in any court having jurisdiction thereof.

Here's another effective way to avoid litigation: *file a lawsuit*. Filing suit (and sometimes just believably *threatening* to do so, especially if you send a copy of the complaint—the document that, along with summons, begins a lawsuit—that you are ready to file) will likely have a big impact. It will show the other party that you are intent on proceeding with the dispute and will demonstrate that if ADR is not chosen, the other side will be sure to experience all the burdens of litigation.

The strategy of filing or threatening to file suit makes sense only if you can file or threaten a *valid* lawsuit. That doesn't mean your suit will definitely win, but that it has a reasonable chance of winning and therefore will not result in *your* getting sued for malicious prosecution.

After you file suit or send an unfiled complaint, the other side may decide that ADR doesn't sound so bad after all, especially if it has already been suggested. If the other party doesn't initiate ADR, you can always write the other party a letter similar to the one above—or, in the unlikely event you feel like it, give the other side a phone call—even though litigation is under way.

Filing suit might well move the case into ADR even if the other party has sworn that he or she will never try mediation or arbitration or any other form of ADR. That's because an increasingly large number of courts now routinely refer many of their cases, or all cases seeking money damages under a certain figure, to ADR, usually arbitration, with the arbitration award being appealable to the court.

Of course, the strategy of filing suit to promote ADR is not without risk. You may find that you have inflamed the other side into a passionate commitment to winning in litigation. You may find that the other side has consulted an attorney who either has stirred the party's passion for a fight or has given the party confidence that the lawyer can represent him or her in a successful countersuit.

Even if one of these scenarios arises, all is not lost. Emotions often cool over the months of a lawsuit and if you later want to drop the suit, you can.

The current dispute may make you want to avoid finding yourself in a future conflict with no way to ensure that the problem will be resolved through ADR. Unless you prefer to retain the option of litigation (there are excellent reasons to do so), you may decide to try to give your business only to firms that are committed by contract or policy to ADR. You can also write an ADR clause into contracts you negotiate. The American Arbitration Association suggests the following clause for contracts dealing with a business relationship:

> Any controversy or claim arising out of or relating to this contract, or the breach thereof, shall be settled by arbitration in accordance with the Commercial Arbitration Rules of the American Arbitration Association, and judgment on the award rendered by the arbitrator(s) may be entered in any court having jurisdiction thereof.

Before agreeing to AAA arbitration, call the AAA office in the major city nearest you and request and read its rules, which include its charges. If you want arbitration but by another specified service, refer instead to that service and its rules. If you want mediation, an effective adaptation of the AAA clause would be:

> Any controversy or claim arising out of or relating to this contract, or the breach thereof, shall be submitted to mediation. The matter shall be mediated by [write name of mediator or write "a mediator provided or suggested by (give name of organization, such as the American Arbitration Association)"] under [give rules, such as "the Commercial Mediation Rules of the American Arbitration Association," the rules of another organization, or "rules to be determined by the mediator"]. If, 60 days after the appointment of a mediator, either party demands to terminate mediation and demands arbitration, the controversy shall be settled by arbitration in accordance with the Commercial Arbitration Rules of the American Arbitration Association, and judgment on the award entered by the arbitrator(s) may be entered in any court having jurisdiction thereof.

Before agreeing upon a particular arbitrator, mediator, or organization, check on the rules and fees that such a person or organization would apply. Note that the American Arbitration Association charges significant administrative fees ($300 minimum); the arbitrators and mediators it suggests often charge their own, additional fees.

This clause may also be modified, and changing it will be particularly easy if you simply want to change the time limits or change the arbitration service. If you want to avoid the financial pitfalls of mediation or arbitration that goes beyond one day of hearing, it might well be wise to add this language to all of the clauses above:

The parties shall notify any mediator and any arbitrator of their intention to limit the mediation session and any arbitration hearing to one day each and shall limit their presentations and otherwise cooperate so that the mediation session and any arbitration hearing are completed in this period. If the session or hearing is not completed within one day, the mediator or arbitrator shall determine whether one of the parties is chiefly responsible for the continuation into a second day, and, if so, the party held responsible shall pay all costs incurred for and because of the second day of hearing, including any reasonable charges incurred by the other party for legal representation, food, lodging, and transportation.

# Lawsuits, Lawyers, and Joint Action

# 6

---

# Litigation and Lawyers

I was never ruined but twice
—once when I lost a lawsuit,
once when I won one.
                    —*Voltaire*

I must say that, as a litigant,
I should dread a lawsuit beyond
almost anything else short of
sickness and death.
                    —*Judge Learned Hand*

## LITIGATION

For some types of disputes and some types of disputants, litigation is the
best course. But generally it is to be avoided.

Litigation can be a black hole right here on Earth, absorbing most of
one's time and tens of thousands of one's dollars, so that even a victorious

litigant regrets ever getting involved. As of this writing, in large American cities, simple cases that go to trial consume $10,000 to $20,000 in legal fees and expenses, including travel, witness fees and expenses, phone calls, overnight delivery services, local messenger services, transcripts, and photocopying—lawyers like to charge 20 to 50 cents a page. Some firms even charge for word processing. Not uncommon are cases that take $50,000 to $100,000 in fees and expenses and five or more days of trial.

Cases do more than absorb time in trial. They absorb time coming to trial. In big cities the wait is *usually* three to five years. Even in rural areas, it is common to wait a year or more. Before the trial opens, plaintiffs and defendants spend great amounts of time—and money and anxiety—on pleadings (complaints, answers, and so on), motions, depositions (answering questions orally, with a court reporter recording the proceeding), and interrogatories (answering questions in writing). Even cases that don't go all the way to trial often are settled only after the extensive and expensive work of the above type has been performed.

Why does this happen? Part of the problem is the American legal system. Majestic in many respects, the result of centuries of British and American court and legislative experience and adjustment, it nevertheless provides lawyers with procedural options that can make the client's pretrial experience far more time-consuming, expensive, and vexing than the trial itself. Everything from a motion to dismiss to a five-day deposition can put every other aspect of your life on hold: forget about getting any work done, forget about spending time with your family, forget about your vacation plans.

Part of the problem is the explosion of civil litigation and criminal prosecutions (especially for drug offenses) despite limited government budgets. The number of court cases has grown far faster than the number of courtrooms. The result is backlog.

To make things worse, litigation proceedings are often highly combative, inducing in parties such emotions as anxiety, hostility, and fear and provoking such fantasies as killing the other side's lawyer, the client's own lawyer, or all lawyers in general. And even after paying the financial and emotional price of litigation, *you may lose.*

## LAWYERS AND JUDGES

Ralph Nader is a lawyer. So was Gandhi. Not all lawyers meet their standard. In fact, although lawyers as a group are part of the solution rather than part of the problem, lawyers are properly blamed for much of the cost, delay, and emotional pain of litigation.

Most lawyers are reasonably competent and reasonably ethical. Often, a lawyer will turn out to be just about the best friend a client has ever had. Nevertheless, lawyers are often justifiably criticized for arrogance, inattention to client needs, wanting to win at *all* costs, unreasonably high fees, incompetence, delay, undue aggressiveness, and plain old unethical conduct (lying, embezzlement, and the like).

How can incompetent or unethical lawyers stay in business? Isn't there regulation of lawyers? Yes and no.

A lawyer is just someone who has (in almost all cases) gone to law school and passed a bar exam. (Wisconsin admits all graduates of two schools in that state.) But in all states the clear majority of those taking the bar exam pass, and in some states almost everyone makes the grade. If a candidate flunks, he or she can take the exam as many times as is necessary to pass (a few have passed after a dozen tries). Although states make some effort to prevent admission of bar applicants of low moral character, the effort tends to be cursory: a superficial background check and a multiple-choice ethics exam that tests memorization, not morality. Once lawyers are admitted to practice, most states do a poor job of disciplining those who are incompetent or unethical. Disbarment is extremely rare.

What about judges? Although some are elected, most judges are political appointees. Republicans by and large appoint Republican lawyers who have given a lot of money or other help to Republican campaigns or who have been voted out of office and need a job. Democrats appoint Democrats with the same (but Democratic) attributes. Some political appointees turn out to be brilliant, sensitive jurists. In general, however, judges are not a great deal more able than lawyers as a whole. (But because they are under greater scrutiny, they are in general more ethical than lawyers as a whole.)

## JUSTICE

One might argue that while litigation is indeed painful, expensive in dollars and in time spent, and full of delays before a decision is reached, it at least guarantees justice. Unfortunately, this is by no means true.

Most lawyers are reasonably competent and reasonably ethical, and so are most judges, but even cases handled by such attorneys and jurists often yield unjust results. A judge's misreading of the law, a lawyer's inattention to one pivotal fact, a loophole in a statute—any number of factors can lead fair lawyers and fair judges to unfair decisions. In particular, a citizen may be morally right but be unable to prove it or unable to find a statute or previous case on which to rely.

Do you want to entrust your dispute to litigation, with its costs and delays, with its lawyers and judges, with its inability to guarantee justice? Sometimes you have no choice, and sometimes when you have a choice the answer should be yes. But when you have a choice, you owe it to yourself to inspect the alternative: ADR.

## LITIGATION: SOMETIMES THE BEST CHOICE

Litigation is an easy target. Lawyers are an easy target. Even so, sometimes litigation is the only course or the best course. It's the only course when: *you've* been sued, the court in which the case has been filed does not have a program in which it refers some cases to ADR, you cannot move the case to another court, or the plaintiff will not agree to any other way to resolve the dispute.

Even when you have a choice, litigation is sometimes the best course. When? When everything (including your sense of public duty) indicates it is in your best interests to use it. The advantages—and disadvantages—of litigation have been sketched in previous chapters in such sections as "Arbitration Versus Litigation" and "Mediation (and Conciliation and Med-Arb) Versus Litigation." Here's a review plus a bit more:

Litigation is appropriate—though not the only alternative—whenever a dispute requires maximum inspection, especially when the party who will prevail may depend on the consideration of hundreds of pages of documents or dozens of witnesses or both.

Litigation is the *only* alternative when the aggrieved person wants or needs to put maximum pressure on the wrongdoer in order to get the wrongdoer to do what the aggrieved person wants. Litigation means the defendant will almost certainly have to hire a lawyer and pay thousands of dollars in legal fees and expenses. Litigation means that even before any trial the defendant will probably have to have his or her deposition taken and therefore—under the dual burden of telling the truth but not saying anything that will hurt his or her case—have to answer questions posed by a lawyer whose sole purpose is to find weaknesses in the defendant's case.

Litigation means that if the case is not settled, it will go to trial, in which the defendant again will have to answer precisely questions posed by an adversarial attorney, only this time in public. Even when not testifying, the defendant will suffer the pressure of a spectator at a sporting event in which almost anything can happen and in which his or her financial security or reputation is at stake. Before and during the trial, the defendant will have to put his or her professional life on hold, missing work in general and key meetings and phone calls in particular.

The defendant's personal life will also suffer, as vacations are canceled and anxiety about the case creeps into life at home. As the plaintiff, you may suffer all these horrors yourself, although litigation is likely to be easier on the plaintiff than on the defendant, who must answer allegations against him or her and who is in the proceeding involuntarily.

One exception to the rule that litigation is the best way to pressure the other party into a fair settlement is the situation in which the most effective kind of pressure is the pressure of a prompt decision. For instance, if your adversary has been resisting your settlement overtures because he or she is temporarily unable to pay the amount you seek, litigation in a big city with a five-year backlog of cases is a good way to *allay* your opponent's worst fears.

Litigation is a powerful way *to hold the other party accountable*. If the other party has treated you poorly but has gotten away with it, never having to answer for his or her wrongdoing, a court and pretrial procedure will demand his or her attention. The defendant will have to show up in certain rooms at certain times and will have to answer your questions (presumably posed by your attorney).

Similarly, litigation is the *only* choice when you have a dispute with someone (and a dispute involving more than the dollar limits that apply to small claims court) and that person refuses to respond or refuses to respond substantively and in good faith to your demand for resolution of the conflict. You can't force the other person to negotiate with you, and you can't force him or her to go with you to arbitration (unless you have an arbitration clause in a contract with him or her) or to mediation. But you can force him or her to go to court. Litigation *requires* the other party to reply to you, and to reply promptly and substantively; in particular, the initial complaint, which, along with the summons, begins the lawsuit, typically must be answered in about 30 days.

Litigation is also the best move if it is important to you to establish a legal precedent on which people with future disputes like yours can rely. When an arbitrator makes an award or a mediator helps two parties reach a settlement, there is no official public record of the decision, and the decision is not binding on future disputants. When a state appeals court makes such a decision (this assumes your case is appealed, but most are not), all state trial courts whose cases might be appealed to the appeals court must follow that decision in similar cases. This has an effect not only on future cases but on future disputes that do not reach trial, as lawyers and others settle the disputes based on what they believe a court would decide if the disputes turned into lawsuits. It is therefore important for you to consider whether litigation in your case would help others.

Litigation may also be the best route to take if you want to begin a dispute resolution process but do not want a decision in the near future; if you are in this position, the delays of litigation can work in your favor. Delays can come in at least three forms: delays due to backlog in the courts; delays caused even when the court calendar is light (depositions, interrogatories, and even settlement meetings can take a great deal of time, particularly because busy lawyers find it difficult to find a time when both they and any necessary witnesses can sit down together); and delays either side can easily cause by undertaking procedures that are not absolutely necessary but are not prohibited: various kinds of motions, depositions of witnesses whose testimony might be useful but is unlikely to be pivotal, and so on.

Finally and most ironically, litigation can be the best way to move the case toward settlement negotiation or toward one of the means of alternative dispute resolution. The worse aspects of litigation—the costs it entails, the time it demands, the vexation it causes—are often its greatest assets. Because people want to avoid litigation, the threat or the filing of a lawsuit very often leads to settlement or to alternative dispute resolution processes such as arbitration and mediation.

Lawyers estimate that 90 to 95 percent of lawsuits are settled (this includes cases settled by negotiation and by other means such as mediation) or otherwise end before trial; therefore, although you may well benefit from raising the specter of litigation that proceeds all the way to a verdict, chances are your case will never go through a complete discovery process; if it does go that far, chances are still strong that it will be settled just before trial (deadlines have a way of getting people to do things they could have done months or years before). Even if a trial begins, the case may be settled between sessions in court.

So litigation has many advantages. If your dispute has some of the earmarks of a case that should be litigated, give litigation serious consideration.

## HOW TO SUCCEED

Do you want to know how to succeed in litigation? In most cases the simple answer is: hire a lawyer. Nevertheless, there are cases in which nonlawyers successfully represent themselves in litigation. Often they do so with the aid of self-help books. In almost all cases, however, these successful nonlawyers are involved in small claims court or traffic court. Appearing in these courts is a far cry from representing yourself in a complicated dispute in which you will be opposed by a competent attorney.

If you think you are one of the rare people who can act pretty much like a lawyer without being one—even in a complex, high-stakes case—

bone up on your task and check reality by doing two things. First, spend at least half an hour with the best, most ethical lawyer you can find (preferably one who doesn't need a single new client). Ask this lawyer whether you are capable of handling the particular case you are considering and ask what work you will have to do. Explain the facts and raise the key legal issues as you perceive them; the lawyer will discuss the legal issues as he or she sees them and will tell you what must be done—factual research, legal research, discovery, preparation of witnesses, conduct at the trial itself assuming there is one—given the specifics of your case.

If the lawyer has not dissuaded you from representing yourself, the second thing you should do is to go to a law library, become *very* good friends with the librarian, ask to see the best books on legal research, and from those books try to figure out how to do the research on the procedural and substantive law that relates to your case. Don't forget the "pocket parts" in the back of reference volumes: these bring the books up to date (actually, up to *year*). Before each key crossroads in the case— filing the complaint, deciding which witnesses to depose and what to ask them, and, if necessary, going to trial—check your strategy with the lawyer you met with in the first place.

# 7

---

# Should I Hire a Lawyer?

Except for matters handled in small claims court or traffic court, almost every litigated dispute demands representation by a lawyer. This is a good reason to try to move your case into one of the types of alternative dispute resolution described in this book. Even in ADR, however, it may be best to hire a lawyer.

Whether you are likely to be in litigation or in ADR, the question of whether you should represent yourself can best be answered only after you have considered your own abilities, the type of dispute resolution that will be undertaken, the substantive issues, and what is at stake.

On the other hand, you will in all probability need a lawyer if, for instance, you don't think well on your feet or feel that your emotions may take over in this particular dispute; if the case will be handled by binding arbitration that will involve depositions and interrogatories and, in the hearing, closely follow court rules of evidence (rules that determine what you can and cannot bring to the attention of the judge or arbitrator to prove your case); if fully understanding the issues requires expert knowledge of medicine or engineering or some other area about which you know no more than most people; or if the other side wants a large amount of money from you. The right lawyer can deal well with all the areas in which you are weak, including your lack of factual (not just legal) expertise: many lawyers have developed extensive knowledge in nonlegal areas such as medicine, product defects, and economics; they also know where to find and how to question expert witnesses.

Despite the importance of carefully examining your own strengths and weaknesses in a given dispute, the best single way to decide whether you need a lawyer—even in an ADR case—is to meet with a lawyer and ask the lawyer.

Certainly you want to consult a lawyer who is competent, and certainly you want one who is ethical. Equally important when all you want is brief advice on whether you need legal representation is to ask this advice of a lawyer *who does not need your business.* Nevertheless, try to find somebody who will be available if it turns out that the initial consultation is the first of many meetings.

So far, the discussion has focused on whether you *need* a lawyer. Still, there are nuances to be considered.

## YOU MAY NEED A LAWYER BUT BE UNABLE TO USE ONE

The rich can afford lawyers; the poor—depending on how poor they are and what kind of case they have—can sometimes get free legal assistance. Free legal assistance is offered mostly by legal services offices, sometimes called legal aid offices. To see if you and your case qualify for free legal help, check the white pages of your phone book under "Legal Services" or "Legal Aid." You might also ask the nearest bar association, listed in the white pages under the name of your county but not in the county government listings. An example would be "Kings County Bar Association."

If your income places you in the lower to upper middle class, you may not be able to afford a lawyer, particularly if legal fees and expenses are likely to be high and the amount (if any) you recover from the case is likely to be low. If you are not sure you can afford standard legal fees, ask the bar association and any nearby law schools whether nonprofit programs or for-profit legal clinics are available that may offer adequate legal assistance at lower than average rates.

If you conclude you need a lawyer but cannot afford one, you do not qualify for free legal assistance, and you cannot find a reduced-rate program or clinic, don't give up. There are at least three ways you may be able to continue with your case:

1. If you have sustained a personal injury or you have been harmed by the death of a close relative, and the injury or death has been caused by someone's negligence (lack of due care under the circumstances), you

have the type of case that almost always is handled "on contingency": the lawyer's fee is contingent on your winning some money and is almost always a percentage, usually 30 to 40 percent of the *net* amount won.

The net amount is the amount the other side is required to pay you, minus the legal expenses (costs such as deposition transcripts, photocopies, phone calls, and expert witnesses). In some states, statutes limit the amount of contingency fees; in some of these states, the percentage goes down as the amount recovered goes up.

It is important to note that *lawyers sometimes take cases on contingency even if they do not involve personal injury or wrongful death*. The main reason lawyers will take a personal injury case on contingency is that it is likely to bring in legal fees. This is usually because it is clear that somebody is responsible for and able to pay for the injury, and the main question is how much the injured party will collect. Therefore, when a lawyer decides whether to take any other kind of case on contingency, the key issue is whether the case will likely result in substantial damages and, therefore, a substantial contingent fee. If you have a clear-cut breach of contract case for high damages against someone with the ability to pay, you will be able—though perhaps only after a lot of searching—to find a lawyer who will take the case on a contingency basis. (Remember: if you happen to *lose* a contingency case, the lawyer may expect payment for all legal expenses.)

**2.** You may be able to get a lawyer to agree to "scale" his or her fee—to reduce it in light of your limited financial circumstances—or even to charge you no fee at all. Some lawyers and law firms have a policy of scaling fees; some that lack such a policy may still scale fees in a given case, depending particularly on how much time the case will involve, whether the subject matter is of professional interest to them or might bring an important benefit to the public, whether they like you (many attorneys have represented relatives and friends for free), and whether business is a little slow. Your case may fit within the tradition of *pro bono* representation, in which lawyers represent the poor or the public interest for free or at significantly reduced rates. A final, somewhat remote, possibility is that you have something of value to a lawyer that you can trade for services. Even if you do persuade a lawyer to take your case for a scaled fee or without charge, do not be surprised if you don't get as much effort or as much courtesy as those clients who are paying the normal hourly fee.

**3.** If you win a lawsuit, you may be able to recover your legal fees and expenses from the defendant or the government. In the early 1970s, the U.S. Supreme Court dramatically limited the kinds of cases in which legal fees can be recovered. Nevertheless, if a statute (a law enacted by the state or federal government) or contract specifically mentions the awarding of legal fees or expenses, you may be able to get them.

Even where a statute does not mention legal fees or expenses, some states provide for their award (by the state government) in cases where the plaintiff has acted as a "private attorney general": has undertaken a lawsuit that helps the public. Finally, some states permit you to recover attorney's fees and expenses if you are suing the other side for bad faith, such as when you sue your own insurance company for failing to pay you a fair amount for an auto accident for which your policy covered you.

If your case has a strong chance of resulting in the court's ordering the defendant or the government to pay you attorney's fees and expenses, you may be able to get a lawyer to represent you on contingency, for a scaled fee, or for free, with the understanding that the lawyer gets paid if you are awarded fees and expenses. Even if a lawyer will not agree to such terms, you may believe you can afford to hire a lawyer because you are likely to be reimbursed at the end of the case for the fees and expenses you pay.

## YOU MAY NOT NEED A LAWYER BUT SHOULD HIRE ONE

The fact that you are *competent* to represent yourself (for instance, in mediation or arbitration) does not mean that you *should* represent yourself.

A lawyer can save you a lot of time. If you are able to represent yourself—even to represent yourself as well as a good lawyer would—but your time must be spent elsewhere or could be spent more productively elsewhere, you may well want to hire a lawyer.

But there is more to it than that: turning the case over to a lawyer does not *eliminate* the time and work you must put into the case; it only substantially *reduces* this time and effort. If it would take you, say, 100 hours to handle your case and you turn it over to a lawyer, you will not save 100 hours. You must take into account the hours you still will have to put into the case. Consider this point when you evaluate how much money (in lost income) and how much trouble a lawyer can save you.

You will still have to talk and meet with the lawyer, find and organize documents and other evidence, show up when your testimony is needed (for instance, in depositions or at a hearing or trial), and *supervise* the lawyer. "Supervising" means that without being intrusive or otherwise offensive, you will have to make sure the lawyer is remembering the key points of the case, your own personal needs (for instance, for a decision or a settlement by the time you must pay certain bills or make a specific purchase), and the various deadlines that will arise (for instance, for filing a lawsuit before the statute of limitations has run out, or for answering a complaint).

And there are even more complications: (1) You will presumably have to pay taxes on your income from the hours you stay on the job instead of working on your case. (2) If yours is a business dispute, your legal fees and expenses will be deductible as a business expense, reducing your net legal costs. (3) Even if you represent yourself, there will be some legal expenses, such as for photocopying and phone calls. They may not be as high as if a lawyer represented you, because you will not undertake unnecessary expenses—as lawyers sometimes do out of a sense of caution—and because you will not charge yourself for profits (you will charge yourself five cents for a five-cent photocopy; a lawyer might bill you a quarter a copy or more).

On the other hand, a lawyer can save you more than money and time. He or she can save you a great deal of anxiety. In particular, the lawyer can handle most of the decisions that a layperson might make correctly but only after great difficulty in balancing the issues and only after great anxiety in worrying whether the decision is right. Typically, the lawyer will "handle" the decisions (be aware they must be made and carefully evaluate what decision to make) rather than *make* them, because most big decisions in the case should be brought to the attention of the client before they are made. Nevertheless, sometimes for better and sometimes for worse, lawyers generally like to "run" cases themselves, making as many decisions as possible and persuasively advising the client how to decide the questions that should be reserved for the client (such as whether to settle the case and how much to settle it for).

Hiring a lawyer also allows you to avoid dealing directly with the other party or, if the other party has hired a lawyer, with the other party's lawyer.

In grappling with all the issues that determine whether you will be represented by a lawyer, remember: even if you cannot or should not hire a lawyer, you may be able to gain many of the benefits of a lawyer without having one represent you. Even if a lawyer does not *represent* you, the same lawyer can *advise* you. The lawyer's involvement can range from discussing the case for half an hour to regularly consulting with you by phone and in person and attending any hearing or trial with you.

Similarly, a lawyer can represent you inexpensively if you ask the lawyer to make only one or two limited contacts with the opposition. Plenty of people of modest income have benefited from having a lawyer make a single phone call or having a lawyer send a single letter.

# 8

How Do I Find and Work with a Good Lawyer?

## FINDING THE LAWYER

It is easy to tell somebody to hire a good lawyer. It is much harder to find that lawyer.

Although fees and expenses are very important, the main things you want to know about a lawyer are whether the lawyer is highly competent in the area involved in the case, whether the lawyer is ethical, and whether you can get along with him or her.

You can interview a lot of lawyers and ask them whether they are competent to handle your type of case, but too many lawyers think they are fully capable of dealing with cases that would be handled much more effectively by someone with more raw ability or someone with more experience in the area in question. Yes, ask lawyers about themselves but, more important, carefully check out lawyers before you ever meet with them.

How? The fastest, easiest, and probably most accurate way is to ask people whose judgment you trust and who have had some experience with lawyers. As when checking out arbitrators, tell your sources that you will keep their advice strictly confidential, and follow through on your promise.

Ideally, ask lawyers about lawyers. If you want to check out a specialist lawyer, ask lawyers in the same specialty. Even if you want a plaintiff's lawyer (a lawyer who usually represents those making claims, not those defending against them), ask both plaintiff's and defense lawyers about the attorneys you are considering. A fellow plaintiff's lawyer may have formally or informally assisted in a case with your candidate; a defense lawyer may have faced your candidate in a negotiation or arbitration. If possible, also check with former or current *clients* of the lawyer.

Ask about overall skill and ask about experience in your kind of case. Your kind of case is a function not only of the *legal area* at issue, such as landlord-tenant or family or personal injury, but also of the *dispute resolution process* you believe will be used. If your case will go to mediation, you want a lawyer who has effectively represented clients in mediation; if your case will go to trial, you want a trial lawyer with a strong win-loss record; even if your case will likely require no more than a lawsuit that will be settled before trial, you still want a lawyer who has won a lot of trials. Your attorney's successful record in court may spur the other side to settle with you on attractive terms to avoid having to tangle in the courtroom with such a skillful lawyer.

Ask people you know about the lawyers who have represented them. What was the case about? What was the outcome? What did the lawyer predict about the case regarding outcome, how fast it would be resolved, and what the legal fees and expenses would be? How accurate did the predictions turn out to be? Did the lawyer ever lie to or deceive the client or the other side? Did the lawyer show up on time for meetings, depositions, hearings, and other events? Was the lawyer hard to reach by phone? If the client ever asked the lawyer about his or her strategy, did the lawyer give a good explanation?

Once you have some lawyers' names, you can do superficial research in the *Martindale-Hubbell Law Directory.* You can find it in any law library and in many general libraries. It lists virtually every lawyer in the United States; each volume's biographical section contains detailed information on lawyers who pay to be listed in that section.

As superficial as the *Martindale* information tends to be, it can tell you a lot. The year of first bar admission is worth noting. On complicated cases or cases requiring narrow legal expertise, you will generally want a lawyer who has practiced 10 or more years. If all else is equal, most lawyers will tell you to choose a graduate of a prestigious law school over a graduate of a law school you've never heard of. Some of the country's best-known lawyers, however, have come from some of the least-known law schools. Also, in some areas, graduates of local law schools have extensive contacts and other advantages.

It is important to find out what you can about skills not evaluated by the grades and Law School Admission Test scores that determine who gets into the top schools: skills in interviewing a client, counseling a client, researching a case, negotiating a settlement, representing a client in a mediation or arbitration or trial.

You will find little about these abilities in *Martindale*. At most, you will find a bit of information in the biographical section about certification in a legal specialty, articles published, or memberships attained; such information may indicate an interest or expertise in a particular area.

Just as you must consider the net financial impact of a lawyer in determining whether to hire one in the first place, you must consider this in deciding which lawyer to choose. Assuming your focus in the case is chiefly on your financial outcome, hire the lawyer who in the end will present you with the most money gained or the least money lost.

Far more complicated is figuring out what the net financial impact of hiring a particular lawyer will be. The lawyer with the lowest fee quite possibly is not the best choice. To find your best option, you must consider two main questions:

1. At the end of his or her representation of you in this case, how much will the lawyer have billed you in fees and expenses?
2. At the end of the case, how much money (and what else of value) are you likely to receive (or give up)?

To find the answer to the first question, ask each lawyer candidate how much he or she charges per hour. But that's only part of the picture. If, like most lawyers, the lawyer you talk with does not practice alone but is in a law firm, you must also ask whether other lawyers there would be involved in representing you and, if so, what their hourly fees are.

It's cheaper to pay $200 an hour for 10 hours than $100 an hour for 40 hours. So you must ask how many hours each lawyer at the firm will likely spend on the case.

You may end up wanting a specialist, and total fees are one reason. A lawyer who specializes in, for instance, entertainment law may be able to handle a case on copyright infringement much more quickly than a competent general-practice lawyer who has never represented a client in such a dispute. The entertainment specialist will know the fastest route to take; the general practitioner may try the same techniques he or she applies to other cases, only to find through dozens of billable hours of trial and error (and perhaps eventual consultation with an entertainment law specialist) that there is a more efficient way to proceed.

The specialist will previously have prepared briefs on the law of copyright, and coming up with a brief for your case may well be more a matter of word processing than mind-bending legal research. Similarly, the specialist may know right away whom to call as an expert witness, while the general-practice lawyer may take many hours finding the same expert.

In addition to fees, there are expenses. Ask the lawyer what will be needed in this case that will entail expenses, and what those expenses will be. Examples are court filing fees, transcripts of depositions, photocopies, phone calls, overnight delivery services, messenger services, travel by the lawyer, travel for out-of-town witnesses, and fees and expenses of expert witnesses.

Take notes on the more important information the lawyer gives you, and don't hide your note taking from the lawyer. The fact that you are taking notes may, in a relatively inoffensive way, make clear to the lawyer that you expect him or her to stay in at least the general vicinity of the estimated fees and expenses and that you have some evidence of what the estimates are. If you ever want to remind the lawyer of the estimates or want to protest a bill, your notes will give you a basis.

Unless you are on unusually good terms with the lawyer, you will probably lose more than you gain by asking for a written estimate. A lawyer is very unlikely to offer to give you a written estimate of fees and expenses, and many lawyers would be surprised if not offended to be asked to do so. Many would see the request as a sign of distrust. Often it is impossible to predict with precision the total fees and expenses in a particular case. In many instances, these depend to a great extent on events beyond the lawyer's control, such as what actions the other side takes and what information the lawyer turns up in the course of researching the law and facts of the case.

On the other hand, if you happen to have a good relationship with the lawyer, you might try to get the lawyer to write a short memo or letter to you outlining the lawyer's planned efforts (such as letters, filing of a lawsuit, and depositions), and fees (not just per hour, but total) and expenses for the case. If the lawyer wants to express his or her estimates in terms of a range of figures (such as "legal fees, $10,000 to $15,000"), that's more than many lawyers will give you and is a lot more precise than no estimate at all. Be tactful in making your request.

The analysis changes if you have a case likely to run up high legal fees and expenses, particularly $20,000 and up. Then you have more need and more right to ask for a written, reasonably precise estimate of fees and expenses. Ideally, this will be a budget, showing anticipated activities, hours for each, and fees and expenses for each. In addition, in more expensive cases, it is important to ask for a monthly accounting of fees, expenses, and activity. Similarly, you should ask the lawyer to let you know each time fees and expenses increase by a certain amount (for instance, every $5,000 or $10,000).

Let's now turn to the second question you must consider when calculating the net financial impact of hiring a particular lawyer: at the end of the case, how much money (and what else of value) are you likely to receive (or give up)? If you are taking action against someone else, you generally want to gain as much as possible, especially in money damages or in agreements to do or refrain from doing something. If someone else is coming after you, you generally want to lose as little as possible, preferably nothing at all (and you may want to make a claim against the party who has initiated an action against you).

The amount you receive or pay at the end of the case is likely to be much bigger and therefore much more important than the lawyer's fees and expenses. Would you rather receive $50,000 and pay the lawyer $15,000 or receive $25,000 and pay the lawyer $10,000?

Again, you must question the lawyer. What are the possible outcomes of the case? What are the chances of each outcome? Has the lawyer had other cases like this? Does the lawyer specialize in this sort of case? What sort of damages were paid in other cases like this?

It is possible that in replying to your questions the lawyer will speak in legal jargon or other terms unfamiliar to you. It is critical at this and all other stages of dealing with the lawyer that you know exactly what the lawyer is talking about. Tactfully ask what the lawyer means.

Don't limit your questions to money and expertise. Also ask how quickly the case is likely to get resolved. This will elicit information about the case and about the lawyer. If you need your case to be resolved in a timely manner and a lawyer says he or she will be glad to take your case but won't be able to move on it for two or three months because he or she has four trials back to back, you'd better find someone else. If the meeting gets a little conversational, ask the lawyer if he or she enjoys practicing law. If the answer is that it's gotten to be a real grind and that if the lawyer could make the same money doing something else, he or she would do so, the lawyer may dislike the profession enough to do as little as possible on your case (and pass it off as a fine job).

When you're in the lawyer's office, learn what you can from sources *other than* the lawyer. Look around. Look at the framed certificates. Where did the lawyer go to school? What awards has he or she won? What about memberships in professional organizations?

What about certifications in specialties? You may also learn something from the books on the shelf, the pictures on the wall; at least you may get some idea as to whether you and the lawyer have anything in common.

Regardless of what you've heard and otherwise learned about the lawyer, don't hire him or her until you've met with the lawyer long enough to confirm that he or she is right for the case and to confirm that you feel comfortable with the lawyer. This is someone with whom you may well spend many hours, on whose judgment your financial or family future may depend, whom you will have to trust with information you want to keep private. Only through a personal meeting, not a phone call, can you tell whether you are going to feel comfortable entering such a relationship with this particular lawyer.

What about legal clinics? These are the high-volume law offices, often operating as a chain, that in many cases advertise on TV. They usually charge substantially less than prestigious firms but deal chiefly in very routine matters, such as wills, divorces, purchases of homes, auto accidents, traffic citations, and bankruptcies. Clinics tend to provide lawyers who only several years ago were in classrooms rather than courtrooms. If your case is outside the routine areas or is in these areas but has unusual characteristics, be especially careful to check out the clinic *and the particular lawyer there who may represent you,* both through questioning others and questioning the clinic lawyer. Have the clinic and the lawyer handled many cases like yours (remember, this includes both the legal area and the dispute resolution process)? How many? With what results?

What about legal services or legal-aid groups? These generally charge no fee and are available only to the poor. They tend to handle only specified kinds of cases. Offices vary, but they usually handle matters such as landlord-tenant disputes, welfare problems, Social Security issues, consumer "rip-offs," and domestic violence. They usually refuse to handle disputes over matters such as auto accidents and contracts. In recent years, the quality of legal assistance provided by legal services offices has improved to the point where it is similar to that available in private firms. More than most private firms, legal services offices rely heavily on paralegals to handle tasks that do not require a lawyer's attention.

What about prepaid legal plans? These present a dramatic new trend. Almost unheard of 10 years ago, they now "cover" more than 30 million Americans, 17 million of whom are covered without further charge as members of the AFL-CIO. These plans are marketed to the general public mostly by large banks, credit card companies, and retailers.

Plans vary a great deal, both in cost and in coverage. Although those sold at low monthly rates to members of a group—such as holders of credit cards issued by a particular bank—imply in their advertising that they furnish good legal protection, this is hardly the case.

Prepaid legal plans marketed to the public tend to provide very limited coverage. They generally offer consultation, letter writing, will preparation, and little else, unless the subscriber pays for each additional service. Most plans severely restrict the subscriber's choice of lawyers: he or she generally must go to a member of the plan's "panel," but the panel may include only a few dozen lawyers in a sizable city and none at all in the smaller towns in which some subscribers live. If, however, the client cannot find an acceptable panel member, most plans will attempt to find a nonpanel lawyer who is acceptable.

The main advantage of the plans is that most restrict the fees of the panel lawyers for services not provided free. One plan, for instance, limits fees to $50 an hour, which will mean a huge savings for subscribers who need many hours of legal work in cities where typical fees are $100 to $250 an hour. On the other hand, depending on the plan, coverage may not be instant and may take too long to be activated for someone already involved in a dispute.

When considering a prepaid legal plan, do not sign up until you are sure that the panel includes one or more highly competent lawyers who practice in your city or nearby and who have successful experience in any legal areas and dispute resolution processes that concern you or may soon concern you. Furthermore, you should check to see whether the plan excludes representation in any legal areas that concern you or any dispute resolution processes (in particular, litigation) that you prefer to use. Also look for any exclusion for disputes and other legal matters that existed before you joined the plan.

What about lawyers who advertise on TV or in big display ads in the newspaper or phone book? Years ago, advertising was banned by state bars. Lawyers could be disciplined for taking out ads. Ads—beyond minimal listings in the Yellow Pages, under "attorneys" or "lawyers" and under legal specialties—are still shunned by most prestigious lawyers. Nevertheless, some very well regarded lawyers take out sizable ads in the Yellow Pages. Relatively few well regarded lawyers advertise on TV or in newspaper display ads. Anyone who knows how many offices some TV-advertising lawyers have knows that it is extremely unlikely that the handsome, confident lawyer you see on the tube is going to represent you personally. If you call the lawyer's office, in all likelihood you'll be referred to some other lawyer who will not inspire as much confidence as the TV celebrity.

## WORKING WITH THE LAWYER

Once you have made a choice, keep an eye on your lawyer. Talk with the lawyer frequently enough to keep him or her up to date on developments he or she may need to know and often enough to spur him or her to keep moving on the case.

If you have not yet received a bill, from time to time ask how much in fees and expenses you have thus far incurred. If the figures are higher than you expected, ask the lawyer to notify you each time fees and expenses aggregate to an additional amount of money, such as $500 or $1,000.

If the case seems to be costing more than estimated, immediately bring this up with the lawyer, courteously ask why, and ask what his or her *current* estimate is for total fees and expenses by the end of the case. If the estimate is unacceptable to you, say so. Be ready to explore alternatives, such as dropping the case, having the lawyer handle the case differently (perhaps less aggressively), having the lawyer assign more of the case to the lawyers in his or her firm whose hours are billed at a lower rate, and changing lawyers or law firms entirely. (Unless another lawyer can pick up where the first left off, however, changing lawyers might well increase your overall fees.)

Whether you are discussing the law and facts of the case or are asking questions about fees, always be totally honest with the lawyer and also be as candid as possible. Avoid statements that do not directly relate to the case and that would ruin your relationship with the lawyer (such as negative remarks about the lawyer). But if the lawyer is to handle your case effectively and in a way that pleases you (not exactly the same thing), he or she must have no false or misleading information from you and should have as much significant information from you as possible.

In particular, be candid concerning your special characteristics and those of your case about which the lawyer may not know but that he or she *should* know in order to help you as much as possible. Don't be penny-wise and pound-foolish, figuring you can't afford the lawyer's fees you will run up by adequately explaining your case.

If your current dispute is part of a long-standing bad relationship between you and the other party or between your family and the other person's, tell the lawyer. If you need money at maximum speed more than you need maximum money, tell the lawyer.

If you are a morning person and the lawyer wants to schedule an arbitration hearing that might extend to 6:00 P.M., tell the lawyer you'd make a better witness at 9:00 A.M. If you have a two-year-old and can find child care only in the afternoon, tell the lawyer that you would prefer to avoid scheduling a mediation session in the morning.

Do not phone the lawyer so frequently as to become a nuisance. Once every couple of weeks is about right for a case in which there may have been some recent change in the lawyer's efforts or your own experience but in which nothing critical is yet happening. If the lawyer seems annoyed with the frequency of your calls and if he or she consistently and for good reason has nothing to report—for instance, if you have chosen litigation, the case won't come to trial for a year, and there is no reason to expect a settlement offer from the other side—back off and call less frequently.

Write a list of the more critical points about your case, including factual issues, legal issues, and evidence. Many lawyers have more than 100 cases and can benefit from occasional reminders, particularly about things the lawyer has agreed should be done. Don't bring up too many points in one phone call or meeting, and, if possible, don't make it obvious you're using a list.

Bring up points on your list without suggesting that you fear the lawyer has forgotten them. If, for instance, you have a personal injury case but want to be sure the lawyer remembers you suffered not a new injury but rather the worsening of a preexisting condition, don't say, "You haven't forgotten that this is an exacerbation, have you?" Say instead, "Does the insurance company understand that we're not claiming I had no previous injury?"

Be considerate of the lawyer's schedule and the pressures of his or her career. If you call and your lawyer says she can only give you a minute because she has a trial the next day, don't say, "Listen, I pay you just as much as they do." Say, "I won't even take a minute. I know a trial takes a lot of preparation. Why don't you call me when you're done?" When she does call, ask her how the trial went. This way you avoid seeming like a pain and you come across as a client who is interested in the lawyer for more than how big a settlement check she can get for you.

Lawyers are human beings, and as such they respond about the way most people do. They work a little harder for and speak a little more frankly to people they like, and they are more likely to do the minimum—or less—for somebody they wish had never walked into their office. Unfortunately, like most experts, lawyers have ways of keeping you from knowing whether they are working hard and carefully on your behalf, ways of explaining delays as being the fault of the court or opposing counsel, ways of passing off bad results as inevitable results. If you establish a friendly relationship with your lawyer, you can have more confidence that when the lawyer is working outside your view he or she is working with real dedication to your interests.

The world often treats lawyers with great callousness. Clients frequently push them for results they may not be able to deliver and for hard and urgent work their schedules simply may not permit. Then, at the end of all the pushing, the same clients are likely not to offer a word of appreciation, figuring the fee will do quite well enough. Most lawyers can take it, but most warm a little or more than a little to the client who shows gratitude.

Often the best thing you can say to a lawyer is *Thanks!*

## If Things Go Wrong

What if you choose a lawyer and then things don't work out? If you simply have a personality conflict, you should pay the lawyer for his or her time, at the fees quoted. If the lawyer is behaving incompetently or unethically, you should fire the lawyer and, depending on circumstances, should probably pay only part of the bill or nothing at all. The best way to fire a lawyer is gently, because even an incompetent, unethical lawyer can cause a lot of trouble for somebody he or she doesn't like—trouble in the form of a lawsuit. If you're not sure a lawyer is acting competently or ethically, ask the opinion of another lawyer whom you have reason to trust.

You can also ask the local or state bar association (in some states called the state bar), and probably can do so without even mentioning the lawyer's name. At your request, the state bar association and probably the local bar association will send you a copy of the state bar's code of ethics, which you can use to evaluate your lawyer's conduct.

If your relationship with the lawyer is at an end and you think the lawyer has behaved incompetently or unethically, you may get something for your trouble (such as a return of fees) and may help other citizens if you make a formal complaint to the state bar association. The state bar association can take disciplinary action against the lawyer, although in most states the state bar disciplinary process is dominated by lawyers and very rarely takes strong action against unethical attorneys. If the lawyer has committed a crime, you should consider complaining not just to the state bar but to the police or the district attorney's office. Your duty to do so increases with the severity of the crime and how likely it is that the lawyer will continue his or her criminal conduct.

You went to the lawyer in the first place as part of your effort to resolve a dispute, but now you may have a dispute with the lawyer. Here, too, there is often a role for ADR. In particular, many bar associations offer mediation or conciliation of fee disputes.

These, however, may present you with new problems. In particular, if the program has lawyers as mediators, these lawyers may be all too sympathetic to a brother or sister attorney. Avoid entering a program dominated by lawyers if it is binding upon you. If it is nonbinding, you might want to give it a try.

If you have been badly harmed by the unethical or negligent conduct of your lawyer, you should consider hiring another lawyer. In fact, you may need *two* additional lawyers. One might handle your original case more effectively—if it's not too late. The other might represent you against your first lawyer. It is not easy to find a lawyer who will sue another lawyer for malpractice, but such specialists do exist, particularly in big cities.

# 9

## Small Claims Courts

If your dispute involves damages (money that might be paid by one party to compensate another party) of about $2,000 or less, if you're irrevocably angry at the other party, and if you have no patience with trying to find a more amicable form of dispute resolution, small claims court is the place for you. It may also be the place for you if you have tried something more friendly that has not worked. Small claims court does not deal with disputes involving more than a certain dollar amount, which ranges from $1,000 in several states to $15,000 in parts of Tennessee but is most commonly from $1,500 to $2,500.

Small claims court is the fast-food outlet of American justice. It has no time for complicated cases that require discovery, motions, or lots of evidence. Other than that, small claims court offers almost all the advantages of litigation and no possibility of extreme expenditures of time or money. In recent years, many states have dramatically increased their small claims limits (many by $500 to $1,000 or more), so small claims courts are becoming a better alternative for citizens with disputes involving substantial amounts of money but not enough money to make it reasonable to hire a lawyer and sue in "regular" court.

Small claims courts offer many benefits:

- You pay a filing fee that is modest—less than $20; in some states, less than $10.
- The trial will probably occur within two months of service of the complaint on the defendant and may well happen within one month.
- You do not have to hire a lawyer; in fact, some states *prohibit* attorneys.
- You do not have to amass a mountain of evidence; the court has no time for more than a molehill.

Although it deals with small claims, the court is often the scene of large amounts of anger and loud outbursts by the parties. If you want to take the bad guy to court, and your claim does not exceed a certain dollar amount, this is the ADR alternative for you. But if you want to get along with the other side after the dispute resolution process is over, small claims court is a good place to avoid. Try mediation or conciliation or "med-arb" (mediation-arbitration). Even arbitration is likely to be a little less hostile.


## STATUTES OF LIMITATIONS

Before reading further, answer two questions: Do you know what *statute of limitations* applies to your case? Do you meet it? A statute of limitations limits the time in which you can file a lawsuit for a particular kind of legal case. Except in claims against governments, it is rarely less than one year. For instance, in many states, if you have suffered a personal injury you must file within one year, but if you are suing for breach of contract you have four years (sometimes you have more time for a breach of a written contract than for breach of an oral one).

Potential sources of quick information on statutes of limitations include the small claims court clerk, the small claims adviser (assuming one is available in your area), and any attorney friends you may have. The *Martindale-Hubbell Law Directory* (see Chapter 1) has a good summary of statutes of limitations. You can find it in the last of the several *Martindale* volumes.

If you believe you have taken longer than the statute of limitations provides, do not immediately give up. First of all, you may have misunderstood the statute: you may think your year or two began running the day the defendant did something wrong, when in fact the clock did not legally start until you knew or should have known of the wrongdoing. Second, under certain circumstances, the court may grant you an exemption from the statute, but such exemptions are rare. Third, even if you are barred from small claims court (and therefore from other kinds of litigation), you are not excluded from voluntary means of dispute resolution, such as mediation and voluntary arbitration. Even if you cannot threaten the other party with small claims or full-scale litigation, he or she may be motivated to resolve the dispute—to calm the relations between the two of you or to settle once and for all who's right and who's wrong.

Even if you have a long time until the statute of limitations runs out, you generally should file suit promptly. If you take a long time, you, the other party, and witnesses may forget key facts. And the judge may wonder why, if something so terrible happened to you and you are so sure you're right, you didn't file earlier: delaying your filing may damage your credibility.

## PROCEEDING WITH A SMALL CLAIMS ACTION

To start a small claims action, phone or visit the nearest state (not federal) court that has "jurisdiction" over the case and where "venue" is proper. Small claims courts are usually part of what in many states are called district or municipal courts. A court with *jurisdiction* has the following characteristics:

**1.** It is located in the state in which the defendant resides or does business or in which any contract involved in the case was entered into or (in most states) in which any injury involved in the case occurred.

**2.** It hears cases involving damages in the amount you seek (a small claims court does not have jurisdiction in cases seeking money damages in an amount over the state's small claims limit).

**3.** It hears cases involving the type of subject matter that is in controversy in your case (typical small claims matters include breach of contract, claims by creditors against alleged debtors, landlord-tenant disputes, problems between neighbors, and claims for injury to people or property; they do not include divorce cases or tax cases).

**4.** It hears cases in which the plaintiff seeks the kind of result you want to obtain. All small claims courts will consider claims for money damages. Many will not grant other kinds of "relief," be it ordering an eviction; granting "equitable relief," such as "specific performance" of a contract (requiring a party to a contract to do what he or she agreed in the contract to do); or issuing an "injunction" (requiring a party to take or, more commonly, to refrain from, an action).

A court whose *venue* is proper is one that has jurisdiction and is closely tied to the case because of convenience or because of where certain actions took place. Proper venue usually is a court in the city in which the defendant lives or has business headquarters or the city in which any contract involved in the case was entered into or (in most states) the city in which any injury involved in the case occurred.

If you are suing a company whose headquarters are far away (especially if they are out of state), most states allow you to sue in any city in which the company does business. This can be a big advantage: you may be able to sue in your hometown, while a corporation (if it chooses to defend the suit rather than default or settle) will have to fly somebody out or hire a local attorney to represent it.

In your visit or phone call, talk with a clerk or someone else in the small claims division. Ask this person what you have to do to file a small claims suit, and request any materials that are available on how the small claims court works. Chances are the clerk will give you or send you a complaint form as well as basic information for parties in small claims cases.

These documents are designed for average citizens and generally are not hard to understand, though one or two parts of the form may be ambiguous enough that you will have to call the clerk and ask for clarification. As the plaintiff (the person seeking money or other compensation or some action to be undertaken by the defendant), you fill out the complaint form, giving some idea as to what the dispute is about, stating the amount of money you want (assuming you want money), and selecting a means of serving (formally notifying in writing) the defendant (the person from whom you are seeking money or something else) with a summons (a document ordering the defendant to appear in court) and a complaint (a document stating your claim).

Then you send the form back to the small claims court, together with a check for the filing fee and for the type of service you have selected. (Service by certified mail, acceptable in most states, is the cheapest; you can also have a friend serve the summons and complaint or pay for the services of a process server, a sheriff, or a marshal.) Plaintiffs are not permitted to serve papers themselves.

The court will send the summons and the complaint through the mail or to the party you have selected to serve these documents.

Within about a week or two—assuming whomever you select to serve the summons and complaint can find and serve the defendant—you will receive a notice from the court as to the date, time, and location of the trial. The time will probably be the beginning of a morning, afternoon, or evening session of the small claims court, so be prepared to wait along with all the other small claims parties who have been given exactly the same date and time. This can take hours.

Occasionally, a case that starts by being filed in small claims court is referred to other means of dispute resolution. To a growing extent, courts are diverting some small claims cases to alternative dispute resolution processes such as mediation, "med-arb" (mediation-arbitration), or arbitration. If your case is referred, you must try to settle it through the alternative means. If the case can't be settled that way, or if it goes to arbitration and you aren't happy with the award, you can appeal to the court for a small claims court *trial de novo,* a new trial not considering the evidence or results of the mediation or arbitration.

Another circumstance in which a small claims case becomes something else occurs when the defendant gets the case "transferred" out of small claims court into the state court in the same area (often called the district or municipal court; in New York City, called the civil court) that hears claims for dollar amounts above the small claims limit. In most states, the defendant can do this if he or she makes a claim against *you* (called a "counterclaim") for an amount above the limit. Some states require a judge's approval. In New York City, a transfer is allowed if the counterclaim is above the limit and both sides have attorneys; in the rest of the state, it is allowed only with the approval of the small claims court. In some states, a defendant can also get the case transferred if he or she wants a jury trial.

Let's assume your small claims case remains a small claims case.

At the appointed time, you show up in court. The other side may not—this happens in many small claims cases. Absent unusual circumstances, a defendant failing to appear loses by default. If the other side does appear, the court, in the person of a judge or court administrator, hears the case. Usually the judge will ask you to speak first, with the defendant going second. You tell what happened and why you think the defendant should give you what you want.

Some small claims courts rarely award anything but money, but if you want something else, such as an apology or the taking or stopping of some action, there's little harm in politely asking for it. Given how important the dispute is to you, you will have amazingly little time to make your case. It may be one minute; it may be five minutes. If you get wordy or deal with matters that the court does not believe are very relevant (related) or material (significant) to the issues to be decided in the case, the court will likely interrupt you, perhaps in midsentence. If you know the law that applies to your case, cite it. But keep in mind that small claims courts often do not apply the law strictly and may award damages to a person who simply has been treated unfairly, even if the law does not precisely cover this plaintiff's case.

You will be allowed to provide—or may be asked to provide— documents (such as receipts or contracts) to back up your case. You will be permitted to present witnesses who can testify as to what happened that gives you the right to seek money (or something else) from the defendant. Ordinarily, as in more sizable litigation, you will ask questions of the witness. Then the defendant will be allowed to ask questions of the witness. (Some judges require that the questions be on the same subject matter you brought up.)

To a greater degree in small claims court than in "real" court, the judge may ask more questions than he or she permits you to ask. Furthermore, the court will not tolerate a parade of witnesses or witnesses whose testimony will take a long time. In some cases, especially if the judge believes a particular witness has presented no relevant evidence, the judge may save time by not permitting the other side to question the witness.

Next, the defendant will be given a chance to answer your accusations and say whatever he or she wants, but within the same time constraints. The defendant can also present documentary evidence and witnesses at this time.

The whole trial to this point will have taken about 5 to 30 minutes.

Finally, the court will issue a decision. It may render it "from the bench" (that is, right at the end of the trial), or the judge may think about the case and have the clerk mail you the decision, usually within a week.

If you have won a judgment saying the defendant must pay you money, your problems are not over. First of all, some losing defendants appeal the judgment. (In some states, the plaintiff, since he or she has selected small claims court in the first place, is not permitted to appeal. In some states, an appeal may be made only if the amount in question is more than a certain dollar amount. In some states, the appeal may be made to deal only with issues of law, not fact. In some states, no appeal is permitted.) An appeal is unusual but not exactly rare. The appeal in most states results *not* in a review and possible reversal of what happened in the small claims court but in a new trial (as explained earlier) by the district or municipal court itself. If such a trial occurs, you are in real, live litigation and almost certainly should hire a lawyer, at least for advice and maybe—especially if the amount in question substantially exceeds the amount the lawyer says you will have to pay in fees and expenses—for representation.

If you have won the case, and even if there is no appeal, you still must collect the money, and you must collect it from somebody who didn't like you before, likes you a lot less now, and may not have the money. In most cases the defendant will just send you the money, but sometimes you will have to attach the defendant's wages, arrange for a sale of the defendant's property, or take other coercive action.

All this—from filing suit to collecting after a decision—makes sense if you want to, or are willing to, punish the other side not just by winning but through the procedure itself. Suing somebody, even in small claims court, is in most cases an offensive, startling act.

This book treats small claims court as a type of ADR because it is an alternative to full-scale litigation. Nevertheless, it should be clear by now that it is indeed litigation, an aggressive form of dispute resolution that can cause pain and destroy relationships. For this reason, you may want to resort to it only after you have unsuccessfully tried more amicable forms of ADR, such as mediation or conciliation.

## SMALL CLAIMS COURTS VERSUS LITIGATION

This is a self-contradictory phrase, in a sense, because small claims suits *are* litigation. But they are not litigation as people usually think of litigation: there is little in the way of time, expense, and formality, and relatively little in the way of damages (money to compensate you for a wrong) you may receive.

### Advantages

Small claims court is so cheap it's almost free. It is a relatively informal process. Hearings occur promptly and are short. Decisions are made quickly. Unless you think for some reason that your dispute, however small in money at stake, can set an important legal precedent, there is almost no reason for taking to district or municipal court a case that could qualify for small claims court.

### Disadvantages

Small claims court is inappropriate if your case requires complicated or detailed explanation or evidence. It is also the wrong place to go if you seek a binding precedent that will help other plaintiffs in the future: small claims decisions are not published. Neither are district or municipal court decisions, but they are more likely to be appealed to appellate courts, whose decisions are published and are binding on lower courts within their areas.

## HOW TO SUCCEED

The first thing to do is to make the right decision as to whether small claims court is for you. It may at first glance appear not to be right but in fact be right. For example, if you have a dispute worth $3,000 and the small claims limit is $2,000, you may quickly figure that you're outside the court's jurisdiction. But if small claims otherwise makes sense for you, you may do well to make a claim for the jurisdictional limit of $2,000 and write off the $1,000. This makes sense particularly if more amicable means of dispute resolution, such as mediation, have been refused by the other side or seem inappropriate for the case and it would cost you more than $1,000 to have a lawyer represent you in district or municipal court.

Similarly, small claims court may appear to be right but not be. You may be tremendously angry at the other side and unable to imagine that your adversary could agree to settle the case on reasonable terms through negotiation or mediation. Millions of successful negotiations and mediations indicate that you could be wrong. Mediation has a particularly good chance of calming down the parties and encouraging them to settle a case instead of going through even the brief adversarial vexation of a trial.

In evaluating whether small claims court is right for you, remember the key point that although more amicable means of dispute resolution require a settlement to which both parties agree, small claims court requires only that you win; further, keep in mind that you can win even by default; and further, remember that a very large proportion of small claims defendants fail to show up in court and thereby default. (In certain cases, they can prevail upon the court to reschedule the case, but if they didn't show up the first time they probably won't bother with this.)

Also consider that small claims court may work not so much in itself but as a prod to get the case settled. Many people who morally should pay a claim will do nothing until they're forced to. They don't want to pay, or they can't easily afford to pay. But a summons and complaint, even a small claims summons and complaint, compel their attention. You just might get a phone call, from the defendant or his or her insurance company, if an insurance policy does or may cover your damages. You may get an acceptable offer without further effort, or you or the defendant may end up successfully suggesting negotiation, mediation, or some other form of dispute resolution.

Give some thought to the possible date and time of the trial. If you know certain dates are convenient to you, ask the court clerk how you might ensure that you get a particular date. (You may not have too much choice; many small claims courts hear cases only one day a week.) It may be that all complaints received the week you file will be scheduled for trial in, say, three weeks. Such predictability would permit you to wait to file your complaint until a time when cases are being scheduled for a week convenient for you.

Also consider time of day. Many courts at least once a month hold small claims court at night. If an evening trial would be convenient for you, think about requesting that.

Ask the court clerk whether there is more than one judge or court administrator who hears small claims cases. If so, check out the possible judges as to bias (see the discussion of bias in Chapter 1), then ask the court clerk how you might ensure having your case heard by the judge or administrator you think is most likely to decide in your favor. For instance, perhaps the judge you want is the only one to preside over night court trials; you would therefore request night court.

Before the trial, or in filling out the complaint form, you may have questions that the clerk cannot answer or—if you require legal advice (applying current law to the facts of your particular case)—that the clerk will not answer. The clerk should at least tell you—if the materials the clerk gave you do not—whether there is a free small claims adviser service available to you. Now available in only a minority of states, this service, usually staffed by law students, paralegals, or young lawyers, will be able to give you some advice, especially on questions that come up over and over about small claims court procedures.

Learn what you can about the law that applies to your case. Ask friends. Visit a law library, local library, or bookstore, and consult books and articles on your type of dispute. In a law library (these tend to be operated by law schools, counties, and bar associations), you may find a law librarian with the time and inclination to explain how to do basic legal research on your case.

If you want highly specialized advice, or better advice than you may get from a law student or inexperienced lawyer, or legal advice about how current state law (with few exceptions, small claims courts apply state law) applies to your case, go to a lawyer. This is yet another example of where you can benefit from a lawyer without being represented by one. If, as is true in most states, your state permits representation by a lawyer, give some thought to hiring one.

Before the case comes to trial, gather any evidence you need (receipts, contracts, and so forth) and make at least one copy, so you can give it to the court without giving up your only copy. Bring the original to court, particularly to resolve any question as to whether your copy is an accurate copy. In the interest of courtesy and fairness (and especially because your courtesy and fairness may impress the judge) you should make a copy for the defendant as well.

Decide who would make a good witness for you. Don't expect the court to tolerate more than one or two witnesses. Ask the witness to appear on your behalf. If the witness is unwilling and you still want him or her to appear, ask the court or the small claims adviser how to go about subpoenaing the witness (requiring his or her appearance).

For the trial, wear business clothes and ask your witnesses to do the same. Judges are used to being treated with respect, and business clothes imply respect. In addition, most people, fortunately or unfortunately, seem more credible in business attire. Speak in correct English, not slang. Address the judge as "Your honor." If the judge tells you to do something or not do it, follow his or her order unless it's very important to contest it.

If you win and the other party fails or refuses to pay, get advice from the court clerk or the small claims adviser or both as to how you can coerce payment, through wage attachment, sale of the defendant's property, or other means.

See Appendix B for a list of small claims dollar limits in each state.

# 10

---

# Private Court Systems

Private court systems are the new limousines of ADR. New, because among alternative dispute resolution forms they are the newest: few existed before the early 1980s. Limousines, because these for-profit services are rightfully perceived as a way for the affluent to luxuriously cruise the fast lane right past common citizens stuck in traffic in their balky old cars (lawsuits) or taking the bus (high-volume mediation and other ADR services offered at no cost or low cost).

You might also use the common slang and call them "rent-a-judge." This system permits those who can afford to do so to pay for a retired judge—or practicing attorney—to hear and decide their cases. Most cases take one to three hours. Most private court systems also offer mediation.

Sometimes the "courtroom" is in a building owned or rented by the private court system. Sometimes it seems like a "real" courtroom because it is—the private system rents a real courtroom from the county, state, or federal government. Sometimes it is a conference room in the office of a lawyer or insurance company.

If the parties require a jury, private courts can provide that as well. Despite controversy, some states permit private court systems to require citizens to serve on their juries, just as real courts require citizens to serve there. Often, there is no disclosure to the citizen—who is poorly compensated for the time taken from work or other activities—that he or she is serving in a private, not public, court.

Although the parties may agree on abbreviated pretrial proceedings, private courts are available to consider the full array of pleadings and motions and to supervise the full array of depositions and interrogatories.

Private courts issue a written decision. As with real courts, the decision can even be appealed, except that the appeal sometimes is also within the private court system. Such an appeal is heard by a panel of retired judges (often judges with appellate experience) or practicing lawyers or both. Sometimes appeals are heard by the public courts.

Private court systems operate in most of the United States. Perhaps the best known is Judicate, headquartered in Philadelphia, employing more than 600 former state and federal judges in 49 states, and available in most cities in the country. (Judicate will send judges most anywhere; also, litigants can travel to cities in which Judicate judges ordinarily work.) The firm specializes in what it calls "standard judicial hearings": short nonjury trials (usually a single session of three hours or less) in which a Judicate judge presides and in which strict rules of evidence may not be observed.

Also well known is Judicial Arbitration and Mediation Services. It has offices in all major West Coast cities and many smaller ones.

It should go without saying that in trials administered by private court systems, the citizen may be and usually is represented by a lawyer. In fact, because these systems can present the same complications and technicalities as real courts, it is the rare citizen who can present a case in a full-scale or even abbreviated private trial without a lawyer's help. On the other hand, it is important to emphasize that private court systems usually also offer nontrial services such as mediation, and that in such processes a citizen may do well without legal representation.

Private courts are either expensive or cheap, depending on how you look at it. While public courts charge a filing fee, there are no hourly charges. Private courts charge per hour or per session, and they don't come cheap. Judicate charges *each party* $240 for a one-hour session (the most common) and $540 for a three-hour session ($150 per hour plus a $90 filing fee). On the other hand, because private court systems offer abbreviated trials and mediation—both of which take far less time than full-scale trials—the client may save a great deal more in lawyer's fees than he or she pays to the private court system.

If time equals money and if a public or private trial is the only acceptable way to resolve a dispute, the private court system can undeniably save the parties huge amounts of money. If the local courts are sufficiently gridlocked, the private trial will come months or years before the public trial ever could.

## PRIVATE COURT SYSTEMS VERSUS PUBLIC COURT LITIGATION

Private court systems are controversial. The most common criticism is that they are a haven reserved solely for the affluent. Irving R. Kaufman, former chief judge and now senior judge of the U.S. Court of Appeals for the Second Circuit (which includes New York City), puts it this way in his November 1988 article in the *Wall Street Journal*:

> It has been argued that private judging establishes an unfair dual justice system. Often dubbed "Cadillac justice," private judging creates a situation where the wealthy can avoid the burdens of the public courts and purchase speedy and, for them, relatively affordable justice. Can we expect low- and moderate-income Americans to maintain their respect for the rule of law and the fundamental fairness of judicial intervention if we allow justice to become just another commodity?
>
> . . . The unspoken message of a dual system is that while justice is blind and available to all, it is readily accessible only at a certain monetary price.

Prominent San Francisco public interest lawyer Robert Gnaizda says, "It provides a deluxe form of justice to some while condemning the middle class and the poor to an increasingly inferior legal system."

Recognizing that—if both parties agree at the beginning of the case—a private judge's decision can be appealed in the public court system, Gnaizda also complains, "How can you allow someone to get a five-year head start in litigation and in appeal?"

But there are answers to the critics. Former judge Daniel Kelly, co-founder of Judicial Resources (since acquired by Judicial Arbitration and Mediation Services), said the service he helped found was "not just for the rich kids." He cited a 1987 case in which Judicial Resources settled a personal-injury dispute involving 15 plaintiffs. The plaintiffs received $6 million and paid just $1,800 for the company's services.

In early 1989, however, Robert D. Raven, then president of the American Bar Association, saw another problem: that high fees would motivate judges to leave the public courts and hire themselves out as a rent-a-judge. "I believe in alternatives but there needs to be a balance," he said. "People pulling themselves out of the public court system won't have the incentive to work for the reforms that our legal system so desperately needs."

Judge Kaufman raises another troubling objection:

> Especially when it involves cases raising novel legal issues, this
> form of conflict resolution serves only private advantage, not the
> public interest. The law cannot respond to changing times and
> technologies if the disputes these developments engender never pass
> through the courthouse doors. This latter concern may also mar-
> ginalize the role of the courts in our communities. As certain types
> of cases are removed, the public courts could become specialized
> arbiters of law in areas with little tangible impact on a majority of
> the citizenry.

Sidney Wolinsky, another San Francisco public interest lawyer, brings
up still another problem, one that applies not only to private court
systems but to all for-profit dispute resolution firms, including those
specializing in arbitration or mediation: "Poorer plaintiffs are often
pushed too hard by corporate defendants to mediate or arbitrate their
claims, forcing them to either pay mediation fees they can ill afford or let
the other side pay, which leads to bias."

This is a realistic concern. Public court judges do not earn more
money if they are assigned more cases, and their decisions—and therefore their biases—are a matter of public record. But private court systems
and for-profit ADR firms keep their client lists and other information
confidential. The citizen who is asked to trust these firms cannot find out
whether his or her corporate adversary has previously hired the same firm
and whether that adversary has done well in its previous cases there. (Of
course, one wonders how many corporations would go back to a private
service if the service's judges or arbitrators consistently made big awards
to consumers.)

## Advantages

Beyond the controversy, there are definite advantages to citizens, even
nonaffluent citizens, in using private courts. As noted, when the only
alternatives are the private courts or the public courts, private courts can
save a great deal of time. Time can equal money.

Time can also determine whether the dispute can be resolved *at
all.* The saying that "Justice delayed is justice denied" is especially true
when a party or witness is near death or when the future of a business cannot be planned until a decision is rendered by a court or
other neutral. It is more likely that a private trial can be held more
quickly than that a public court will agree to requests to specially
expedite a particular case.

In addition, the quality of judges may be better in the private system than in the judicial system. Public court judges, especially at the trial level, are, of course, usually appointed or elected before they have had any full-time experience deciding cases. They are usually lawyers who have worked on election campaigns, made big campaign contributions, or otherwise gained the gratitude of partisan politicians (especially those who can make appointments).

Private court systems, however, can evaluate a judge's record *as a judge* before engaging him or her. Judges known to be unskilled or highly biased will not likely attract clients to the private court service and therefore are unlikely to be hired in the first place. Moreover, the parties must agree to use a particular private court judge, so a party need not accept one he or she perceives as being incompetent, unfair, or lacking adequate expertise in the subject matter of the case.

Private court proceedings are almost always closed to the public. Some parties will see this as letting them have their cake and eat it, too. You can maintain confidentiality but obtain a judicial hearing and decision. This is a particularly valid objective when confidentiality will protect the parties (as in a divorce case) but not damage the public (which needs to know who is discharging toxic wastes and who is making defective brakes, but does not need to know which party contributed more to the breakup of a marriage).

Another advantage of the private court system is that it can save time not just in shortening the period before a case is heard but in providing a trial that itself is relatively brief. While public courts generally offer nothing but full-scale litigation, private courts specialize in abbreviated trials: the parties can have their dispute decided by a judge, can have the general procedures of a trial, but need not spend a week where an afternoon will do.

It is also important to note that because the parties must agree to use a private court system and must agree on a specific judge, the dispute is often handled in an atmosphere of cooperation and efficiency not usually seen in the public courts, where parties and lawyers often do not know each other and have never agreed on anything, and where much time is often lost in fights over procedural and factual issues not significant to the final resolution of a case.

### Disadvantages

As discussed, it costs more to use a private court system than it does to pursue a case in the public courts. (Nevertheless, private court systems may not mean higher costs *overall,* especially when time is money.) Public-minded litigants may feel embarrassed to use an elite system while others must struggle in the clogged courts. They may also be troubled by the potential adverse impact on the interests society has in the setting of legal precedents and in the strength of the public court system.

The individual faced with the choice between private courts and public courts should typically focus on the following key questions:

1. Are the alternatives really limited to private courts and public courts? Would nonprofit (or for-profit) arbitration or mediation accomplish an equally acceptable result at a lower cost?

2. Given your financial position and the issues (including money) at stake in the case, will the private court, with its high per-hour fees, save you more (money, anxiety, time) than it costs?

3. In view of the specific public courts (and judges) and private courts (and judges) available to you, is one system (because of the quality of judges or a private service's possible bias toward corporate and other regular users of the system) more or less likely than the other to result in a decision favorable to you?

4. Because of the elitism of the private system and its potential adverse impact on the public interest, would you be more comfortable in the public courts?

## HOW TO SUCCEED

How to succeed in a private court system depends on what you mean by success and on the particular service you seek from the private system. Strategies vary greatly, depending on whether the private system will be providing full-scale litigation, an abbreviated trial, or mediation.

If what you seek from the private service is adjudication of full-scale or abbreviated litigation, your biggest concerns will be to find the right lawyer and to work effectively with that lawyer.

# 11

---

# Joint Action

Joint action isn't orthodox ADR. But you need to know all your significant alternatives to typical litigation. And for some disputes, the best move is joint action. Often, however, this joint action involves litigation—not necessarily typical litigation, but, for instance, a class action or a series of small claims actions. Joint action can also take place outside the courts.

Most forms of dispute resolution, traditional and alternative, assume there is one adversary on each side. This is not necessarily the case. A person seeking justice may be more likely to prevail if he or she organizes a group or joins a group fighting for the same cause.

People will join groups if they have been injured in a similar way or if they see a possibility of benefiting in a similar way. Plaintiffs who join forces to file a class action lawsuit seeking damages for similar injuries from the same product are motivated by both reasons.

Joint action *is* a type of dispute resolution. It also *uses* various types of dispute resolution. Examples of joint action *being* a type of dispute resolution occur when citizens get together to strike, picket, boycott, sit in, write letters, make phone calls, issue press releases, lobby government officials, draft legislation for potential passage by legislators and enactment by government executives, draft an initiative for enactment by the electorate, promote a referendum on a legislative issue, or initiate the recall of a public official.

Examples of *using* other types of dispute resolution occur when citizens form or join groups and pursue arbitration, mediation, or litigation (including small claims litigation as well as traditional and private court litigation). The appropriate type of joint action depends on the nature of the problem and on the group of people involved.

When you are faced with a dispute—or just a conflict that might turn into a dispute—ask yourself whether others may be engaged in the same kind of dispute or troubled by the same kind of problem. If this is the case, working with others may well reduce your costs, increase your chances of success, and increase the impact of your success, because more people will be affected and because actions of groups of people are more likely to draw media attention than the actions of individuals.

## CLASS ACTIONS

Class actions are lawsuits brought in the federal or state courts by groups of people who are "similarly situated": people who have suffered similar injuries caused in a similar way by the same defendant or group of defendants. Cases are initiated by a "representative": a plaintiff with a claim similar to that of other members of the class. These members are notified. If they do not take advantage of an opportunity to "opt out" of the class, they are bound by the decision in the case.

Good examples are the class actions brought against major automobile manufacturers by consumers who have had to pay for expensive repairs necessitated by the failure of the same part in the same year and model car.

To qualify as a class action, a case must satisfy four requirements:

1. **Numerosity.** The representative (the person proposing to initiate a class action) must show that the class (the group of prospective plaintiffs) is too numerous for "joinder" to be practical. (Joinder is the uniting of several lawsuits into a single suit.) Because the number of prospective plaintiffs is not the only consideration, courts have certified classes as small as 13 and refused to certify would-be classes of 1,000.

2. **Commonality.** The representative must show that members of the prospective class share identical or similar issues of law *or* fact.

3. **Typicality.** The claims or defenses of the representative must be typical of those of the class. Courts have often stated that the representative cannot use a class action to gain what he or she could not gain alone. The key issue is whether there is a "sufficient nexus" between the

representative's claim and the claims of the class. Various courts have said this phrase means "sufficient homogeneity of interests," "co-extensive interests," sharing a "common element," or having a "common legal grievance."

**4. Adequacy of representation.** The representative must fairly and adequately protect the interests of members of the class. Without this, it would be unfair for parties who are not active in the case to be bound by its results. The court may deny the class if the representative has an interest in not proceeding with the case or in not pursuing benefits for absent class members. Some courts have required that representatives show financial resources adequate to finance the prospective litigation. The representative must show that the lawyer(s) who will represent the class have adequate qualifications, including experience.

Cases involving automobile defects are only one type of the limitless variety of cases that can be brought as class actions. A recent issue of *Class Action Reports* listed cases in these areas:

Antitrust
Attorney's fees
Civil-political rights/liberties
Consumer credit
Consumer fraud/warranty/contract
Derivative actions (suits by shareholders against corporate
    management)
Employment discrimination
Inmate rights
Labor/wage/pension
Legal ethics
Mass accidents/diseases
Securities
Social welfare/entitlements
Taxpayers
Utilities

Beginning in the mid-1970s, U.S. Supreme Court cases have made it harder to qualify as a "class" and more burdensome and expensive to pursue a class action. As a result, the number of class actions filed in the federal courts plunged from 3,584 in 1976 to 610 in 1987. Nevertheless, state courts have taken up some of the slack, particularly in the wake of a Supreme Court ruling that under certain circumstances class actions can be filed in state courts even though they involve plaintiffs from more than one state.

Despite the burdens of class actions, such lawsuits can be worth the effort of the plaintiffs who initiate them. (Plaintiffs who join later and who are not part of the initiation and organization of the case bear far lesser burdens.) Of course, this is especially true if each plaintiff stands to gain large damages.

Despite the greater attractiveness of the case with huge damages, some class actions have succeeded despite claiming very small damages per plaintiff. In an antitrust class action against Rainbo Bakery Products and others, 245,387 consumers received checks averaging $9.60 (restaurants and others also won damages), and the total settlement fund exceeded $6 million.

Although many attorneys argue that cases for small per-plaintiff damages should not be filed because costs of the case may exceed the damages, this is not necessarily true. Of the fund in the Rainbo case, only 23 percent was consumed by attorney's fees ($1,047,925) and claims administration costs ($330,197).

Class actions comprise a highly specialized area of law and should not be entrusted to an attorney who has not successfully litigated them before. To locate such an attorney, ask lawyers or law professors in your area for names of attorneys with class action experience. You may also want to go to a library and read about lawyers in *Class Action Reports* (see Appendix D).

## SMALL CLAIMS COURTS

You might think small claims courts are only for individuals. You might be wrong. First of all, a small claims case can be filed by more than one plaintiff against the same defendant. More important, plaintiffs whose aggregate claim far exceeds the small claims limit ($1,500 to $2,500 in most states) can sometimes file many separate claims. For instance, if 100 neighbors each have suffered $2,000 in damages as the result of noise from an airport, and if they are convinced they must file suit, they still need not endure the burdens of full-scale litigation. Instead of combining their individual claims into a joint claim for $200,000, each can file a $2,000 small claims case against the airport. Even with separate claims, they can help each other by developing and sharing evidence, by jointly hiring a lawyer for advice (you'd be amazed how little a lawyer costs when you divide the fee by 100), and in other ways.

In fact, many neighbors in the vicinity of San Francisco International Airport did sue the airport in a series of individual small claims cases.

They won more than 100 judgments on the same day. And there is nothing that prohibits them from filing again for noise damage occurring after the period for which damages were sought in the original actions.

## INITIATIVES

If you are the victim of or simply concerned about a statewide problem whose resolution might attract the support of a majority of the electorate—a problem such as high auto insurance rates or inadequate state legislative efforts to discourage smoking (and thereby to reduce the state's expenses in caring for those with illnesses caused by smoking)—your best move may be a state initiative campaign. For example, in 1988, California, the state most active in this area, enacted initiatives mandating a reduction in auto insurance rates and requiring an increase in the cigarette tax.

For information on initiatives in your state, contact the secretary of state in your state capital. Find out what is required; in particular, you will find that you must get a certain number of petition signatures by a particular date. The number of signatures is generally a percentage of the number who voted in the most recent state general election.

Many cities also permit local initiatives. If your problem is citywide but not statewide, or if you don't have the resources or the interest to organize a whole state, check with your city hall or county clerk to determine whether initiatives are permitted to enact city ordinances. Find out how to qualify for the ballot: in particular, as with statewide initiatives, you will have to get a certain number of petition signatures by a certain date.

## COALITIONS

Joint action can be action by a group of individuals or by a group of groups. The latter kind of group is called a coalition. The West Coast Regional Office of Consumers Union has prepared a packet of materials for the training of advocates. Although the packet is aimed at coalitions, much of what it says applies equally well to groups of individuals. This packet says that coalitions present three advantages:

**Strength in numbers:** Whether you are educating the public or lobbying public officials, any advocacy project is more effective when there are more people involved.

**Strength in diversity:** Different types of groups (health, parent, religious, etc.) have different bases of public and political support. A coalition is much stronger if it draws together groups not usually seen as partners.

**Broadened skills and expertise:** Different groups also have different talents and knowledge to bring to a project. This gives your effort a broader collection of skills (media, organizing, policy) and a fuller sense of how to address the problem.

The packet proceeds to list five "Tips for Making Coalitions Work":

1. Avoid formal structure unless necessary.

2. Understand each group's constraints: all organizations have internal rules that need to be respected.

3. Delegate responsibility: coalitions, whether of groups or individuals, work best when each member has a specific task for which responsibility is assumed.

4. Make key decisions as a group.

5. Keep everyone informed: maintain a complete mailing list and send out updates on an ongoing basis to keep the broad coalition informed. You will also likely have a core group of key advocates who should meet regularly to steer your project.

## PUBLICITY

Much of the power of joint action lies in the power of publicity. People working together naturally attract more attention than individuals, and the very fact that dozens or hundreds of people are upset about the same problem makes it difficult for the opposition to claim that the complainer is just a lone lunatic. In addition, people working together can afford much more time and money than an individual can to stand on a picket line, prepare and deliver press releases, contact members of the media, hold press conferences, and appear on radio and TV.

Publicity tends to illuminate the issues in a dispute and to end the dispute itself. The bright light of publicity educates and warns the public about the problem you are suffering and may also draw media attention to problems similar to it. And few corporations, small businesses, and government officials will not rapidly act to reduce or end an activity they are undertaking and know is harmful once that activity begins to receive a great deal of attention in newspapers and on news programs.

## JOINT ACTION VERSUS LITIGATION

### Advantages

Costs are dramatically lower in a joint action than in litigation. In fact, there may be no monetary costs at all. Unless you are the leader of the group, time and emotional energy expended will also be drastically less than if you fought the battle yourself. In fact, the *esprit de corps* may make joint action *fun,* while individual litigation is usually a vexing, lonely experience.

Joint action can bring about dramatic change in days, even hours. Litigation that results in settlement rarely is completed so quickly, and litigation that goes to trial generally takes one or more years.

Most important, if the opposition is susceptible to the pressure and publicity created by a group of adversaries, joint action may well be more likely than litigation to bring about the desired result. This, of course, is true particularly when your case is based more on fairness than on a precedent in statutory or case law.

### Disadvantages

A major drawback to joint action is that you do not have complete control over how your case is presented. Even if you founded the group, someone else, well meaning or just ambitious, may take it over and use ineffective strategies, change the purposes, or use the group mostly to promote his or her career or other personal goals. Nevertheless, if this happens, chances are you will still be able to drop out of the group and go your own way, which means you will have lost little but time.

## HOW TO SUCCEED

To ensure that your goals are pursued and that your strategies are used, it is critical to become a leader of your group or to select leaders who not only will do a lot of work but will be worthy of being followed. Too often groups are led by those who have the time or inclination to do most of the work, even if these people aren't qualified to make decisions.

It is also very important to seek group members with whom you are highly compatible and with whom you as a disputant have very similar interests. Otherwise, because of the high stakes and high anxiety often involved in disputes involving groups of people, conflicts will likely arise over what goals should take priority, which firm or agency or individual to attack, what strategies and tactics to employ, how much money to spend, whom to hire (especially whether to hire a lawyer and which lawyer to hire), and other issues. The number and heat of these conflicts will be reduced if you join with compatible people who share your interests.

As with disputes involving individuals, it is critical to choose the right kind of dispute resolution. Don't become so wrapped up in the dispute itself or the governance of your group that you fail to focus on the costs and benefits of traditional litigation versus alternatives such as arbitration and mediation.

For disputes involving governmental processes such as initiatives, referenda, and recall, contact the secretary of state regarding statewide efforts and contact your city hall and county clerk regarding those affecting only your city. Ask specific questions and request general materials, including pamphlets.

## A Note About Initiatives

If you want to mount an initiative campaign and you live in a populous state, you are almost certainly out of your league. Organizing and winning initiative campaigns in big states is extremely demanding, extremely specialized work. This does not mean you should drop out. It means you must contact professional political organizers who have waged credible (and preferably successful) initiative campaigns in your state before. Your secretary of state's office should be able to give you the names and addresses of those who sponsored successful campaigns in the past. If that doesn't work, ask one of your state legislators for help in locating the people behind previous initiatives.

## A Note About Publicity

Key elements of publicity are press releases and press conferences. All too often, inexperienced citizen activists make an impressive argument or mount an impressive demonstration, only to have next to no impact because there is no media coverage.

A press conference is optional, although it is ideal if you want to answer questions. A more visual event, more attractive to TV, may be preferable. A press release can be more critical. If well written, it will help the media understand the issues involved as well as notifying the media of your events.

Several days in advance of your event, contact newspapers, magazines, and radio and TV stations that may be interested in covering it. If possible, direct your press releases (and any phone calls) to specific, named people.

Prepare the press release with letter-quality type. Double-space. At the top write "FOR IMMEDIATE RELEASE" (if the media can print or broadcast the information as soon as it wants) or "FOR RELEASE [for instance] SATURDAY, JANUARY 10, 1:00 P.M." Next, give the name and phone number of a person the media can contact for more information (this person should be capable and *available*). For example, "Contact: Aileen Activist, (312) 555-1234." Then write and underline a heading in the same style as a newspaper headline. For example, "CONSUMERS PROTEST CAR DEALER'S REPAIRS."

Do not write the body of the release in essay fashion. Write it like a news article. That's the way it's done—to do otherwise will look unprofessional. And it's done that way to enable newspapers to print all or part of the release with minimal changes (easy for the paper, good for you). To learn newspaper style, carefully check over newspaper articles. In particular, write in the "inverted pyramid" style: with the most important information at the top, the least at the bottom, all organized so an editor can easily shorten the article simply by cutting from the bottom up. Answer the classic journalism questions: who, what, why, when, where, and how. Make all your paragraphs short, preferably one or two sentences. Keep the whole release no longer than the longest space a periodical could plausibly devote to it. In general, keep it at one to three double-spaced pages. If you have short documents (such as detailed explanations or previous newspaper articles) that persuasively support your case, you can staple them to the release.

To increase the chance of getting your event covered, try to hold it when there is relatively light competition from other news events. If all else is equal, hold your event on a Saturday or Sunday. These are slow news days, and an event that might make page 18 if it is held on a Tuesday might sneak onto the front page if it is held on a weekend.

# Selecting and Succeeding in Dispute Resolution

# 12

---

# Which Type of Dispute Resolution
# Is Right for Me?

Following is a chart that *roughly* summarizes many of the distinctions between the types of dispute resolution emphasized in this book. Along the vertical axis are alternatives for resolving your dispute. Along the horizontal axis are most of the main characteristics that can vary from one type of dispute resolution to another: cost; waiting time until trial, hearing(s), or session(s); length of trial, hearing(s), or session(s); whether a lawyer is permitted to represent—not just advise—you and, if so, whether he or she is likely to be worth the cost or is even essential; whether the result is binding; whether the result is appealable; whether the dispute resolution process holds a real possibility for preserving the relationship between the parties; and whether the process is highly public.

An additional characteristic that is not included here (because it has already been discussed repeatedly) is whether the result of the dispute resolution process may be binding on other courts and other disputants. As you already know, the only means of dispute resolution offering this possibility is public court litigation.

On each axis, lines separate the categories. The lines form boxes, each symbolizing the conjunction of a dispute resolution type (for instance, "mediation") and a characteristic (for instance, "cost: free"). A word or phrase in each box indicates how often the characteristic describes that type of dispute resolution: "always," "almost always," "usually," "occasionally," "rarely," "hardly ever," and "never."

In this chart, "mediation" includes "conciliation" as well as what this book defines as mediation. "Private court litigation" means just that: full-scale or abbreviated trials, not the mediation services that most private court systems also offer.

A chart can give only rough guidance. There are so many dispute resolution programs even of a given type (such as mediation or arbitration) that a particular chart entry (such as "rarely" where it indicates mediation sessions are rarely long) will prove quite inaccurate for some programs. For instance, in a particular divorce mediation program it may by no means be "rare" to have a dozen or more sessions, each lasting an hour or more.

With this chart, you can quickly assess the *usual* characteristics of a type of dispute resolution you are considering for your dispute. Similarly, if you are looking for one or more particular characteristics—for instance, low cost and a substantial chance of keeping the parties on speaking terms—you can look for dispute resolution types that sport an "always," "almost always," or "usually" under "free" or "cheap" and under "may well preserve relationship between parties."

| Cost | | | |
|---|---|---|---|
| Fees and/or expenses paid to lawyer and/or dispute resolver such as court or mediator | | | |
| | Free | Cheap | Moderate | Expensive |
|---|---|---|---|---|
| Public Court Litigation | Rarely | Rarely | Occasionally | Usually |
| Arbitration | Occasionally | Occasionally | Usually | Occasionally |
| Mediation | Usually | Occasionally | Occasionally | Rarely |
| Neighborhood Panels | Almost always | Occasionally | Hardly ever | Hardly ever |
| Small Claims Court | Rarely | Usually | Rarely | Rarely |
| Private Court Litigation | Hardly ever | Hardly ever | Occasionally | Usually |
| Joint Action | Usually | Occasionally | Occasionally | Rarely |
| Negotiation | Usually | Occasionally | Occasionally | Occasionally |

| Waiting Time | | | |
| --- | --- | --- | --- |
| From start to trial, hearing(s), session(s), etc. | | | |
| | Fast | Moderate | Slow |
| Public Court Litigation | Rarely | Occasionally | Usually |
| Arbitration | Occasionally | Usually | Occasionally |
| Mediation | Usually | Occasionally | Rarely |
| Neighborhood Panels | Usually | Occasionally | Rarely |
| Small Claims Court | Usually | Occasionally | Rarely |
| Private Court Litigation | Occasionally | Occasionally | Rarely |
| Joint Action | Usually | Occasionally | Occasionally |
| Negotiation | Usually | Rarely | Rarely |

| Length | | | |
|---|---|---|---|
| Of trial, hearing(s), session(s), etc. | | | |
| | Brief | Moderate | Long |
| Public Court Litigation | Rarely | Occasionally | Occasionally |
| Arbitration | Rarely | Usually | Rarely |
| Mediation | Usually | Occasionally | Rarely |
| Neighborhood Panels | Usually | Occasionally | Rarely |
| Small Claims Court | Usually | Occasionally | Hardly ever |
| Private Court Litigation | Rarely | Usually | Occasionally |
| Joint Action | Occasionally | Usually | Occasionally |
| Negotiation | Usually | Occasionally | Rarely |

| Lawyer as Representative, Not Just as Adviser | | | |
|---|---|---|---|
| | Prohibited Except to Represent Self | Permitted and Worth Cost | Essential to 99 + % of People |
| Public Court Litigation | Never | Almost always | Almost always |
| Arbitration | Never | Occasionally | Occasionally |
| Mediation | Rarely | Occasionally | Rarely |
| Neighborhood Panels | Never | Rarely | Hardly ever |
| Small Claims Court | Occasionally | Occasionally | Rarely |
| Private Court Litigation | Never | Almost always | Almost always |
| Joint Action | Never | Occasionally | Rarely |
| Negotiation | Never | Occasionally | Occasionally |

| Other Factors | | | | |
|---|---|---|---|---|
| | Decision or Settlement Binding | Decision or Settlement Appealable | May Well Preserve Relationship Between Parties | Highly Public |
| Public Court Litigation | Always | Almost always | Rarely | Almost always |
| Arbitration | Usually | Occasionally | Rarely | Rarely |
| Mediation | Usually | Hardly ever | Almost always | Rarely |
| Neighborhood Panels | Usually | Hardly ever | Almost always | Rarely |
| Small Claims Court | Always | Usually | Rarely | Almost always |
| Private Court Litigation | Always | Usually | Rarely | Rarely |
| Joint Action | Rarely | Almost always | Occasionally | Usually |
| Negotiation | Usually | Rarely | Almost always | Rarely |

# 13

---

# What If Someone Comes After *Me*?

Most of this book assumes that the reader has been treated unfairly and has the option of going after the other party or doing nothing, as well as the option of using one type of dispute resolution or another.

Nevertheless, the time may come when, rightly or wrongly, someone will make a claim against you. The other person may talk about ADR, but more likely, the claim will hold the possibility of turning into a lawsuit. Or, like countless Americans before you, you may be surprised by a process server's handing you a summons and complaint when you had little idea that anyone wanted to go so far as to sue you.

Even if you are surprised by a lawsuit, stay calm. Many people sue other people just to get their attention and to move them toward settlement. And a lot of lawsuits are unwinnable or ask for damages that are 10 or 100 times what a court would likely award.

In addition, the parties and lawyers responsible for lawsuits often do not really believe everything stated in the lawsuit (the complaint) or the documents filed in connection with it. In particular, lawyers often make exaggerated allegations that their clients have never fully approved. They also often deny contentions made by the other side that they know are probably true but have not yet been proven; again, in doing so, they do not necessarily represent the thinking of their clients. So if you receive a complaint or other legal document that seems to indicate that a person or individual or company dislikes you or doesn't believe you, the document may not represent the true thinking of either the lawyer or the client.

## DEFENSE STRATEGY

Defendants can commonly benefit from the very characteristics of litigation that most people see as major disadvantages. Cost, time, and vexation discourage claimants from filing lawsuits, from pursuing them with great care and vigor, and sometimes from pursuing them at all.

If you are of limited means but have reason to expect to have enough money in the future to contest the lawsuit, or if you simply don't have time right now but will have time in the future to go to legal war, the delays of litigation will "suit" you well. In other words, the case will likely move slowly even without your making any effort to impede its progress, and every competent attorney knows how to delay a case.

But you must understand that delays often are the enemy not only of the claimant but of the respondent as well. As a respondent, you may want to get rid of the anxiety of the claim, particularly if there is the possibility of having to pay a lot of money or suffer other consequences that would be difficult to bear. You may want to clear your name, a name that may have been soiled by newspaper accounts of charges made against you or of a lawsuit that has been filed.

You may not want to slowly hemorrhage money, a thousand dollars here, five thousand there, as litigation takes its long and winding course. Litigation delays sometimes come free of charge, or free of much charge, as when one side or the other asks to delay a deposition or a court appearance and the other side readily agrees. More often, however, they come at substantial cost. Even to make nothing happen—to get a delay—may cost you fees and expenses as the lawyer makes phone calls, dictates letters, and makes motions to the court.

To delay a case through extensive "discovery" can easily run past $10,000 in lawyer's fees plus expenses ranging from expert witnesses to court reporters. You may have to spend a lot of time in consulting with your attorney, doing research on the case, or appearing at a deposition.

Many state and federal courts have responded to the litigation traffic jam by creating programs that require cases to move very quickly. At this writing, most of these programs are experimental, but the sense is that the experiment has worked. Lawyers and judges therefore expect these programs to be adopted in more and more areas.

Often called "Fast Track," these programs do not so much change the rules as require strict adherence to them. In particular, they make it hard—not easy, as it has been—to get "continuances" (postponements).

If a complaint must be answered in 30 days, absent rare exceptions it must really be answered that fast. If discovery must be started in 60 days, the parties cannot extend this deadline on their own: they must get the judge's approval, and the judge probably won't give it. Cases that could have taken five years now take one year—or less. "Fast Track" makes it hard to use the strategy of delay.

Most people like "Fast Track," but some don't. Among the arguments for it is that it promotes settlement. In the traditional system, parties can present a tough facade but still not spend serious money and time until three to five years later, when the case is about to come to trial. Under "Fast Track," however, parties who don't really want to go to trial must move quickly toward settlement. Among the arguments against "Fast Track," surprisingly, is that it *does not* promote settlement because parties don't have time to carefully consider and reconsider the case as it plods haltingly through each of many stages, and they don't have time to cool off: the lawsuit is filed, and (relatively) suddenly, the parties find themselves in trial.

Whether or not you face a "Fast Track" lawsuit, you may find that the best defense is a good offense. Just because somebody has come after you does not mean you cannot strike back, and strike back with more force than you have felt. So if somebody has sued you, you can sue the other side right back.

Most commonly, this is done not in another suit or another court, but in the context of the same litigation. Let's say the Middlesize Corporation has filed a complaint against you for breach of contract. You file a counterclaim, in some areas called a "cross-complaint," against Middlesize for fraud, breach of contract, and breach of the implied covenant of good faith and fair dealing (a covenant that most courts infer from all contracts). While the company has sued you for general damages of $100,000, you counterclaim for general damages of $1.5 million and punitive damages of $2 million. That should get its attention. But remember that your counterclaim must be reasonable, not something more or less made up for strategic reasons. If your counterclaim is without merit, you could face another suit—for malicious prosecution.

Also remember that in some states there is a "compulsory counterclaim" rule. This means that if you have a "cause of action" against the other party (a basis for suing the other party), and this cause of action stems from the same events or relationship as the original case, you *must* make a counterclaim as part of the same case or forever lose your opportunity to sue the other party for causes of action stemming from the events or relationship.

Even if the case has begun in ADR or moved to it, your best defense may still be a good offense. Suppose Nancy Neighbor thinks you play your stereo too loud, and you've agreed to mediation. There's no reason you can't bring up the fact that she repeatedly parks her station wagon in your driveway *and* that she parties with friends who end up drinking in your front yard at all hours of the night *and* that she promised to mow her lawn frequently but now has grass tall enough to hide a basketball team.

If the other party has gone so far as to file a lawsuit, counterattacks such as these will make especially clear to the other side how much he or she stands to lose from litigation (not just the costs and time and vexation, but also extensive damages from a counterclaim). Once educated in this way, the onetime single-minded plaintiff may begin to see many advantages to ADR, particularly the processes of mediation and negotiation, in which no settlement can be reached without both parties agreeing to it. This is unlike litigation, in which a judge or jury, for good reason or bad, can reach a verdict so costly as to send the party not to the original lawyer but to one specializing in bankruptcy.

## GIVING THE CLAIMANT WHAT HE OR SHE REALLY WANTS

Whether or not you really did anything wrong, you may be able to get out of the claim more cheaply than you think. The claimant will almost certainly settle for less than he or she has originally sought, either because the claim is inflated or because the claimant or the claimant's lawyer will realize that a bird in the hand is worth two in the bush, especially because it costs money and time to go after the two.

Less obviously, the claimant may want something else more than what he or she *says* he or she wants. Usually, people say they want money. And they do. But often they want something else as much or more. And often that something else is something you can give up a lot more easily than money. When people make claims, and especially when they sue or demand arbitration, they often are angry. They may feel they have been insulted. If you can make them feel better, you may be able to get them to drop the claim or to settle for something other than money.

What the claimant may really want is an apology. Maybe you have harmed the claimant, but what really irks the claimant is that you have refused to admit that you were in any way at fault. The words "I'm sorry" or "I apologize" could save you thousands of dollars.

Back in the 1970s, a legendary Hollywood entertainer felt he had been defamed by a major motion picture. He sued for $500,000. The case proceeded to depositions. Even after three years, the entertainer would not settle for less than $250,000. But the lawyer defending the famous director of the film thought the entertainer's wounded pride could be pivotal. On the occasion of the entertainer's seventy-sixth birthday, the lawyer suggested that the director send a card saying that he respected the entertainer, that he meant no offense, and that he apologized for any ill feeling he might have caused. He further suggested that the card enclose a settlement check for $7,600: $100 for each year of the entertainer's life. The director followed the lawyer's advice. The entertainer was happy with the card and accepted the check as settlement of the suit.

Still, be careful with apologies: if you have not already admitted you did something wrong, words such as "I'm sorry" could be held against you. You may want to consult a lawyer. You may prefer to use the words "I regret," which imply you feel bad that something happened but may not imply that you feel you are responsible. Regardless of which verb you use, try to apply it to the subjective experience of the claimant, not to anything you may have done or failed to do. Better to refer to "the anxiety you have felt" or "how much you have suffered" than "the damage to your property that I caused."

What the claimant may really want is respect. Perhaps what really has made the claimant angry is that you have seemingly insulted the claimant or the claimant's family or the claimant's abilities in an occupation or avocation. If so, there are ways to assure the claimant no disrespect was intended. "You really did a terrific job of painting the inside of our house," you might say. "I've seen the work of a lot of painters, and yours is the best. But the reason I feel I can't pay you the full amount you want is that I didn't want the bathrooms painted, only the living room, the bedrooms, and the kitchen."

Still, what the claimant may really want is the very money he or she has requested. Even *here,* there may be alternatives. Perhaps you have some influence in the industry in which the claimant works or wants to work. If your dispute with the claimant has nothing to do with his or her abilities or ethics, you may offer to hire the claimant or to recommend him or her for a position or an assignment that may not only pay as much as the claim but provide the claimant with career advancement (for a discussion of interest-based negotiation, see Chapter 4).

### Communication

Let's say you want to convey your apology or your respect, or you want to offer the claimant a way to make money without taking *your* money, or you more generally just want to find out what's really bothering the claimant and what his or her underlying interests are. It may be best to talk directly with the claimant rather than to the claimant's lawyer or through your lawyer. If you don't have a lawyer, fine. If you do, the other side's lawyer (if any) can't ethically talk directly with you, but you can still talk directly with the other side. The other side may tell you to address all communications to his or her attorney, but if you are gracious at the beginning of your call or visit, you may get your foot in the door.

Just establishing communications can make a revolutionary change in a dispute. It's difficult to intensely dislike someone with whom you're having a civil conversation. You may find the claimant warming to you and making suggestions for ending the dispute. Whether or not this happens, the claimant may react well to your statements of apology or admiration or to your offer of alternative means of compensation. Whether in response to your questions or more voluntarily, the claimant may also explain just what it is that he or she thinks happened and just what it is that really made him or her angry.

Even if you are not prepared to give the claimant anything, it may help you a great deal to communicate with him or her. In particular, it may help both parties if you respectfully ask the claimant to tell you precisely what he or she believes is the problem. You may be able to show that what the claimant thinks happened didn't happen, or that you're not the one responsible, or that you didn't mean any offense. On the other hand, but still helpfully, you may find that the claimant's claim is more valid than you had thought, and that it deserves something in return, from an apology to a payment. Either way, you have improved chances of the claim's being dropped or at least being settled promptly and fairly.

If the claimant won't talk with you, there are still plenty of other ways to find out about the claimant and the claim. Obviously, assuming there are two lawyers, the lawyers can talk. In addition, whether in litigation or formalized arbitration, you can pursue discovery. In a deposition of the claimant, you and your lawyer can likely find out a great deal about whether the claimant has a valid claim and what damages the claimant may be awarded in the event the case is decided by a judge or arbitrator.

Discovery is also an opportunity for you to communicate with the claimant. Although some defense lawyers aggressively contest every request for information, others are very cooperative, particularly if the facts they disclose present a strong defense. They know that, in many cases, the information they provide to the other side will reduce the claimant's anger, confidence in the claim, and resistance to settlement. They also know that they can often trade easy access to the respondent's information (such as financial documents) for easy access to information from the claimant (such as medical records). Further, they know that resistance is most often futile: if evidence is relevant to the case, the judge or arbitrator will usually rule that it must be provided.

Remember that it's one thing to have a valid claim, another to be awarded sizable damages. In more than one celebrated case, including that of National Football League star Joe Kapp against the NFL and the U.S. Football League against the NFL, plaintiffs have, after the expenditure of vast attorney's fees, "won" their lawsuits only to be awarded essentially nothing (Kapp got nothing; the USFL got $1 "trebled" to $3 because its suit was an antitrust case). If the claimant who has sued you says he was disabled for six months and therefore lost $50,000 that he would have gained in his profession, ask for a copy of his 1040 tax forms for the last five years. If he was making $100,000 net per year, his $50,000 claim may be fair. If he was making $10,000 per year, a claim for $5,000 would be more realistic.

## EVEN IF YOU'RE RIGHT, YOU MAY WANT TO SETTLE

It is too easy to say that you will never pay that invalid claim that has been made against you. Perhaps you have talked with the other party, your lawyer has talked with the other party's lawyer, and there have been depositions or interrogatories that have given you details of the other side's claim, but you still know that you did nothing wrong.

Nevertheless, you may want to pay some money to settle the case. If you cannot handle the emotions you will feel if you settle an invalid claim and you can afford the time and money of defending the claim, by all means defend it. But if you are faced with a $5,000 claim and can win it by paying $20,000 in legal fees and expenses (plus extensive time in depositions and trial), but can settle it by paying $3,000, you may want to save yourself $17,000.

In making the decision, consider that in most cases the other side thinks it's right, too. In many cases, the other side is just as committed to its position as you are to yours. In many cases, the other side figures, as you may, that it will persist forever if necessary, but that its opponent (you) will eventually give up.

## GETTING SOMEBODY ELSE TO PAY

If you are in danger of being required to pay somebody for damages he or she believes you have inflicted, your hopes are not limited to disproving the claim. You should also look into the possibility that you can get somebody else to pay.

### Cross-Claims

One possibility is to avoid some or all liability by convincing the other side or a third party (such as an arbitrator or a judge) that someone else is totally responsible, more responsible, or partly responsible. If you are (or were) an employee and caused injury while acting within the scope of your duties, your employer (or former employer) has a duty to pay. If you are a partner in a business, your partners should share the responsibility for problems you have caused. If you were prevented from performing your contractual obligations because someone else failed in his or her contractual responsibilities to you, that person should pay.

The least expensive way to proceed on any of these premises is to communicate the facts to the claimant. If you can convince the other party that you cannot be held legally responsible, the claimant may let you off the hook. If not, and if you are involved in arbitration or litigation, you must convince the arbitrator or the court. In litigation, the procedure for making someone else a party to the lawsuit is called making a *cross-claim,* not to be confused with a cross-complaint. In litigation, another strategy is to try to win the case, but to sue the responsible party either after an unfavorable verdict or even while the original lawsuit is active. Even if you win the original lawsuit, you may want to make a claim against your employer or partner or contractual party for your attorney's fees. Whether you file a cross-claim or a separate suit, be sure to file before the statute of limitations has run out.

### Insurance

If someone has come after you, the most important word you can hear may be *insurance.* Too infrequently, people facing common claims, from personal injury to breach of contract, do not consider insurance (unless their auto policy is involved). Your insurance need not be a business errors-and-omissions policy or a professional malpractice policy. Believe it or not, the typical homeowner's or renter's insurance policy can often be of tremendous help.

This is because typical homeowner's and renter's policies go beyond fire and theft and also have *liability* clauses. Most obviously, they cover you for injuries other people suffer when they are on your property. Less obviously, they also generally cover you and your family if, other than with an automobile, you cause an injury *off* your property. If your child is playing baseball, hits the ball, then tosses the bat aside, unintentionally causing it to strike another child, the policy probably covers you.

Far less obviously, the policy may even cover you for causes of action having nothing to do with the kinds of claims specifically mentioned in the policy itself. In particular, homeowner's and renter's policies have been used to cover defamation, breach of contract, and unfair competition. (Still, they rarely cover intentional wrongdoing. This is not the same as intentional conduct. In other words, if you intentionally wrote something defamatory about another person, but did not do so with the intent to defame, you may be covered.)

"Sure," you say. "So the policy may help me out once I've lost a suit and paid my lawyer $20,000 to defend me. So what? I don't have $20,000."

Okay, more good news: an insurer's willingness to defend often exceeds an insurer's willingness to indemnify. In English, this means that an insurance company sometimes will furnish you with legal representation even in cases in which, if you are found liable, the insurance company will not pay the claimant or reimburse you.

This is partly a matter of law and partly a matter of common sense. Sometimes the law requires the insurer to provide you with a lawyer even though the insurer will not have to pay if you lose. Often, however, the insurance company will provide representation as a matter of informed self-interest. If you are a lucrative client of the insurance company, or if the insurance company just plain likes you, it may want to help you out and retain your business. More commonly, the insurance company will not be too sure whether or not the policy covers the claim (it may also fear that the claim will change slightly and therefore be more clearly covered by the policy) and will prefer providing a lawyer and winning the claim rather than having you lose the claim and then demanding that the insurance company pay the award.

If you face a claim, valid or not, and if there is any possibility that any of your insurance policies will cover that claim, you should probably contact your insurance carrier. If you are on good terms with the agent or broker who sold you the policy, start there rather than with the company's claims department. Perhaps the agent, who benefits from your premiums but loses nothing when you make a claim, can prevail on his or her contacts in the company to help you out by representing you or by paying the claim without any dispute resolution process.

Be careful, however, if the limits of your policy are much lower than the maximum amount the claimant might be awarded. Once it seems the other side will win an amount equal to or greater than your policy limits, the lawyer provided by your insurance company will have limited incentive to fight hard to keep an over-limit award or verdict as little over the limit as possible. You are, of course, liable for the amount of an award that exceeds the policy limits. Therefore, in cases in which damages substantially in excess of your limits may be awarded, you may want to hire your own counsel.

If the insurance company says no, and a significant amount of money is at stake (in the claim against you or in the cost of a lawyer or both), take your insurance policy to a lawyer and ask the lawyer whether the policy covers the claim or at least your legal defense. Don't take the policy to just any lawyer: ideally, go to one who is experienced in insurance law.

If your insurance company is required to defend you but refuses to do so, or if it is required to pay a claim against you but refuses, you are not out of luck. You just have another potential dispute on your hands. This one you should take to a lawyer specializing in "bad faith" claims against insurance companies. If you can prove your company should have provided representation or paid the claim, you can recover what you have lost. If you can prove the company acted in bad faith, you may be able to recover many thousands of dollars in punitive damages.

# 14

## How to Succeed in Dispute Resolution

You are in a dispute. You have selected a type of dispute resolution that seems appropriate for your case and your needs. You have decided the question of whether or not to hire a lawyer. You have done your best to get a good neutral. *Now* what?

Success and winning are related but not identical. When one party wins and the other loses, it may well be that the "winner" has not succeeded. Success means resolving a dispute in a way that in both the short term and long term is acceptable to you. If you win and the other party loses and as a result you lose the other party's friendship or business, or if the other party retaliates and causes you harm, the resolution may end up not being acceptable to you.

So focus not on winning but on an acceptable resolution. Realize that there is not just win-lose negotiation and win-lose resolution, but plenty of situations that can end with a *win-win* result. Focusing on win-win is very current in the dispute resolution movement. It is near to the heart of those who promote "interest-based" negotiation.

Still, in the real world, sometimes a win-win resolution is impossible or will not present a result that is acceptable to you. Then the only option is between winning and losing.

Whether you seek a result that is win-win or win-lose, you *can* succeed. You can succeed even against prominent opponents and their formidable lawyers. The key is to use five basic principles: honesty, discipline, psychology, thinking like a lawyer, and effective writing.

## HONESTY

If you want to succeed in resolving your dispute, be honest. Not sort of honest, not honest most of the time. Be completely honest all the time. Honesty is not only right; it is also in one's self-interest.

If you are always truthful, you will never be caught in a lie during a dispute. Being caught in just one lie can ruin months of careful work to resolve your case: it can completely derail the train to success you have been constructing in dozens or hundreds of hours of painstaking research and writing and negotiation. Why? Because if the other side, perhaps suspicious of you anyway, finds you have lied once, it will never trust you as much again and may never again trust you at all.

Once you have been caught in a lie, just try threatening litigation. Just try saying $20,000 is your final offer. Just try saying you have an expert who will testify in your behalf. The other side will think you're bluffing.

Ruining your credibility is only one problem with being dishonest. Another is the pressure you put on yourself. Unless you have a computer built into your head, it will be anywhere from difficult to impossible to keep track of your lies and your truthful statements. The more lies you have told, the more random access memory your onboard computer will need to have. Not only will you have to remember whether in various instances you lied or told the truth; you will also have to remember the exact information you communicated in each lie.

When your true annual income was $31,000 in 1989 but you exaggerated it to make it seem as if your lost time was more valuable than it really was, you had better remember whether you said your income was $35,100 or $42,500 or $44,622. Because if you said $42,500 four months ago and you say $45,000 now, the other party may very well catch you in the lie, especially if the other party is or was represented by a lawyer, because lawyers take a lot of notes.

One reason Davids sometimes knock out Goliaths is that the Davids try harder, try more creatively, try more passionately. They perform better than the Goliaths because they are fighting a righteous crusade against an evil foe, or at least a foe who has done something wrong. If you have lied, just how passionate will you be? Will you work as hard or as well, knowing that as a liar your moral standing may be no higher than that of the landlord who is trying to wrongfully evict you, the auto manufacturer who will not replace its new but unsafe car, the neighbor who doesn't give a damn if his stereo wakes you up every night after four hours of sleep?

Because it is the right thing and because it is the right *tactic,* always tell the truth.

But amid all this sweetness and light, a dark but necessary caution: honesty and candor are not the same thing. Always be honest; don't always be candid. To disclose everything can be fatal to your case. Be as candid as you can be; candor helps to make relations between disputants as amicable as possible, enhances credibility, and may lead to settlement as each party understands the interests of the other and moves to meet them. But to tell the other side of evidence that will severely damage your case, or to let the other side know that you must get the case over with by a certain date, or that you fear the courtroom too much to go through litigation, can be dispute resolution suicide. Don't volunteer damaging information. Even if you are asked a question whose answer might badly hurt your case, and the setting (such as a mediation) does not require that you answer, respectfully decline to do so. You might say, "I'm not prepared to go into that at this time."

### Lies from Your Adversary

Although you will be honest, you must be ready for the opposite from your adversary. The more there is at stake, the more likely it is that people will lie. In disputes, a huge amount is often at stake. In disputes, people who may go days and weeks of normal life without lying will lie, and will lie repeatedly and convincingly.

Unless the other side has demonstrated that even during the dispute it is going to be unflinchingly truthful, be prepared for lies. Check out the opposition's case in advance, so you can compare your research to what the opposition says. If the other side tells you something that helps it but whose accuracy you do not know, try to find a way to check it out (perhaps by calling other people). In a hearing in which the other side has testified and said something that is important to the case but that may or may not be true, ask the other side questions to see if the other side can support what it said. (Of course, if the other side seems convincing on this point, get off the issue quickly or you will overemphasize one of its strengths.) Particularly if the hearing is only part of the process and not the final stage, check out testimony even after it has been given.

## DISCIPLINE

To succeed consistently in dispute resolution, you need the discipline and endurance of a marathon runner intent on finishing the race, no matter what. The other side will test your discipline, will assume you cannot endure. Endure. Compete like the most serious athlete, intent on doing your best.

In many cases, the longer you can endure the better you will do. In particular, once you have made clear—through your words or your actions or both—that you will never quit, your opponent will almost always take you more seriously than before. Chances then will be much higher that your adversary will do what you want.

If you make a claim against another party, be prepared for the first response to be one that is harshly and coldly uncooperative. Many cases, especially cases by individuals against large corporations, begin with the individual making a claim that is answered by a lawyer who "stonewalls." The lawyer says in so many words that you don't have anything approaching a valid case, that you are foolish, and that you are wasting everyone's time. The lawyer may add frosting to the sour cake: if you file suit against us, the lawyer will say, we will sue you for malicious prosecution.

You may persist past this discouraging point only to hear more of the same. If you believe that the lawyer may be right, perhaps you should reevaluate whether to proceed with your claim. Whether or not you must review your case, follow the words of Davy Crockett: "Be always sure you're right—then go ahead."

Endurance means more than putting up with unpleasant experiences and abusive people. It means not getting discouraged by long delays. It means not giving up if the case takes a turn for the worse. It means making financial sacrifices in order to stay in the battle.

And discipline means more than finishing the race. It means *preparing* for the race. If all else is equal, the better-prepared party will win. This is because he or she will have the material to present a more convincing case. Further, it is because the third party—whether a judge or arbitrator who will decide the case or a mediator who will merely influence the case—will tend to be more impressed by, and will therefore tend to favor, the party who has prepared well. After all, the well-prepared party seems to take the proceeding more seriously (this shows respect for the third party) and seems to have worked harder on the case (people like to reward people who have worked hard, and hard work may imply a righteous, highly credible sense of having been wronged).

As much as possible, know the facts of the case, the law that applies, and the rules of the dispute resolution process you are using. Rehearse the hearing or other session, at least in your mind. Bring in convincing documents and, if useful, convincing witnesses; interview the witnesses before the session. ("A good lawyer never asks a question whose answer he or she doesn't know.") Visit the session site and, if possible, observe other sessions. Learn about your adversary and his or her case. Request copies of documents the other side claims support his or her case. As further preparation, bring notes to the session that are easy enough to read and well enough organized that you can find what you need in a few seconds. (On the other hand, do not write out long speeches: speak from notes or no notes; you will be more convincing than if you read and will be more likely to retain the third party's attention.)

Bring plenty of copies of all key documents (at a minimum, one copy for yourself, one for each opposing party, and one for each third party). If possible, also bring originals of all documents (this will defeat questions of authenticity, of whether somebody "doctored" a photocopy). Organize the documents so you can find them fast. If the media are interested in the case, consider whether you should make copies for them or create press releases or other documents for them. If the media are not already interested, consider contacting them.

### Don't Be Intimidated

A big part of dispute resolution discipline is keeping yourself from being intimidated. One reason many people avoid dispute resolution or do badly in dispute resolution is that they allow themselves to be unduly frightened by the process, the other side, the other side's lawyer, or the neutral—or all four. Sure, sometimes each of these *should* be intimidating. But find out what you can about them. If you become familiar with them, you may find they are not as impressive as you thought they'd be.

If, for instance, you're frightened of small claims court, sit in on a session in your local courthouse. Pretty informal, isn't it? The parties are not Rhodes scholars, but they do all right, don't they?

If you are intimidated by an adversary you've never met—such as an executive with some far-off corporation—do some research. Perhaps you know someone who knows something about the executive. Perhaps you can find some information on the executive by going to the library and reading articles on the corporation and the executive; you can find these by using the indexes to newspapers and magazines. Remember, behind that embossed stationery and that big title is a human being.

If you are scared by the other side's lawyer, remember that it's not particularly hard for a reasonably intelligent person to become a lawyer, and all lawyers make mistakes. If your case goes on long enough, chances are substantial that the lawyer will make one or more mistakes of which you can take advantage.

What about those imposing folks called judges and arbitrators? Acting intimidated may help you get along with these people, especially those who may revel in their authority. But just remember that among all dispute resolvers, the judge towers above the mediator and the arbitrator in power and authority. Further remember that underneath the robes of the judge there is a lawyer.

Another thing that shouldn't intimidate you about the other side is the other side's "rules" and "policies." Some company employees cite company rules and policies as though they are law. Rules and policies can be changed, exceptions can be made, and when companies insist too strongly on following their rules, they can be taken to court, or arbitration, or even mediation, where they will find that laws beat rules every time.

### Be Prepared for Delays

Intimidation can discourage you at the outset of a dispute. Delays can wear you down much later. Know what you're up against: any kind of dispute resolution process can incur surprising and amazing delays, and, as a rule, the more formal the process, the more extensive the delays. A neighborhood mediation will generally be done in less than a month, but an arbitration (including agreeing on one or more arbitrators, setting the hearing date, holding the hearing, awaiting the award, and getting paid) can easily take six months, and in big cities litigation often takes five years from filing to trial.

Try to find a dispute resolution process whose delays you can endure. Try to fight unnecessary delays by the other side, without making too clear that you can't wait much longer. Try to hang in there through the long and surprising delays that all too often happen; in particular, if the dispute is important enough, make sacrifices elsewhere in your life to find the time and money to be there until the process has run its course.

### PSYCHOLOGY

Even if you didn't major in psychology and even if you didn't go to college, you may already know enough about people and their personalities to use psychology to help resolve your disputes. If you have common sense and good judgment, you probably already understand people well enough and can predict their behavior well enough to succeed in dispute resolution. Even so, if you have found yourself in disputes before and believe you may find yourself in disputes in the future, it may be worth your while to read or skim a basic psychology text.

Recognize that when someone is angry with you or you are angry with someone, the cause is always frustration. Further, realize that it may be that the angry person initially was angry with someone else but could not safely express anger at that person and therefore is using you as the target.

If you are angry at your neighbor, ask yourself whether the problem is mostly with your boss, whom you dare not yell at or threaten with litigation. Asking yourself this question could keep you from needlessly engaging in a long dispute resolution process against your neighbor and may help you focus on the part of your life that has more need for change.

If your neighbor is angry at you, ask yourself whether the real cause is not you but the neighbor's problems in the workplace, in marriage, with money, or with health. Perhaps these problems will go away; perhaps if you treat your neighbor courteously, the dispute will vanish as his other problems are solved. Perhaps you can in some way reduce the frustration the neighbor is feeling in other areas, thereby reducing the neighbor's aggression and maybe gaining his or her gratitude as well.

Take psychology into account when assessing whether you really should engage in a dispute. It is possible that in some potential disputes the conflict or imperfection lies more within yourself than between yourself and another party. Are you using the other side as a target for frustration the other party has not caused? Are you dwelling excessively on a problem you would prefer to forget? Would your time be better spent not on attacking something that has upset you but rather in understanding yourself better?

## Threats and Warnings

By considering psychology and by doing research on the other side—and dealing with him or her (especially if the other side is an interest-based negotiator who believes in frankly disclosing his or her underlying interests)—you can learn what the other party wants to get and what it wants to avoid. In the often unpleasant world of dispute resolution, a claimant must generally use implicit and explicit threats of harm much more often than implicit or explicit offers of benefit. As a claimant you therefore in most cases should determine the other side's most vulnerable point and direct your attack there.

Without doing much research, you can figure that almost any adversary wants to avoid litigation. So if you can credibly threaten a plausible lawsuit, you may get what you want. Take care, however; many people see litigants in the same light as they see burglars—as people doing something very wrong. Through threats of litigation you can derail an ongoing relationship or can turn a lukewarm dispute (perhaps one efficiently resolvable through ADR) into a red-hot one that must go to court.

Threats do work. But don't go too far with them. If you make a fist, and tell the other side to pay you right then and there or you will slug him or her in the nose, you could conceivably be imprisoned for assault or even attempted robbery. If you threaten the other side with future physical harm or with disclosure of private information (or certain other kinds of information), you might well be imprisoned for extortion.

But it's very effective to threaten the other side with a dispute resolution process that you can compel the other side to endure. These processes are pretty much limited to public court litigation (including small claims court suits) and to arbitration. The other side can be required to enter arbitration when there is an arbitration clause in a contract or when the other party has agreed to have disputes against it handled by a particular arbitration system; this is true of most or all firms in many industries, most notably the automotive industry. You won't be successfully prosecuted or sued for your threats if you are making your claim in good faith and with a significant chance of prevailing and if you make your threat *implicitly* rather than *explicitly*. Don't say, "Unless I receive $5,000 from you within 15 days, I will sue you." Say, "Unless I receive an adequate settlement offer within 15 days, I will be forced to take immediate action to protect my legal rights." The other side will get the picture.

## How Will They React to Your Words?

Beyond the specific use of psychology in understanding the other side and in understanding what's important to the other side, use psychology in each specific step of dispute resolution. In particular, in your oral and written communications with the other side, with your lawyer if you have one, and with any neutral who may become involved in the case, think very carefully about how those who hear or read your words will react to them.

When there is time, go over in your mind what you are planning to say, and pretend you are the person who will hear your remarks: try to hear them as that person would. Similarly, after you have written a draft of a letter or other document, let it sit for a day, then read it as if you were the other party, your lawyer, or, for instance, a mediator. Consider their specific personalities, their specific careers, the specific pressures they are under to do this or that, and their specific interests. Predict how people will react to certain words, information, and arguments. Change your oral and written communications—by choosing different words and by adding and, especially, deleting information—so that the people who will hear and read them will respond favorably to what you are saying. Even when speaking without preparation, keep the other people in mind as you plan your words, even if you will be speaking the words only a fraction of a second later. Speak and write to them, not to yourself.

## Be Likable

It is very important to avoid offending the other side or the neutral. If you offend people on the other side, they may become more interested in your case than you would like: they may make every effort to defeat you, every effort to carefully prepare for any hearing or trial. In addition, they may resist negotiated settlement or any other means of dispute resolution except those that leave you in total defeat.

Stick to your allegations and state them clearly and persuasively. But you need not yell or swear or insult. If you must bring up an action that can make the other side look like a terrible person, in negotiation and sometimes in third-party processes, you will come across better if you criticize the action more than the person. You might say, "Mr. Nextdoor has always been a good neighbor, but when his basement flooded, water ran into my yard and killed $300 worth of plants." This comes across better than, "Mr. Nextdoor killed my plants with his damn water."

One of the best ideas in the negotiation book *Getting to Yes* is to avoid undue offense by staying away from the word "you." Its authors suggest that complaints be cast in terms of how you feel rather than what the other party did to you. You might say, "I feel let down" rather than "You broke your word"; "We feel discriminated against," not "You're a racist."

Certainly there are exceptions to the general rule that you should be likable. If the other party seems as though he or she will not take you seriously unless you take aggressive action, you may have to file a regular or small claims lawsuit. If the other party repeatedly insults you during a phone call, you may be able to gain his or her respect the same way you can sometimes get the respect of any bully: by striking back. You, too, can make an angry remark or two, but make accurate statements and try to sound firm and formidable, not agitated and unprofessional. In a given setting you might say, "I'm sorry, but I'm getting very tired of these questions about my integrity. I always tell the truth, and I'm telling you now that the product never worked right."

Just as you may want to depersonalize accusations, you may benefit from *personalizing* complimentary remarks: "You do terrific work"; "I appreciate your willingness to talk about this"; "That's a good point you made."

Perhaps as important as avoiding offense is encouraging the other side and the neutral to *like* you. It is by no means impossible to get the other side and its representatives, even in the very midst of the dispute, to like you. In this connection, you may have particular success with the other side's lawyer.

The lawyer usually has far less at stake than the party he or she represents. Unless the lawyer is handling the case on a contingent-fee basis, the lawyer will get a fee (or salary check) even if the client does not do so well; if the lawyer settles the case, it won't be the lawyer's own money that must be paid. In most cases, the lawyer was not involved in the circumstances that caused the dispute and so has little or no anger toward you (especially if you have not insulted the lawyer or caused him or her a lot of trouble). And more often than you might guess, the lawyer representing Ms. Thompson or Mr. Murray or the General Engines Corporation intensely dislikes Ms. Thompson or Mr. Murray or GEC: for one thing, many clients give their lawyers many more demands than thank-yous.

So when you deal with the lawyer, in negotiation or any other setting, direct your attacks not at the lawyer but at the client (and, most safely, at the client's conduct). Be reliable: quickly return calls; promptly send documents. Save the lawyer time when you can. If things get conversational, as they often do, ask the lawyer about himself or herself, at least about career and possibly about personal life. Most people love to talk about themselves, and lawyers—unless under time pressure—love to talk, period.

Try to get along with anyone else who is representing the other side or is part of the other side. This advice applies not only to intense disputes involving an opposing lawyer, but also to those cases where you as a consumer are unhappy with a product or service. Let's say you want to take an appliance back to a department store because it doesn't work as well as you expected it to, or that you want some money back from a hotel because there were no towels in the room and it took housekeeping an hour to get you some (meanwhile you couldn't shower and were late for an appointment).

Don't think that when you talk to the saleswoman or the desk clerk that you are talking to a big, imposing corporation looking to make every cent it can. In fact, you are talking to a human being who happens to work for the corporation. The department store employee may not only be bound by corporate policy to take back most anything and be nice about it, but she may also want to help you more than she wants to help her employer. And the hotel clerk may want to knock $20 off your bill or upgrade you to a bigger room not only to please you and get you out of his hair, but also to retaliate in a tiny way against his employer.

If you have a sense of humor, use it. (If you don't, a dispute is no time to try to acquire one.) A sense of humor can put the other side at ease, can reduce its aggression, can make you seem more human, more attractive. Don't pepper people with one funny statement after another, but fit in humor here and there. The amount should vary with the formality of the setting and the subject matter.

Don't tell jokes unless someone else tells one first; instead, use humor in the midst of normal dispute resolution dealings, from negotiations to arbitrations and even to trials. If possible, try to be self-deprecating: if you have made fun of yourself, you may seem less the threatening aggressor, and you may sap the hostility felt by the other party, who may feel you have already attacked yourself and therefore that there is no need for him or her to attack you. Unless the proceeding is quite informal, start seriously—you don't want anyone to get the first impression that you're a jokester rather than someone who has been injured or someone justifiably resisting a claim.

## Gang Up

Let's say three college students rent the house next door to you. They are bright, and you've had pleasant conversations with them. But they are used to living among other college students rather than in an adult neighborhood such as yours. They play their stereo loudly during the evening and sometimes past midnight. The noise distracts you and your family when you are engaged in a quiet activity, and it often awakens you and your wife in the middle of the night. It also disturbs other neighbors.

When the problem began, you courteously asked the college students if they wouldn't mind keeping the noise down and avoiding late night noise. They said they would try. But the problem continued with little improvement.

You needed to put some pressure on the situation. You wrote a letter to the neighbors' landlord, outlining how much trouble the noise had caused. You politely but firmly insisted that the landlord find a way to stop it or find other tenants. The landlord came up with the idea that the dispute be mediated by a man from the housing office at the university the students attend.

You agree to mediation. You and your wife do not want to be outnumbered, three to two, by the college students. And because noise is to some extent a subjective matter, you do not want to appear to be a hypersensitive complainer who would be annoyed or awakened by a pin dropping. The smartest thing you can do is to ask the other suffering neighbors to show up at the session, as informal witnesses.

Two of the neighbors are willing to come, partly to protect their own interests and partly just to help out. At the mediator's suggestion, the mediation is held in the living room of the students. In the face of criticism from you, your wife, and the two neighbors, the three college students back down. The noise problem declines dramatically.

Particularly if your credibility or possible hypersensitivity may be at issue, try—whether in a proceeding as informal as a noise mediation or in one as formal as a rigid arbitration—to get other people to attend who will speak in favor of your position.


## THINKING LIKE A LAWYER

In law school, the professors tell the student they're going to teach him or her to "think like a lawyer": beyond all the principles they will teach in their courses, they will also change the way the student's mind works. And the professors are right. After three years in the very narrow and unusual environment of a law school, a student who came in as a fairly normal college graduate comes out thinking about a lot of things the way a lawyer does.

If you're involved in a dispute, especially a legal dispute, and especially a legal dispute that will involve full-scale litigation, small claims court, or arbitration that includes legal procedure, you would do well to think like a lawyer.

A lawyer thinks a lot about *precedents*. (Courts are heavily influenced and sometimes *bound* by decisions made by others in similar cases. These cases and their decisions are called precedents.) If you can find disputes like yours that have been decided in favor of a party in your position, you may have made it most of the way toward victory.

A law student also learns to *distinguish cases:* to find differences, sometimes seemingly very small ones, that cause one case to be decided for the plaintiff while a very similar case is decided for the defendant. Perhaps in both cases the defendant driver rear-ended the plaintiff driver, with both plaintiffs being stopped at a stoplight, with both defendants speeding and not stopping fast enough, and with both plaintiffs suffering whiplash injuries. But in one case the plaintiff had an opportunity to get out of the way and didn't take it, and in the other case the plaintiff had no such opportunity. So try to be sure that your case not only is similar to cases that you believe stand as precedents for your position, but also that there is nothing to *distinguish* those would-be precedents from your case. Similarly, if you find a case, or your opponent finds a case, that at a glance seems to be a precedent for the other side, look for ways in which the facts of that case differ from the facts of yours.

And a law student considers whether, in a particular hypothetical or real-life situation, there is a *cause of action:* a basis for suing. You can't successfully sue somebody unless you have been the victim of the kind of wrong that courts handle. If you are angry at your friend for liking someone else, you may have been harmed, you may in fact feel terrible, but you have no cause of action.

There are in fact plenty of causes of action. Among the classics, stemming from the common law—court cases decided in England and the United States—are negligence (for instance, in auto accidents and professional malpractice), intentional and wrongful damage to a person (for instance, battery or intentional infliction of emotional distress) or property, trespass, breach of contract, breach of express or implied warranty, misrepresentation, conversion (similar to theft), and defamation (libel and slander). There are many other common-law causes of action, and there are also those created by state and federal statutes.

The good news here is that, generally (but unfortunately not always), if somebody has done something that most people would believe is wrong, there is a cause of action. You may need to go to a lawyer to find a name for it, but it's there. If someone has cheated you out of money by lying to you, very likely it's fraud or misrepresentation or a violation of a state statute. If someone has caused you a physical injury through his or her careless disregard of your safety, chances are it's negligence. If someone agreed to pay you to do something and then refused to, you probably have a case for breach of contract.

In addition, the law student learns to consider whether certain information makes for *admissible evidence.* In litigation and sometimes in arbitration, the judge or arbitrator will not permit just any old fact to be weighed as evidence in the case. To be "admitted," evidence must be *relevant* and *material.* If it's relevant, it relates to the issues to be decided in the case, including the cause of action and the damages. If it's material (that's an adjective), it's significant enough that it may help prove or disprove a point that is at issue.

Even if evidence is relevant and material, a judge or arbitrator may refuse to admit it on the ground that its admission would violate another rule of evidence. Other than objections about relevance and materiality, the most widely heard objection to evidence is that it is "hearsay": an out-of-court (or out-of-hearing) statement used to prove the "truth of the matter stated." If you, Paula Plaintiff, are suing Daniel Driver for running into your car and you try to testify that you heard Wilma Witness say, "I saw Daniel run right into Paula's Pontiac," the defense lawyer will object to the admission of this evidence on the ground that it is hearsay: you are trying to bring in Wilma's out-of-court statement for the purpose of proving that what she said is true: that Daniel ran into your car. The judge will sustain the objection. (If the statement were to be used to prove that Wilma was present at the location of the collision, it might be admitted for that purpose.)

The rationale behind the hearsay rule is that it is more difficult to assess the credibility of an absent witness than that of one who can be cross-examined and whose demeanor can be observed. There are plenty of exceptions to the hearsay rule (especially admissions against interest, dying declarations, and other statements that by nature are unusually believable).

What does any of this have to do with you if you happen to be a nonlawyer representing yourself in a type of dispute resolution other than full-scale litigation? Plenty. First of all, you may well be in a type of dispute resolution (such as small claims court and many arbitrations) in which the third party decides the case and where the third party is a lawyer. Lawyers tend to follow the rules of evidence, and some will follow it strictly.

Second, even if the process is not so legalistic, it's simply *in your interest* to generally follow the rules of evidence. This is because these rules are not arbitrary; rather, they are designed to provide a court with the most important, most believable evidence. If your evidence is relevant and material and not in violation of the hearsay rule or other rules of evidence, it is much more likely that it will be of value to the decision-making process. In addition, ADR processes, far more than full-scale litigation, offer the parties a limited time in which to make their cases. In an arbitration you may have two hours, in mediation one hour, in small claims court five minutes. You do not want to waste this precious time on the irrelevant or the immaterial. Similarly, you may not want to spend it on a statement made outside the trial or hearing or session, especially if a witness can be brought in to testify.

A lawyer must also find out about the *statute of limitations*. Statutes of limitations come up infrequently in the academic discussions of the law school classroom. But in the first minutes of talking with a prospective client, the lawyer will ask, "When did this happen?" If it happened too long ago, it's too late to sue. (That's not to say you can't still succeed through ADR, especially if you have something other than the threat of litigation with which to prod the other party.) Find out what statute of limitations applies to your case (see Chapter 9).

The lawyer, much more than the law student, will also pay attention to *damages*. Yes, law students learn about damages, but they rarely know much about how to realistically evaluate how much a given case is worth. A lawyer will quickly get into this subject. If you have a cause of action not barred by the statute of limitations, it's still not worthy of a lawsuit unless you are likely to receive a substantial amount in damages.

With one main exception, damages are the amount a court orders the defendant to pay in order to compensate the plaintiff for his or her loss. The main exception is punitive (or "exemplary") damages, awarded to punish the defendant for wrongdoing. For a court to award punitive damages, the wrongdoing generally must be malicious or involve fraud or oppression. Punitive damages can be in the hundreds of thousands of dollars, even where the compensatory damages in the same case are only a small fraction of such amounts.

How do you assess what your case is worth? Certainly your most objective opinion of your losses—how much it will cost to fix your car or treat your injury, how much income you or your business lost—may be a good estimate. But the best index is how much judges and juries (or arbitrators) in your area have awarded in cases like yours. Lawyers are very familiar with what cases are worth in their areas, and they must be: the value of cases varies greatly from area to area. Generally, courts in big cities will award a lot more money than courts in small towns, particularly in negligence cases. So, particularly if you need some legal advice anyway, ask a lawyer what your case is worth. You might also ask a law librarian for a copy of any local publication that lists recent jury verdicts.

In addition to all the other factors they weigh, lawyers will rapidly want to know what *proof* there is of the wrong and the resulting damages. It's a shame that the woman from out of town agreed to buy your business, causing you to take it off the market and lose the chance to sell it, and then went back on her word. But if you have no written agreement, can you prove your case?

What if your car was struck by another car? Do you have witnesses? Is the damage to your car consistent with the other party's being negligent? It's pretty hard to deny negligence if the other car has damage to its grille and yours has a badly dented back bumper. But what if everyone agrees your car was struck, but nobody agrees your personal injuries were due to the accident? Perhaps there are credible doctors who will testify that you weren't injured before, that your injuries stem from the accident, and that the costly treatment you have undergone was necessary.

And what if everything is in place—you have a cause of action for substantial damages that is not barred by the statute of limitations, and you can prove what happened and prove how badly you were damaged— but the other person can't be found or has no money? Early in your initial consultation with the lawyer, the lawyer will have asked you about the other party: can you identify the party and find the party (if not, you can't "serve" him or her)? Does the other party have assets or income that cannot be protected from seizure in the event of a court judgment and an unwillingness to pay? The poor are called "judgment-proof": sure, they can be sued, but no judgment for money can be collected from them because they have no money to pay. So, just as the lawyer would ask you, ask yourself: *Could a judgment be collected?*

### Avoid Admissions Against Interest

The concepts discussed above are the ones people usually cite when they talk about "thinking like a lawyer." Another principle that is second nature to lawyers is: *avoid admissions against interest*. If you are inclined to tell the other side something that can be used against you, stop yourself. There are exceptions to this rule. In interest-based negotiation, frankness may be more valuable than secrecy, although even there some information should be held back: if it's enough to blow your case out of the water, don't be the one to bring it up. Another exception is when you are testifying in a deposition or arbitration or trial and you are asked a question whose truthful answer will damage you. In such a situation, you must tell the truth. But even the truth can be told in many ways, so tell it the way that harms you the least.

In the adversarial world of lawyers and courts, the other side will use against you almost anything it can. Don't think you will get away with saying something that harms your case: the other side will value it like a jewel and use it when it hurts you most. A good lawyer will say nothing or almost nothing that can possibly be used against his client.

When you communicate with the other side, especially in writing, be very careful to avoid admissions against interest. Follow the same precaution in dispute resolution involving a neutral. This is especially true in adversarial settings—full-scale litigation, small claims court, and the formal types of arbitration.

Being careful to avoid admissions is important not only in the hearing or trial, but in previous parts of the process, particularly depositions and interrogatories. Remember, when the other side takes your deposition, it is almost for the sole purpose of getting you to make statements it can use later to defeat you and to reduce the amount of any damages you might be awarded. From your own perspective, in a deposition, *you are not there to win: you are there not to lose.*

In a deposition or any other setting where the other side is asking you questions aimed at finding weaknesses in your case, answer almost every question as briefly as you can. You need not respond with only a "Yes" or "No" to every question, but limit yourself to "Yes, I did" or "That's correct" or "No, that's not accurate"—and nothing more. Detailed explanations of why you did something will hurt you more often than they help you—by giving the other side more material, by showing your concern about the issue, or by emphasizing the issue in the mind of the opposition or the third party.

Avoiding admissions against interest is not so important in processes such as mediation and negotiation, where you can walk away if you don't like the result. Still, even if you are in what seems to be an unthreatening mediation, ask the mediator whether what you say can be used in any later arbitration or lawsuit.

Be careful not only about statements that definitely would hurt you but also about statements that are not as clearly damaging but just might later be used against you. Your financial situation is a prime example. If you let the other side know you're wealthy, it may see you as a "deep pocket." If it finds out you have little money, it may figure you can't afford litigation and it may therefore file suit. Another key example is any deadline you have for resolving the dispute: among other things, experienced negotiators know that parties often make heavy concessions just before their deadline. Also avoid disclosing that you're too busy for a full-scale battle or that you fear publicity of information that might come out in the course of certain dispute resolution processes.

### Ask for More Than You Will Accept

One more aspect of thinking like a lawyer is thinking like a veteran negotiator. In any traditional negotiation, each party begins with a position more extreme than what it will accept. The same holds true for dispute resolution, and people who are experienced in this area expect opening positions to be subject to change. If you go to an arbitration or mediation asking for $100,000, the other side as well as the neutral will probably figure you believe the claim is worth less and that you will be satisfied with less. Therefore, as in negotiation, you have two choices. The first choice is to start high—to compensate for other people's expectations and also in the hope that you can get a lot more than the minimum you would find satisfactory. Even if you start high, be sure to have evidence for the position you take; you just might get the amount you ask for, and you certainly should not appear to be making a claim for an insupportable amount. Because of the almost inevitable expectations of the other parties, this is the safer option.

The other choice is to start at the amount you think is fair and make absolutely clear that this is no inflated position. You must make this clear in words and tone and by presenting strong evidence.

## EFFECTIVE WRITING

You could work your whole life trying to write compellingly and creatively, but it is much easier simply to write clearly. Consider this quotation, source unknown:

> Some people write so that they may be understood. I write so that I cannot be misunderstood.

In dispute resolution, that is how you should write. It is not enough for you to write so that your letter or other document is a good record for yourself of what you wanted to say. You must write so that another person — of different background, of different values, from a place where the words you use may mean something different from what they mean to you — can fully and precisely understand what you mean to say.

Still, there is more to effective writing than lack of ambiguity. You must avoid words that will needlessly offend the other side or that will make you look silly. A good tip is that if you are uncomfortable with a certain sentence or paragraph but still want to keep it in, you should probably throw it out.

Then there is the question of length. Good writing and effective dispute resolution writing are not the same thing. Good writing is always tight: just about as brief as it can be while communicating what is needed. Yet some very effective dispute resolution writing is verbose.

Concise writing is, however, usually better even in dispute resolution. It makes you look professional. It leads to short letters. The recipient may well read a short letter in its entirety but only skim a letter of more than a page or page and a half.

On the other hand, part of your task in dispute resolution may be to implicitly show the other side that you are serious and that dealing with you will not be easy. If you send the other side a long, wordy letter, it helps make these two points clear.

If you need to communicate a lot of details but still want to write a short letter, the trick is to write a very brief letter, perhaps less than a page, and in that letter refer to an accompanying document (called a "statement," "list of complaints," "summary of issues," "memorandum," "addendum," whatever you prefer). That document can then go on for miles and miles.

Length and verbosity are not the same thing. A one-page letter can be verbose (it can say in a full page what could have been communicated equally well in half that space); a 50-page letter can be concise (expressing its content as briefly as possible). So, unless you want to give the other side a sense that you are a little awkward, a little strange, somebody who perhaps cannot be dispatched as easily as a buttoned-down professional, even your long, accompanying "statement" should be concise.

If good writing is your goal, concentrate not just on short letters but on short sentences. They are easier to follow. Really.

Another hallmark of good writing is use of the active voice. Say, "The car hit me," not "I was hit by the car." Writing in the active voice makes you seem stronger. It also holds the reader's attention. Nevertheless, there *are* times for the passive voice. If you don't want to be too accusatory, instead of saying "You breached the contract," you might say "The contract was breached."

Another way to make your writing strong and persuasive is to avoid language that makes something appear to be your opinion instead of a fact. Try to avoid saying "I feel my property has declined in value." Instead say "My property has declined in value."

Start writing your letter a few days before it must be sent. Write the letter but *don't* proofread it. Instead, wait a day and *then* read it over. This will help you read it more as the recipient will read it: freshly, without knowing what it contains. When you do read it, read it pretending you *are* the recipient. Do you—as recipient, not writer—understand exactly what the writer meant to say?

If you are anything but a very accomplished writer (and perhaps even if you are such a writer), you will have to revise your letter after reading it over. Even so, if the letter is quite important, that's not enough.

Have *someone else* read it. Although it is preferable for this reader to be similar to the recipient in significant ways, a spouse or friend will do. Just the fresh analysis by someone unfamiliar with what you have written may identify a disastrous set of words and change your letter into an effective device of persuasion.

If all the efforts you make to write clearly and concisely and persuasively do not produce a letter that you believe will strongly help your case, ask somebody else to write the letter for you. It is not necessary for this person to be a lawyer. Just find somebody who writes well enough, ask him or her to rewrite what you have written, then review his or her work until the letter makes the points you need to get across.

### Paper, Print, and Sending the Letter

For effective writing to have the proper impact, it must be professionally presented. An effectively written document takes more than good writing and good content. It takes the right kind of paper and the right kind of printing.

Unless you are in an informal dispute, you must send a letter that does not stand out as amateurish when contrasted to business and professional correspondence the other party may receive. Use printed stationery suitable for business. Use a letter-quality computer printer or a typewriter with a carbon ribbon. Use pica, not the smaller elite, type. Follow the form of a standard business letter. Some dictionaries provide examples.

Photocopy all letters and other documents you send to the other side or the neutral or anyone else involved in the dispute. Keep copies even of those documents to which you do not expect to refer in the future: you may end up needing the copies.

If the dispute is informal, it may suffice to use first-class mail. But if you want to be able to prove that the other party got your letter, you must send it by a means that provides documentation. The cheapest way is to use "certified mail, *return receipt requested*" (which will show who signed for the letter and the date it was received).

If you want to get the letter to the other party quickly and the other party is nearby, consider local messenger services, particularly if they appear professional and provide documentation of delivery. If you want the letter to reach the other party quickly and the other party is or is not nearby, a national overnight service is an excellent move. Before using such a service, find out how to get documentation of delivery.

Whether you use certified mail, return receipt requested, or a faster service, the other party probably will know or figure that you will be able to prove delivery. Although certified mail, return receipt requested is by far the cheaper of the two, it is the more effective for making absolutely clear to the recipient that you want to be able to prove delivery. This may be the most effective way to show the other party that you envision and are preparing for a time (such as a trial or arbitration hearing) when you will need to prove that he or she received what you sent.

### Addressee

In most cases, you know the name of the person to whom to send your letter and other documents. But if you have a problem or dispute with a corporation, you may not. If you have been dealing with a particular person in the corporation and believe that writing to that person may get results, you will probably save time by writing to him or her. But if there is no particular person you expect to help you, it is often best to go all the way to the top: to the chairman of the board or, if you prefer, the president.

You can go to the library and check reference books for the names of these officials, but the references are not up to the minute. It is better to make a one-minute phone call to the company and ask for the name of the executive to whom you want to write.

It is important to get the attention of the highest-ranking person who will take the time to deal with your correspondence. The higher a person's rank, the more authority he or she has to settle disputes. In all likelihood, you will not hear directly from the chairman or president. Nevertheless, this official's office will in almost all cases refer the letter to the right department, and to the top person in that department who will take the time to deal with the letter.

Another reason why writing to the chairman or president is a good idea is that it implies you are forceful and not a person who is easily intimidated. In addition, an employee handling your letter may justifiably be afraid that if he or she does not handle your complaint promptly and to your satisfaction, you may write again, making sure the chairman is informed.

## Letter Copies

If you want to put maximum pressure on the addressee, it's often a good idea to send copies of your letter to other people and institutions and to inform the addressee that you have done so by noting the copies in the "cc" section at the bottom of the letter. Examples are the addressee's direct supervisor or the head of the firm; state and federal regulatory agencies that may deal with the kind of problem you have had; prosecutors (attorneys general, district attorneys); legislators; national and local public interest groups; and local newspapers, radio stations, and TV stations.

Ideally, enclose a cover letter with copies you send to people other than the primary addressee. Some people feel a photocopy need not be answered: after all, it is addressed to someone else.

The small amount of effort required to send a photocopy may result in a large amount of help. In particular, there is a good chance that legislators representing you at the state and federal levels will take an interest in your case. If you want their help and these people don't respond within a couple of weeks, give them a call. The first priority of virtually every legislator is reelection, and reelection depends to a large extent on service to constituents. All legislators who have sizable staffs have "caseworkers," people whose job it is to respond to constituents with problems. The legislator's office may contact the person or company that is giving you trouble, may refer you to agencies that can force the wrongdoer to change its ways, or may provide dispute resolution services.

There may be a further benefit. By bringing the problem or dispute to the attention of the government and the media, you may help show that there are many cases like yours and that what is needed are new laws, or better enforcement of existing laws. Furthermore, publicity of your problem may help others by warning them to avoid the product or service or by giving them an idea of how to get satisfaction.

Note that if your leverage over your adversary stems largely from his or her fear of publicity, you may want to *refrain* from sending copies. It is unlikely the other party will make concessions to you out of fear of publicity if significant publicity has already occurred.

## THREE MISCELLANEOUS POINTS

### Self-Help

"Self-help" is a legal term meaning the protection of one's person or property by one's own actions and without use of a dispute resolution process, especially without use of the courts. Generally speaking, if your neighbor has borrowed your lawn mower and refused to return it, and if you are on his or her property with permission, you can take back the lawn mower. If you have given a firm the right to take collateral if you default on a promise to pay for goods or services, the firm generally can take the collateral (as when a finance company repossesses a car) as long as it does not breach the peace in doing so. If you have paid for a product that immediately after the sale fails to work or fails to work right, you generally can stop payment on your check or get your credit card company to refuse to pay the merchant who sold you the product.

Self-help can work before problems develop into disputes, and it can work once a dispute is well under way. But two basic problems may arise: your effort may be illegal or otherwise wrongful, exposing you to criminal prosecution or a lawsuit; and your effort may provoke the other party to attack you physically or in other ways. Be sure you're right, try to take action when someone else will not oppose it, and, most important, get legal advice before you proceed.

### Pick Your Shots

Enough things go wrong in life that, if you wanted to, you could find yourself in a new dispute almost every week. This is no way to spend most of your time. Disputes should generally be reserved for those grievances that involve an amount of money that can make a difference in your life, or that concern something else—such as a principle—that is of pressing importance to you.

Often it's best just to turn the other cheek. This is not so much a religious concept as a matter of saving yourself for what to most people are more important than most conflicts: the major pleasures, the major obligations, and, yes, the major *disputes* of life.

### Be an Athlete

Many lessons from sports apply to disputes. Lessons like teamwork, preparation, focusing, discipline, never quitting, being confident, and taking risks. An even more direct relationship between sports and disputes is found in the need to take care of your physical side. If a taxing, high-stakes dispute resolution process lies weeks or months in the future, get in shape if you aren't already. Before an important negotiation phone call and in particular before an important mediation session, arbitration hearing, or trial, get some sleep and eat properly.


## YOUR OWN KIND OF SUCCESS

"Success" is defined in many ways. It may be winning and making the other side lose. It may be winning and helping the other side win at the same time. It may be finding a settlement that is acceptable to you, regardless of its impact on the other side.

There are too many conflicts and too few disputes. Conflicts arise when claims have been denied. It's a shame that so many citizens have been harmed and must make claims in an attempt to gain justice. But it's also a shame that so many citizens, once their just claims have been denied, just walk away rather than proceed with a dispute that might well have been worth the trouble. They walk away out of a lack of will or out of a lack of knowledge about how to resolve a dispute, especially how to resolve a dispute without litigation and lawyers. They walk away swallowing their pride, their humiliation, their anger, their sense of justice, and their losses. A diet like that can give you ulcers; worse, it can drain your idealism and break your spirit.

Good-faith disputes are in the public interest. They discourage wrongdoing. More clearly, they can give great personal satisfaction. The process can be as satisfying as the result; this is a good reason to pick your process carefully. There are many disputants who have won their cases and ended up unhappy because of their dissatisfaction with the process they've had to endure. There are many other disputants who have lost but have walked away pleased because they were satisfied with the process.

With techniques they have learned and with a dedication to succeed, many people before you have found the right type of dispute resolution and have done their best within it. Many feel a great satisfaction, a great self-respect, from having gone forward, having held the other party accountable, and having received a hearing of their case. Many gain a favorable verdict, award, or settlement.

So can you.

# Epilogue: How to Prevent Disputes

Preventive dispute resolution medicine is not limited to establishing alternative dispute resolution as the means of dealing with certain kinds of future conflicts. You can also try to prevent disagreements and can try to keep disagreements from turning into disputes.

When establishing a new relationship or embarking on a new project with others, take the time and ask the questions necessary for the parties to come to a "meeting of the minds" in which they fully understand and fully agree on what will take place. To achieve this understanding and agreement, it is important for all parties to be frank: let each other know not only the benefits of the undertaking but its burdens and possible pitfalls. Also discuss alternate ways of pursuing the same goal, so that no one will come back months later and say, "I would have wanted to do it differently if only you had told me it was possible."

It is obvious that you should try to get a fair deal for yourself. What is not so obvious is that you should also try to ensure that the other party is satisfied and will remain satisfied with the arrangement. Whether it's you or the other person, a party who is unhappy with the original agreement is especially likely to be unhappy enough later to initiate a dispute. In particular, a party who believes he or she was treated unfairly in the agreement will likely be unforgiving if the other party technically or substantively breaches it.

Once a meeting of the minds has taken place, get the results in writing. If the other party resists, explain that this is not a matter of distrust, but something you do on every project to assure that everyone has the same understanding.

Avoid getting into projects with people who are litigious. As a customer or client, seek out stores, manufacturers, professionals, and technicians with good reputations for high-quality products and services and for fair dealing, who have been in business for years, and who put their representations (especially their warranties) in writing.

Before committing to an expensive product or service, check it out in periodicals and books that have reviewed it. If reasonable to do so, rent a similar or identical product before committing to an expensive purchase. Try to buy products and arrange for services that are of either high quality or low cost. High quality tends to satisfy. Low cost tends to reduce expectations: if a five-dollar watch fails, you probably won't be upset. In making a purchase, carefully check the seller's policy on returns. Will it take back the product if you are merely dissatisfied with it and it is in salable condition? Will the seller refund your money or give you only a store credit?

If you require services from a doctor, lawyer, or other professional and the services involve danger or high expense, get a second opinion.

If you are about to buy an expensive product or arrange for a service that may turn out to be unsatisfactory, try to be billed rather than paying upon receipt. If you must pay right away, try to pay with a credit card, which, in the event you are dissatisfied, would give you the maximum time in which to prevent payment to the party who sold you the goods or services. (Before a purchase, ask your credit card company about any limitations on its ability to "charge back" a purchase to the seller: some may refuse to do this if the purchase was for $50 or less or if it was not made in your home state or within 100 miles of your mailing address.)

If you can't use a credit card, use a check: you will probably have one or more days in which to stop payment. Avoid large cash purchases, and be suspicious of anyone who demands that a large purchase be made in cash. Don't pay in full for expensive services until all services have been rendered.

If you are entering a contractual relationship and want to ensure that any dispute that arises will be handled by ADR rather than litigation, seek a mediation clause or arbitration clause in the contract. If the contractual relationship breaks down, try—on your own or through a representative such as an attorney—to negotiate a settlement before even invoking the ADR clause.

In phone calls with people with whom you are in a business relationship or people who are providing you with a product or service, always take notes, even when you don't think they will be necessary. One reason is that notes will often prove necessary even in relationships that once seemed simple and pleasant: a difference of recollections may arise, and there may be an attempt to misrepresent recollections. Another reason you should always take notes is that if in a dispute you must refer to those notes, they will be more credible if you can say you always take notes, rather than having to say you were taking these particular notes because you were anticipating a dispute and wanted them available as evidence. Your notes should show the date of the call, the time it began, the time it ended, and key statements made. If a particularly important statement is made, try to quote it exactly.

If a disagreement arises, try hard to keep it from intensifying into a dispute. A few hours of unpleasant work at this stage may save you a hundred even more unpleasant hours later. Try to see the other party's side of the story: hardly anyone *thinks* he or she is acting unfairly, so it is likely the other party has at least a halfway reasonable basis for his or her actions or omissions.

If you remain angry for a long period, ask yourself whether at least some of the problem is your own personality, not what was done to you. It is not abnormal to be angry, but, absent unusual circumstances, it is abnormal to become obsessed with a particular wrongful act. Remember that anger almost always hurts the angry person more than the object of the anger: you may be lying awake at night seething while the other party hasn't even thought about the problem for days.

If, after imagining yourself in the other party's shoes and after examining your own anger, you still cannot tolerate what he or she has done, consider calling or meeting with the other party. Life is full of misunderstandings, and if you and the other party can talk (or even write) frankly, precisely, and *courteously* as soon as an apparent disagreement has arisen, the two of you may find that most of the problem stems from a failure of communication. If there is a true disagreement, one of you may nevertheless come around to the other side's position. Even if this does not occur, both of you may feel much less angry than you did before you discussed the problem.

Even if you remain angry, work hard to avoid angering the other side. Many disagreements have flamed into disputes, and many disputes have become unnecessarily contentious and costly because someone was personally offended by behavior he or she thought was discourteous, belittling, or insulting.

# Appendix A
# Agencies and Industry Groups Offering
# Alternative Dispute Resolution Services

## AGENCIES

Until recently, there was no extensive list of agencies in the United States that offer alternative dispute resolution services as such are traditionally defined (in particular, arbitration, mediation, "med-arb," and conciliation). The first list of this nature was prepared in 1989 by the National Center for State Courts under funding from the State Justice Institute. An updated version appears below. It includes the results of NCSC's survey of some 1,000 agencies that conduct court-ordered or court-referred ADR. In some states, no agency returned a survey form. Therefore, some states are not represented in the list.

Those who seek ADR services should check with listed agencies to determine exactly what type of ADR services they offer. Do not rely exclusively on the following list. It does not include all ADR centers even as of the time when the list was compiled. Given the rapid growth of ADR, many new ADR centers will be established even in a matter of months after the publication of this book. Also, this list emphasizes only agencies, not individuals. For individuals (and centers) not on the list, look in the Yellow Pages of your phone book under "arbitration," "mediation," and "dispute resolution." Also check with local people and organizations who often deal with disputes or who refer people to dispute resolution services. These include lawyers, bar associations, court clerks, the police, the district attorney's office, members of the clergy, and the "consumer action" telephone lines operated by some radio stations, TV stations, and newspapers.

Also missing from this list are the names of most major national arbitration and mediation organizations and major private court systems. Refer to chapters 1, 2, and 10, respectively, for the names of some. National arbitration organizations often provide not only arbitration but also mediation and other services. Private court systems often provide not only private versions of public litigation but also mediation. To contact one of these firms, first check the phone directory for the nearest large city. If no office is listed there, call directory assistance for the city in which the firm is headquartered (these cities are cited in the chapters).

Despite these omissions, this list is of particular value because its compilers have sought to include every court-annexed ADR program in the United States that provides court-ordered ADR. These most commonly offer arbitration, though some provide mediation or med-arb, in which cases are first mediated and then, if no settlement is reached, arbitrated. The advantage of court-ordered programs is that they offer a party in a dispute the opportunity to be all but absolutely certain that his or her dispute will be handled by ADR: if a disputant files suit in a court with a court-ordered ADR program, and if the court has jurisdiction, if venue is proper, and if the case fits the rules under which the ADR program operates (in particular, if damages the plaintiff seeks are below a certain dollar amount), the case almost certainly will be referred to the ADR program. Check with your local courts to learn of local rules that determine which cases are referred to court-ordered ADR.

Publication of this list does not constitute an endorsement of any center on it.

At the end of most addresses, please note one or more capital letters. Each letter denotes a legal subject area handled by the center. Be sure to check with the center to confirm that it is still handling the subject area(s) indicated in the list.

*Legal Subject Areas*

A. Custody/visitation
B. Child support
C. Spousal maintenance
D. Property division
E. Visitation enforcement
F. Child abuse and neglect
G. Domestic violence

H. Minor criminal
I. Contract
J. Tort (chiefly negligence)
K. Small claims
L. Landlord/tenant
Z. Other (especially neighborhood, bad check, family other than divorce, and school-related)

ALABAMA

Birmingham Dispute Settlement
   System
Birmingham Municipal Court
City Hall, Room 100
710 N. 20th St.
Birmingham, AL 35203
Tel. (205) 254-2011
GHZ

ALASKA

PACT
2nd Judicial District
Box 749
Barrow, AK 99723
Tel. (907) 852-7228
AHK

ARIZONA

Conciliation
Coconino County Superior Court
County Courthouse
Flagstaff, AZ 86001
Tel. (602) 779-6598
A

Counseling (Mediating)
Coconino County Superior Court
County Courthouse
Flagstaff, AZ 86001
Tel. (602) 779-6578
A

Arbitration
Coconino County Superior Court
County Courthouse
Flagstaff, AZ 86001
Tel. (602) 779-6578
I

Arbitration
Pinal County Superior Court
Clerk of the Superior Court
P.O. Box 889
Florence, AZ 85232-0889
Tel. (602) 868-5801 Ext. 296
IJZ

Ex Parte Wage Assignment(s)
Pinal County Superior Court
Clerk of the Superior Court
P.O. Box 889
Florence, AZ 85232-0889
Tel. (602) 868-5801 Ext. 296
BC

Family Law Referee/Commissioner
Pinal County Superior Court
c/o Pinal County Courthouse
P.O. Box 889
Florence, AZ 85232-0889
Tel. (602) 836-8002
B

Probate Registrar
Pinal County Superior Court
Alma Jennings Haughts
P.O. Box 889
Florence, AZ 85232-0889
Tel. (602) 868-9621 Ext. 296

Conciliation Services of Pinal County
Conciliation Court of the Superior
   Court
P.O. Box 1759
Florence, AZ 85232
Tel. (602) 868-5801 Ext. 680
A

Community Mediation Program of
   Terros
Phoenix Municipal Court
301 E. Bethany Home Rd., Room
   A119
Phoenix, AZ 85012
Tel. (602) 230-2567
ABCDHKLZ

Conciliation Services
Superior Court for Maricopa County
201 W. Jefferson
Phoenix, AZ 85003
Tel. (602) 262-3296
AB

Court-Annexed Arbitration Program
Superior Court of Ariz.
Superior Court for Maricopa County
201 W. Jefferson
Phoenix, AZ 85003
Tel. (602) 262-3204
IK

Judicial Supervision Program
Superior Court, Maricopa County,
    Domestic Relations Division
201 W. Jefferson
Phoenix, AZ 85003
Tel. (602) 256-5701
AE

Ariz. Attorney General, Community
    Relations/Mediation
Maricopa County Justice of the Peace
1275 W. Washington
Phoenix, AZ 85027
Tel. (602) 542-4192
HIKLZ

ARKANSAS

UALR—Pulaski County Mediation
    Program
Municipal Court, Pulaski County
College Arts, Humanities & Social
    Sciences
2801 S. University, UALR
Little Rock, AR 72204
Tel. (501) 569-3234
GHKL

CALIFORNIA

Modoc County Probation Dept.
Modoc County Superior Court
201 S. Court St.
Alturas, CA 96101
Tel. (916) 233-3939
A

Family Mediation Service
Santa Cruz County Superior Court
6233 Soquel Dr., #E
Aptos, CA 95003
Tel. (408) 476-9225
A

Humboldt Mediation Services
Courts of Humboldt County
3260 West End Rd.
Arcata, CA 95521
Tel. (707) 826-1066
ABCDGHJIKLZ

Judicial Arbitration Program
Kern County Superior Court
1415 Truxtun Ave.
Bakersfield, CA 93301

Family Conciliation Services, Kern
    County, Probation
Kern County Civic Center
1415 Truxtun Ave.
Bakersfield, CA 93301

Berkeley Dispute Resolution Service
1771 Alcatraz
Berkeley, CA 94703

Mr. Richard C. Berra
Mr. McClellan Carr
216 Park Rd.
Burlingame, CA 94010

Catholic Charities
2525 Stanwell Dr.
Concord, CA 94520

Battered Women's Alternatives
P.O. Box 6406
Concord, CA 94524

Landlord-Tenant Mediation Board
City of Culver City
9696 Culver Blvd., Room 100
P.O. Box 507
Culver City, CA 90232
Tel. (213) 202-5768
L

Sierra County Probation Dept.
Sierra County Superior Court
P.O. Box 67
Downieville, CA 95936
Tel. (916) 289-3277
AE

Community Dispute Res. Center
Roybal Medical Center
245 S. Fetterly, Room 2017
East Los Angeles, CA 90022

North Coast Mediation & Arbitration
    Center
Superior Court, San Diego County
4401 Manchester, Suite 202
Encinitas, CA 92024
Tel. (619) 436-8392
ABCDIJKL

Child Custody Mediation Team
Humboldt County Superior Court
2002 Harrison Ave.
Eureka, CA 95501
Tel. (707) 445-7401
A

Family Court Services
Solano County Superior Court
Hall of Justice
600 Union Ave., 2nd Fl.
Fairfield, CA 94533
Tel. (707) 429-6686
A

CASP
208 Dana St.
Fort Bragg, CA 95437

CAARE, Inc.
461 N. Franklin St.
Fort Bragg, CA 95437

Arbitration Program
777 9th St.
Fortuna, CA 95540

Arbitration Hearing Program
39439 Paseo Padre Pkwy.
Fremont, CA 94538

Family Court Services
Fresno County Superior Court
2220 Tulare, Suite 1111
Fresno, CA 93721
Tel. (209) 488-3241
AZ

Gardena Rent Mediation Board
1700 W. 162 St.
Gardena, CA 90247

Community Dispute Resolution
   Center
Glendale Municipal Court
600 E. Broadway
Glendale, CA 91206

Claremont Dispute Resolution Center
333 W. Foothill Blvd.
Glendora, CA 91740
Tel. (818) 963-3969
ABCDEFGHIJKLZ

Mediation/Child Custody/Visitation
Kings County Superior Court
Kings County Probation Dept.
1424 Forum Dr.
Hanford, CA 93230
Tel. (209) 582-3211 Ext. 2850
A

Metro-Harbor Fair Housing Council
25324 Frampton Ave.
Harbor City, CA 90710

Echo Housing
Alameda County Superior Court
770 A St.
Hayward, CA 94541
Tel. (415) 581-9380
LZ

Civil Arbitration Program—Municipal
   Court
Mt. San Jacinto Judicial District
800 N. State St.
Hemet, CA 92343

Dept. of Industrial Relations
6430 Sunset Blvd., Suite 301
Hollywood, CA 90028

Christian Conciliation Services of Los
   Angeles
Municipal Court Los Angeles
Northwest Division
1800 N. Highland, #507
Hollywood, CA 90028
Tel. (213) 467-3331
ABCDEHIJKL

Hollywood–Mid Los Angeles Housing
   Council
6565 Sunset Blvd., Room 515
Hollywood, CA 90028

Family Conciliation
Riverside County Superior Court
Law Library Building, Room 3100A
46-209 Oasis St.
Indio, CA 92201
Tel. (619) 342-8205
A

Mediation Program
Superior Court
255 N. Forbes St.
Lakeport, CA 93546

Fair Housing Foundation of Long
   Beach
2023 Pacific Ave.
Long Beach, CA 90806

Dispute Resolution Services, Inc.
Los Angeles County Bar Assoc.
617 S. Olive St.
P.O. Box 55020
Los Angeles, CA 90055

Calif. Lawyers for the Arts
315 W. 9th St., Suite 1101
Los Angeles, CA 90015

Family Court Services/Mediation and
  Conciliation
Los Angeles County Superior Court
111 N. Hill St., Room 241
Los Angeles, CA 90012
Tel. (213) 974-5524
AG

Hearing Officer Program
210 W. Temple St., Room 17-404
Los Angeles, CA 90012

Arbitration Forums, Inc.
680 Wilshire Pl., Room 408
Los Angeles, CA 90005

American Arbitration Assoc.
443 Shatto Pl.
Los Angeles, CA 90020

Dependency Court Mediation
Los Angeles County Superior Court,
  Juvenile
210 W. Temple St., Room 12A
Los Angeles, CA 90012
Tel. (213) 974-5861
F

M.L.K. Dispute Resolution Center
Los Angeles County Superior Court
4182 S. Western Ave.
Los Angeles, CA 90062
Tel. (213) 295-8582
ABCDEGKLZ

Bureau of Electronic Appliance Repair
Dept. of Consumer Affairs, State of
  Calif.
107 S. Broadway, Room 8040
Los Angeles, CA 90012

Voluntary Mediation Service
1102 Crenshaw Blvd.
Los Angeles, CA 90019-3198

Los Angeles County Dispute
  Settlement Services
Los Angeles County Municipal Courts
500 W. Temple St., Room B-96
Los Angeles, CA 90012
Tel. (213) 974-0825
IJKLZ

Western Law Center for the
  Handicapped
Loyola Law School
1441 W. Olympic Blvd.
Los Angeles, CA 90015
Tel. (213) 736-1031
LZ

Los Angeles County Bar Assoc.
  Dispute Resolution Services
East Los Angeles Municipal Court
  Mediation Program
Box 55020
Los Angeles, CA 90055
Tel. (213) 627-2727
K

Los Angeles County Bar Assoc.
  Dispute Resolution Services
Long Beach Municipal Court
  Mediation Program
Box 55020
Los Angeles, CA 90055
Tel. (213) 627-2727
L

Los Angeles County Bar Assoc.
  Dispute Resolution Services
Los Angeles Municipal Court
Barristers Landlord Tenant Settlement
  Office
Box 55020
Los Angeles, CA 90055
Tel. (213) 627-2727
L

Los Angeles County Bar Assoc.
  Dispute Resolution Services
Long Beach Superior Court
  Settlement Office
Box 55020
Los Angeles, CA 90055
Tel. (213) 627-2727
IJ

Los Angeles County Bar Assoc.
  Dispute Resolution Services
Santa Monica Municipal Court
  Mediation
Box 55020
Los Angeles, CA 90055
Tel. (213) 627-2727
JL

Los Angeles County Bar Assoc.
  Dispute Resolution Services
Los Angeles Superior Court Central
  District
Joint Assoc. Settlement Office
  Program
Box 55020
Los Angeles, CA 90055
Tel. (213) 627-2727
IJL

Los Angeles County Bar Assoc.
  Dispute Resolution Services
Pasadena Municipal Court Mediation
  Program
Box 55020
Los Angeles, CA 90055
Tel. (213) 627-2727
H

Los Angeles County Bar Assoc.
  Dispute Resolution Services
Los Angeles Municipal Court Central
  District
Los Angeles Municipal Court
  Settlement Office
Box 55020
Los Angeles, CA 90055
Tel. (213) 627-2727
IJLZ

Los Angeles Bar Assoc. Dispute
  Resolution Services
Pasadena Superior Court Settlement
  Office
Box 55020
Los Angeles, CA 90055
Tel. (213) 627-2727
IJ

Jewish Family Service of Los Angeles,
  Divorce Mediation Program
Los Angeles County Conciliation
  Court
6505 Wilshire Blvd., Room 614
Los Angeles, CA 90048
Tel. (213) 852-1234 Ext. 2626
ABCD

Mediation/Family Law
Superior Court
209 W. Yosemite Ave.
Madera, CA 93637
Tel. (209) 675-7739
A

Arbitration Settlement
Superior Court
209 W. Yosemite Ave.
Madera, CA 93637

Institute for Dispute Resolution
Pepperdine University School of Law
Malibu, CA 90265

Dispute Resolution Center of the
  Eastern Sierra
P.O. Box 2535
Mammoth Lakes, CA 93545

Family Court Services
Alpine Superior Court
P.O. Box 145
Markleeville, CA 95120
Tel. (916) 694-2192
AEG

Contra Costa Superior Court
Courthouse
P.O. Box 1110
Martinez, CA 94553
Tel. (415) 372-2950

Family Court Services
Contra Costa Superior Court
724 Escobar St.
Martinez, CA 94553
Tel. (415) 646-2681
AG

Mediation Services for Mariposa
  County
1750 Cypress Way
Merced, CA 95340

Civil Arbitration
Merced County Superior Court
2222 M St.
Merced, CA 95340

Arbitration Program
Superior Court, Stanislaus County
P.O. Box 3488
Modesto, CA 95353-3488

Mediation Program
Superior Court, Stanislaus County
P.O. Box 3488
Modesto, CA 95353-3488

Arbitration Program
Old Courthouse
825 Brown St.
Napa, CA 94559

Conciliation Court
Old Courthouse
825 Brown St.
Napa, CA 94559

Fair Housing Council of San
  Fernando Valley
12444 Victory Blvd.
North Hollywood, CA 91660

Norwalk Consumer Rental Mediation
Board
Downey Calif. Municipal Court
12700 Norwalk Blvd.
Norwalk, CA 90650
Tel. (213) 864-3785
LZ

Family Court Services
Superior Court of Alameda County
1221 Oak St.
Oakland, CA 94612
Tel. (415) 272-6030
AG

Conciliation Forums of Oakland
Municipal & Superior Courts,
Alameda County
672 13th St.
Oakland, CA 94612
Tel. (415) 763-2117
LZ

Victim Offender Reconciliation
Program
Juvenile Probation
Catholic Charities
433 Jefferson St.
Oakland, CA 94607
Tel. (415) 834-5656
H

Judicial Arbitration, Alameda County
Superior Court
1225 Fallen St., Room 205
Oakland, CA 94612
Tel. (415) 272-6069
IJ

Inland Mediation Board
420 N. Lemon Ave.
Ontario, CA 91764
Tel. (714) 984-2254
LZ

Fair Housing Council of San Gabriel
Valley
1020 N. Fair Oaks Ave.
Pasadena, CA 91103

Community Dispute Resolution
Center
Pasadena Municipal Court
200 N. Garfield, Room 209
Pasadena, CA 91101

Community Dispute Resolution
Center
330 S. Oak Knoll Ave., Room 11
Pasadena, CA 91101

Family Mediation
El Dorado County Superior Court
495 Main St.
Placerville, CA 65667
Tel. (916) 621-6459
AFG

Conflict Resolution Panels
Contra Costa County
P.O. Box 23227
Pleasant Hill, CA 94523
Tel. (415) 935-4249
LZ

Family Court Services/Mediation
Plumas County Superior Court
P.O. Box 10258
Quincy, CA 95971
Tel. (916) 283-6200
A

Early Settlement Program
P.O. Box 10686
Quincy, CA 95971

Arbitration Program
P.O. Box 10686
Quincy, CA 95971

Child Custody Mediation
Plumas County Superior Court
P.O. Box 10258
Quincy, CA
Tel. (916) 283-6200
A

Probate and Family Court Services
Shasta County Superior Court
1558 West St., Suite 1
Redding, CA 96001
Tel. (916) 225-5707
A

Arbitration Program
Superior Court
401 Marshall St.
Redwood City, CA 94063

Judicial Arbitration
Superior Court
Hall of Justice
Redwood City, CA 94063

Mediation Program
Community Services
300 Bradford
Redwood City, CA 94063

Family Court Services
San Mateo Family Court
401 Marshall St., 7th Fl.
Redwood City, CA 94063
Tel. (415) 363-4561
AEG

San Mateo County Community
  Services Mediation Program
San Mateo County Municipal Court
300 Bradford St.
Redwood City, CA 94063
Tel. (415) 363-4889
IKLZ

Richmond Housing Community Board
551 S. 26 St.
Richmond, CA 94804
Tel. (415) 237-3276
GLZ

Custody Mediation Services
Placer County Superior Court
700 Sunrise Blvd.
Roseville, CA 95661
Tel. (916) 783-5003
A

Human Rights/Fair Housing
  Commission
2131 Capitol Ave., Suite 206
Sacramento, CA 95816

Family Court Services
Sacramento County Superior Court
800 9th St.
Sacramento, CA 95814
Tel. (415) 440-5633
A

Sacramento Mediation Center
Sacramento Municipal Court District
P.O. Box 5275
Sacramento, CA 95817
Tel. (916) 731-5511
ABCDHIJKL

Sacramento Mediation Center
Superior Court, County of
  Sacramento
P.O. Box 5275
Sacramento, CA 95817
Tel. (916) 731-5511
AHIJKLZ

Property Mediation Program
San Bernardino County Superior
  Court
County Clerk, 351 N. Arrowhead
  Ave.
San Bernardino, CA 92415-0240

Arbitration Program
San Bernardino County Superior
  Court
Courthouse, 351 N. Arrowhead Ave.
San Bernardino, CA 92415-0240
Tel. (714) 387-3881

Dispute Resolution Office
City Attorney's Office
1010 2nd Ave., Room 300
San Diego, CA 92101

Presbytery of San Diego Mediation
  Service
8825 Aero Dr., Room 220
San Diego, CA 92123

Judicial Arbitration & Mediation
  Services, Inc.
401 B St.
San Diego, CA 92101

American Arbitration Assoc.
525 C St., Room 400
San Diego, CA 92101

Judicial Arbitration & Mediation
  Program
401 B St., Room 2000
San Diego, CA 92101

Mediation & Dispute Resolution
  Center
225 Broadway, Room 900
San Diego, CA 92101

Domestic Settlement Program
Superior Court
P.O. Box 2724
San Diego, CA 92112

Arbitration Program
Superior Court
220 W. Broadway, Room 3107
San Diego, CA 92101
Tel. (649) 531-3448
IZ

Better Business Bureau
525 B St., Suite 301
San Diego, CA 92101

Community Mediation of San Diego
San Diego Superior Court
2150 W. Washington St., Suite 112
San Diego, CA 92110
Tel. (619) 238-1022
ABCDEHIJKLZ

Family Court Services
Superior Court, San Diego County
1501 6th Ave.
San Diego, CA 92101-3246
Tel. (619) 557-2100
AG

Community Boards of San Francisco
149 9th St.
San Francisco, CA 94103

Mediation Service—San Francisco
    District
Attorney's Office, Consumer
    Protection
732 Brannan St.
San Francisco, CA 94103

Community Relation Service
U.S. Dept. of Justice
211 Main St., Suite 1040
San Francisco, CA 94105

Calif. Community Dispute Services
445 Bush St., 5th Fl.
San Francisco, CA 94108

San Francisco Human Rights
    Commission
1095 Market St., Room 501
San Francisco, CA 94103
Tel. (415) 558-4901
L

American Inter. Services
Telesis Tower, Suite 2100
1 Montgomery St.
San Francisco, CA 94104

St. Peter's Housing Committee
1049 Market St., Suite 200
San Francisco, CA 94103

Early Settlement Program
Superior Court of Calif., City &
    County of San Francisco
Bar Assoc. of San Francisco
685 Market St., Suite 700
San Francisco, CA 94105
Tel. (415) 764-1600
EJLZ

San Francisco Rent Arbitration Board
170 Fell St., #16
San Francisco, CA 94102

San Francisco County Superior Court
313 City Hall
400 Van Ness
San Francisco, CA 94102
Tel. (415) 554-4110

Small Claims Legal Adviser
Municipal Court of San Francisco
City Hall, Room 163
San Francisco, CA 94102
Tel. (415) 554-4526
IJKLZ

Arts Arbitration & Mediation Services
Bldg. B, Room 300
Fort Mason Center
San Francisco, CA 94123
Tel. (415) 775-7715 or 7200
DIJKLZ

Family Court Services
San Francisco Superior Court
463 City Hall
San Francisco, CA 94102
Tel. (415) 554-5080
A

Calif. Community Dispute Services
San Francisco Municipal Court
30 Holing Pl., Suite #302
San Francisco, CA 94111
Tel. (415) 434-2200
ADHIKLZ

Alternative Dispute Resolution
Auto Line, BBB
505 Meridian Ave.
San Jose, CA 95125

Santa Clara County Superior Court
292 N. 1st St.
San Jose, CA 95113
Tel. (408) 299-2964

Family Court Services, Santa Clara
    County
Santa Clara County Superior Court
191 N. 1st St.
San Jose, CA 95113
Tel. (408) 299-3741
A

Victim/Offender Mediation Program
551 Stockton Ave.
San Jose, CA 95126
Tel. (408) 295-6033
H

Family Court Services
San Luis Obispo County Superior
  Court
County Government Center
San Luis Obispo, CA 93408
Tel. (805) 549-5423
A

San Luis Obispo County Superior
  Court Arbitration
County Government Center
Courthouse, Room 355
San Luis Obispo, CA 93408
Tel. (805) 549-5473
DIJLZ

Judicial Arbitration
Municipal Court-Central
800 N. Humboldt
San Mateo, CA 94401

Peninsula Conflict Resolution Center
177 Bovet Rd., Suite 230
San Mateo, CA 94402
Tel. (415) 571-0367
LZ

Superior Court Arbitration
Marin County Superior Court
Hall of Justice
San Rafael, CA 94903
Tel. (415) 499-6072
IJ

Marin County Consumer Protection
  Division
Superior & Municipal Courts
Hall of Justice, Room 183
San Rafael, CA 94903
Tel. (415) 499-6482
IJKL

Family Mediation Service
Marin County Superior Court
1450 Lucas Valley Rd.
San Rafael, CA 94903
Tel. (415) 499-6659
A

Arbitration
Marin County Municipal Court
Civic Center Hall of Justice
Marin County Municipal Court,
  Room 191
San Rafael, CA 94903
Tel. (415) 499-6211
LZ

Marin Mediation Services
Municipal, Superior Courts Marin
  County Judicial
Civic Center, Room 412
San Rafael, CA 94903
Tel. (415) 499-6190
DIJKLZ

Arbitration
Orange County Superior Court
P.O. Box 1994
Santa Ana, CA 92701
Tel. (714) 834-3766
IJL

Mediation & Investigative Services
Orange County Superior Court
700 Civic Center Dr. W., Room
  D301
Santa Ana, CA 92701
Tel. (714) 834-4791
AFGZ

Alternative Dispute Relief Program
Orange County Superior Court
P.O. Box 1994
Santa Ana, CA 92701
Tel. (714) 834-3766
IJL

Arbitration Program
Santa Barbara Municipal Court
118 E. Figueroa St.
Santa Barbara, CA 93101

Rental Housing Mediation Task Force
1136 Montecito St.
Santa Barbara, CA 93108

Legal Aid Foundation
1032 Santa Barbara St.
Santa Barbara, CA 93105

Family Custody Services
Superior Court, County of Santa
  Barbara
1100 Anacapa St.
Santa Barbara, CA 93101
Tel. (805) 568-3175
A

Mediation/Arbitration Program
701 Ocean St., Room 200
Santa Cruz, CA 95060

Santa Monica Municipal Court
1725 Main St., Division I
Santa Monica, CA 90401

Santa Monica/West Los Angeles
Office
2330 Pico Blvd.
Santa Monica, CA 90405

Center for Dispute Resolution
1337 Ocean Ave.
Santa Monica, CA 90401
Tel. (213) 451-1615
ABCDEFGIJKLZ

Long-Term Care Ombudsman
  Program
Los Angeles City/County, c/o Wise
  Senior Service
1320 3rd St. Promenade
Santa Monica, CA 90401

Sonoma County Rental Information &
  Mediation Services, Inc.
Municipal & Small Claims Courts
324 Santa Rosa Ave.
Santa Rosa, CA 95404
Tel. (707) 575-8787
L

Arbitration Program
San Joaquin County Superior Court
222 E. Weber Ave., Room 303
Stockton, CA 95202
Tel. (209) 944-3642
IJZ

Family Court Mediation
San Joaquin County Superior Court
222 E. Weber Ave., Room 370
Stockton, CA 95202
Tel. (209) 944-2101
A

Arbitration Program
Tahoe Judicial District Court
P.O. Box 5669
Tahoe City, CA 95730

Family Mediation
Mendocino County, Superior Court
  #1
Courthouse
Ukiah, CA 95482
Tel. (707) 463-4484
A

Ventura County ADR Program
Ventura County Superior Court
800 S. Victoria Ave.
Ventura, CA 93009
Tel. (805) 654-2670
IJ

Consumer Mediation Unit
Office of the District Attorney
800 S. Victoria Ave.
Ventura, CA 93009
Tel. (805) 654-3110
IKLZ

Superior Court, Family Court
  Services, State-Mandated Mediation
Ventura County Superior Court
800 S. Victoria Ave.
Ventura, CA 93009
Tel. (805) 654-5021
A

Rent-a-Judge
Municipal Courts Hall of Justice
800 S. Victoria Ave.
Ventura, CA 93009
IJ

Custody
Municipal Courts Hall of Justice
800 S. Victoria Ave.
Ventura, CA 93009
A

Family Mediation & Conciliation
Tulare Superior Court
Tulare County Probation Dept.
Visalia, CA 93291
Tel. (209) 733-6207
AE

Housing Alliance of Contra Costa
  County
1963 Tice Valley Blvd.
Walnut Creek, CA 94595

Family Court Services
Trinity County Superior Court
P.O. Box 1258
Weaverville, CA 96093
Tel. (916) 623-1369
AE

Civil Arbitration Program
311 4th St.
Yreka, CA 96097

Siskiyou County Court Mediator
Siskiyou County Superior Court
322 W. Center St., #6
Yreka, CA 96097
Tel. (916) 842-8107
A


COLORADO

Court-Annexed Arbitration
20th District Court
Boulder Justice Center
1777 6th St., Box 471
Boulder, CO 80306
IJ

Office of Dispute Resolution, County
    Judicial Dept.
21st District Court
1301 Pennsylvania St., Suite 300
Denver, CO 80203
Tel. (303) 837-3672
ABCDEFGIJKLZ

Office of Dispute Resolution, County
    Judicial Dept.
20th District Court
1301 Pennsylvania St., Suite 300
Denver, CO 80203
Tel. (303) 837-3672
ABCDEFGIJKLZ

Office of Dispute Resolution, County
    Judicial Dept.
17th District Court
1301 Pennsylvania St., Suite 300
Denver, CO 80203
Tel. (303) 837-3672
ABCDEFGIJKLZ

Office of Dispute Resolution, County
    Judicial Dept.
19th District Court
1301 Pennsylvania St., Suite 300
Denver, CO 80203
Tel. (303) 837-3672
ABCDEFGIJKLZ

Office of Dispute Resolution, County
    Judicial Dept.
2nd District Court
1301 Pennsylvania St., Suite 300
Denver, CO 80203
Tel. (303) 837-3672
ABCDEFGIJKLZ

Office of Dispute Resolution, County
    Judicial Dept.
4th District Court
1301 Pennsylvania St., Suite 300
Denver, CO 80203
Tel. (303) 837-3672
ABCDEFGIJKLZ

Office of Dispute Resolution, County
    Judicial Dept.
18th District Court
1301 Pennsylvania St., Suite 300
Denver, CO 80203
Tel. (303) 837-3672
ABCDEFGIJKLZ

Office of Dispute Resolution, County
    Judicial Dept.
1st Judicial District
1301 Pennsylvania St., Suite 300
Denver, CO 80203
Tel. (303) 861-1111
ABCDEIJL

Office of Dispute Resolution, County
    Judicial Dept.
7th District Court
1301 Pennsylvania St., Suite 300
Denver, CO 80203
Tel. (303) 837-3672
ABCDEFGIJKLZ

Office of Dispute Resolution, County
    Judicial Dept.
8th District Court
1301 Pennsylvania St., Suite 300
Denver, CO 80203
Tel. (303) 837-3672
ABCDEFGIJKLZ

Office of Dispute Resolution, County
    Judicial Dept.
9th District Court
1301 Pennsylvania St., Suite 300
Denver, CO 80203
Tel. (303) 837-3672
ABCDEFGIJKLZ

Office of Dispute Resolution, County
  Judicial Dept.
10th District Court
1301 Pennsylvania St., Suite 300
Denver, CO 80203
Tel. (303) 837-3672
ABCDEFGIJKLZ

Office of Dispute Resolution, County
  Judicial Dept.
14th District Court
1301 Pennsylvania St., Suite 300
Denver, CO 80203
Tel. (303) 837-3672
ABCDEFGIJKLZ

Court Settlement Conference Program
La Plata County District Court
1301 Pennsylvania St., Suite 300
Denver, CO 80203-2416
Tel. (303) 861-1111
IJZ

Mandatory Arbitration Program (Pilot)
La Plata County District Court
1301 Pennsylvania St., Suite 300
Denver, CO 80203-2416
Tel. (303) 861-1111
Z

Domestic Relations Mediation
  Program
La Plata County District Court
P.O. Box 3340
Durango, CO 81302
Tel. (303) 247-1301
A

Court-Annexed Arbitration
18th District Court
Arapahoe County Justice Center
7325 S. Potomac St.
Englewood, CO 80112
IJ

Mandatory Arbitration, 8th Judicial
  District
8th District Court
P.O. Box 2066
Fort Collins, CO 80522
Tel. (303) 221-7917
Z

Mandatory Arbitration
1st District
Hall of Justice
1701 Arapahoe St.
Golden, CO 80401-6199
Tel. (303) 278-6197
IJZ

Court-Annexed Arbitration
7th District Court
Montrose County Courthouse
309 S. 1st St., Box 368
Montrose, CO 81401
IJ

Court-Annexed Arbitration
14th District Court
Routt County Courthouse
522 Lincoln Ave., P.O. Box 73117
Steamboat Springs, CO 80477
IJ

Court-Annexed Arbitration
3rd District Court
Las Animas County Courthouse,
  Room 304
Trinidad, CO 81082
IJ

CONNECTICUT

Attorney Trial Referee
Superior Court
75 Elm St.
Hartford, CT 06106
Tel. (203) 722-5838
DIKLZ

Arbitration
Superior Court
75 Elm St.
Hartford, CT 06106
Tel. (203) 722-5837
DIJKLZ

Housing Mediation
Superior Court
75 Elm St.
Hartford, CT 06106
Tel. (203) 722-5838
IKLZ

Factfinding
Superior Court
75 Elm St.
Hartford, CT 06106
Tel. (203) 722-5838
IK

Magistrates
Superior Court
75 Elm St.
Hartford, CT 06106
Tel. (203) 722-8538
HKZ

Family Services Unit, Connecticut
    Superior Court, Family Division
Connecticut Superior Court
28 Grand St.
Hartford, CT 06791
Tel. (203) 566-8187
ABCDEHLZ

Juvenile Matters Unit, Connecticut
    Superior Court, Family Division
Connecticut Superior Court
28 Grand St.
Hartford, CT 06106
Tel. (203) 566-8187
FZ

DELAWARE

Family Court of Del. Mediation Unit
Family Court of the State of Del.
900 King St.
P.O. Box 2359
Wilmington, DE 19899
Tel. (302) 571-2215
ABCEFZ

Superior Court Compulsory
    Arbitration Program
Del. Superior Court
The Public Building
11th & King Sts.
Wilmington, DE 19801
Tel. (302) 571-2343
IJKLZ

Family Court of Del. Arbitration
P.O. Box 2359
Wilmington, DE 19899
Tel. (302) 571-2215
HJZ

DISTRICT OF COLUMBIA

Multi-Door Small Claims Mediation
    Program
Superior Court of the District of
    Columbia
500 Indiana Ave., N.W., Room 1235
Washington, DC 20001
Tel. (202) 879-1549
K

Multi-Door Dispute Resolution
    Division/Citizen Intake
Superior Court of the District of
    Columbia
500 Indiana Ave., N.W., Room 4242
Washington, DC 20001
Tel. (202) 879-1478
KLZ

Multi-Door Accelerated Resolutions of
    Civil Dispute Program
Superior Court of the District of
    Columbia
500 Indiana Ave., N.W., Room 4242
Washington, DC 20001
Tel. (202) 879-1478
IJZ

Multi-Door/Expanded Mandatory
    Non-Binding Arbitration
Superior Court of the District of
    Columbia
500 Indiana Ave., N.W., Room 4242
Washington, DC 20001
Tel. (202) 879-1478
IJZ

Multi-Door—Settlement Week
    Program
Superior Court of the District of
    Columbia
500 Indiana Ave., N.W., Room 4242
Washington, DC 20001
Tel. (202) 879-1549
IJZ

Multi-Door Dispute Resolution
    Division/Domestic Relations
    Mediation Program
Superior Court of the District of
    Columbia
500 Indiana Ave., Room 1235
Washington, DC 20001
Tel. (202) 879-1549
ABCDE

Multi-Door Dispute Resolution
Division, Civil II Mediation
Program
Superior Court of the District of
Columbia
500 Indiana Ave., N.W., Room 4242
Washington, DC 20001
Tel. (202) 879-1549
IJZ

Mediation Service
Superior Court of the District of
Columbia
Building A
515 5th St., N.W.
Washington, DC 20001
Tel. (202) 724-8215
ABCDGHIKLZ

FLORIDA

Citizen Dispute Settlement
Pinellas County Court
418 S. Fort Harrison Ave.
Clearwater, FL 34616
Tel. (813) 462-4946
HKLZ

20th Judicial Circuit Court Mediation
1700 Monroe St.
Fort Myers, FL 33901
Tel. (813) 335-2884
IJZ

20th Judicial Court Family Mediation
1700 Monroe St.
Fort Myers, FL 33901
Tel. (813) 335-2884
ABCDE

Citizens Dispute Settlement Program
20th Judicial Court, Lee County
1700 Monroe St.
Fort Myers, FL 33901
Tel. (813) 335-2884
HIKL

Court Mediation & Arbitration
Program
17th Judicial Circuit
Court Administrator's Office
516 S.E. 5th St.
Ft. Lauderdale, FL 33301
Tel. (305) 765-4491
HIKLZ

Family Mediation & Conciliation
Program
17th Judicial Circuit
507 S.E. 6th St., 2nd Fl.
Ft. Lauderdale, FL 33301
Tel. (305) 765-4012
ABCD

Okaloosa County Citizens Dispute
Settlement Program
Summary Claims, Okaloosa County
Court
917 Holbrook Circle
Fort Walton Beach, FL 32548
Tel. (904) 862-7735
KL

Family Mediation Program
8th Judicial Circuit Court
201 E. University Ave., Room 410
Gainesville, FL 32608
Tel. (904) 374-3648
ABCDE

Family Mediation Program
4th Judicial Circuit of Fla.
1283 E. 8th St.
Jacksonville, FL 32206
Tel. (904) 630-0987
AE

Family/Divorce Mediation for the 10th
Judicial Circuit
1835 N. Gilmore Ave.
Lakeland, FL 33805
Tel. (813) 683-5701
A

Alternative Dispute Resolution
Program
County Court of Brevard County
Brevard County Courthouse
50 S. Nieman St., Bldg. C
Melbourne, FL 32901
Tel. (407) 727-9719
GHKL

Family Mediation Unit
11th Judicial Circuit
Dade County Courthouse
73 W. Flagler St., Suite 2201
Miami, FL 33130
Tel. (305) 375-1650
A

Arbitration
11th Judicial Circuit
Mediation & Arbitration Division
Dade County Courthouse, 73 W.
  Flagler St.
Miami, FL 33130
Tel. (305) 375-5225
IJ

Mediation Unit
County Court of Dade County
73 W. Flagler St., Room 1700
Miami, FL 33130
Tel. (305) 375-3864
ABCDIJKL

County Mediation
Collier County Court
Mediation/Arbitration Programs
Collier County Courthouse, Room 63
Naples, FL 33942
Tel. (813) 774-8704
K

Mediation/Arbitration
20th Judicial Circuit
Mediation/Arbitration Programs
Collier County Courthouse, Room 63
Naples, FL 33942
Tel. (813) 774-8704
ABCD

Civil Mediation
20th Judicial Circuit
Mediation/Arbitration Programs
Collier County Courthouse, Room 63
Naples, FL 33942
Tel. (813) 774-8704
IJZ

Family Mediation Program
Circuit Court, 1st Judicial Circuit
Judicial Bldg.
190 Government Center
Pensacola, FL 32501
Tel. (904) 436-5733
A

Citizen Dispute Settlement
12th Judicial Circuit
Courthouse
2000 Main St.
P.O. Box 48927
Sarasota, FL 34239
Tel. (813) 951-5778
IKL

Family Mediation
12th Judicial Circuit
Sarasota County Courthouse
2000 Main St.
Sarasota, FL 33577
Tel. (813) 951-5700
A

Arbitration Services
6th Judicial Circuit
150 5th St. N.
St. Petersburg, FL 33701
Tel. (813) 892-7583
ABCIJZ

Family Mediation
6th Judicial Circuit
150 5th St. N., Room 217
St. Petersburg, FL 33701
Tel. (813) 892-7803
A

Leon County Citizens Dispute
  Settlement Program
County Court of Leon County
197C Villas Ct., S.E.
Tallahassee, FL 32303
Tel. (904) 385-8863
K

Arbitration Program
13th Judicial Circuit
Mediation & Diversion Services
800 E. Kennedy Blvd., Courthouse
  Annex
Tampa, FL 33602
Tel. (813) 272-5642
IJ

Circuit Court Civil Mediation &
  Diversion Services
Courthouse Annex, Room 206
800 E. Kennedy Blvd.
Tampa, FL 33602
Tel. (813) 272-5680
IJZ

County Court Criminal Mediation &
  Diversion Services
Courthouse Annex, Room 206
800 E. Kennedy Blvd.
Tampa, FL 33602
Tel. (813) 272-5642
H

County & Circuit Court Community
   Mediation & Diversion Services
Courthouse Annex, Room 206
800 E. Kennedy Blvd.
Tampa, FL 33602
Tel. (813) 272-5642
KLZ

County Court Civil Mediation &
   Diversion Services
Courthouse Annex, Room 206
800 E. Kennedy Blvd.
Tampa, FL 33602
Tel. (813) 262-5642
KZ

Family Diversion Program
13th Judicial Circuit
Courthouse Annex, Room 206
800 E. Kennedy Blvd.
Tampa, FL 33602
Tel. (813) 272-5642
ABCD

Family Mediation
18th Judicial Circuit
Brevard County Courthouse
518 Palm Ave.
Titusville, FL 32796
Tel. (407) 269-8943
AB

Riese Counseling/Mediation Services
19th Judicial Court
2096 38th Ave., Suite 2
Vero Beach, FL 32960
Tel. (407) 778-2525
ABCD

Summary Jury Trials
19th Judicial Circuit Court
c/o Judge Smith
239 County Courthouse
Vero Beach, FL 32960
Tel. (407) 567-8000
JZ

County Court Mediation
300 N. Dixie Hwy., Room 427
West Palm Beach, FL 33410
Tel. (407) 355-2739
KLZ

Circuit Civil Mediation
15th Judicial Circuit
P.O. Box 1989
West Palm Beach, FL 33402-1989
IJZ

4th District Court of Appeals
   Settlement Conference Project
P.O. Box A
West Palm Beach, FL 33402
Tel. (407) 686-1903
ABCDEIJZ

Family Mediation
300 N. Dixie Hwy., Room 427
West Palm Beach, FL 33410
Tel. (407) 355-2739
ABCDE

County Court Arbitration
300 N. Dixie Hwy., Room 427
West Palm Beach, FL 33410
Tel. (407) 355-2739
IJ

Circuit Court Mediation
300 N. Dixie Hwy., Room 427
West Palm Beach, FL 33410
Tel. (407) 355-2739
IJZ

GEORGIA

Civil Arbitration Program
Superior Court of Fulton County
Fulton County Courthouse, Room 201
136 Pryor St., S.W.
Atlanta, GA 30303
Tel. (404) 730-4551
ABCDEIJKLZ

Neighbor to Neighbor Mediation
   Center (NNMC)
1st Judicial Administrative District,
   Eastern Judicial Circuit
1810 Bull St., Room 101
Savannah, GA 31401
Tel. (912) 236-0918
ABCDEHIKLZ

HAWAII

Waiakea Settlement YMCA Mediation
   Center
Family Court of 3rd Circuit/District
   Court of 3rd Circuit
300 W. Lanikaula St.
Hilo, HI 96720
Tel. (808) 935-7844
ABCDHIKL

Neighborhood Justice Center of
    Honolulu, Inc.
Family Court of 1st Circuit/District
    Court of 1st Circuit
200 N. Vineyard Blvd., #501
Honolulu, HI 96817
Tel. (808) 521-6767
ABCDHIKLZ

Court-Annexed Arbitration Program
1st Circuit Court
777 Punchbowl St., 4th Fl.
Honolulu, HI 96813
Tel. (808) 548-4380
J

Center for Alternative Dispute
    Resolution
Supreme Court of Hawaii
The Judiciary, State of Hawaii
P.O. Box 2560
Honolulu, HI 96804
Tel. (808) 548-3080
Z

Juvenile Monetary Restitution
    Program
1st Circuit Family Court
P.O. Box 2560
Honolulu, HI 96804
Tel. (808) 548-5598
Z

West Hawaii Mediation Services
Family Court of the 3rd Circuit/
    District Court of 3rd Circuit
P.O. Box 1890
Kamuela, HI 96743
Tel. (808) 885-5525
ABCDHIKL

Kauai Economic Opportunity
    Mediation Board
Family Court of the 5th Circuit/
    District Court of the 5th Circuit
2670 Niumalu Rd.
Lihue, HI 96766
Tel. (808) 245-4077
ABCDHIKL

Mediation Services of Maui, Inc.
Family Court of the 2nd Circuit/
    District Court of the 2nd Circuit
J. Walter Cameron Center
95 Mahalani St.
Wailuku, HI 96793
Tel. (808) 244-5744
ABCDIJKLZ

IDAHO

Friends of the Court—Custody/
    Visitation Mediation Program
Magistrate Division of 4th Judicial
    District, Idaho
Ada County Courthouse
Boise, ID 83702
Tel. (208) 383-1209
ABE

The Sounding Board
P.O. Box 246
Boise, ID 83701
Tel. (208) 345-8639
L

Custody/Visitation Mediation Program
Valley County, Magistrate Division
Valley County Courthouse
Cascade, ID 83611
Tel. (208) 382-4150
A

Conflict Resolution Center
410 Sherman Ave., #216
Coeur d'Alene, ID 83814
Tel. (208) 664-9448
ABCDEJK

Bonner County Child Custody
    Mediation Program
Magistrate Division of District Court
Bonner County Courthouse
Sandpoint, ID 83864
Tel. (208) 263-6841
A

ILLINOIS

Children's Home & Aid Society of Ill.
    Youth Service
20th Circuit (St. Clair)
7623 W. Main, Rear
Belleville, IL 62223
Tel. (618) 398-6700
AFHZ

Conflict Resolution Assoc.
11th Circuit (McLean)
McLean County Divorce Mediation
    Program
205 N. Main, Suite 418
Bloomington, IL 61701
Tel. (309) 454-1431

Catholic Social Services
11th Circuit (McLean)
603 N. Center St.
Bloomington, IL 61701
Tel. (609) 829-6307

Department of Children & Family
  Services
7th Circuit (Macoupin)
Carlinville Field Office
532 N. Broad
Carlinville, IL 62626
Tel. (217) 854-2544

Macoupin County Mental Health
  Center
7th Circuit (Macoupin)
100 N. Side Sq.
Carlinville, IL 62626
Tel. (217) 384-3733

Preliminary Conference
2nd Circuit (White)
P.O. Box 566
Carmi, IL 62821
Tel. (618) 382-8520
HZ

NJC of Chicago
53 W. Jackson
Chicago, IL 60604
Tel. (312) 929-7383

Endispute, Inc.
222 S. Riverside Plaza, Suite 800
Chicago, IL 60606
Tel. (312) 648-4343

Leonore Levit
1901 Daley Center
Chicago, IL 60602

Resolve Dispute Management, Inc.
650 N. Dearborn
Chicago, IL 60610-9038
Tel. (312) 943-7477
ABCDEIJ

Marriage & Family Counseling
  Service
Cook County Circuit Court
32 W. Randolph, Suite 1050
Chicago, IL 60601
Tel. (312) 609-8750
A

Sinnisspippi Mental Health Center
15th Circuit (Lee)
325 IL, Rt. 2
Dixon, IL 61021
Tel. (815) 284-7621

Divorce Mediation
11th Circuit (Woodford)
Woodford County Courthouse
Eureka, IL 61530
Tel. (309) 467-3312

NJC of Evanston
Evanston, IL
Tel. (312) 866-2920

Conciliation & Mediation
16th Circuit (Kane)
Office of State's Attorney
P.O. Box 294
Geneva, IL 60134
Tel. (312) 232-3500

McDonough County Juvenile Court
9th Circuit (McDonough)
130½ S. Lafayette St.
Macomb, IL 61455
Tel. (309) 837-2307

Family Service & Community Mental
  Health Center for McHenry County
19th Circuit (McHenry)
McHenry County
5320 W. Elm St.
McHenry, IL 60050
Tel. (815) 385-6400

Piatt County Mental Health Center
  Outpatient Counseling
6th Circuit (Piatt)
125 W. Lafayette
Monticello, IL 61856
Tel. (217) 762-5371
AEFG

Divorce Mediation for Rest of 13th
  Circuit
13th Circuit (LaSalle)
LaSalle County Courthouse
Ottowa, IL 61350
Tel. (815) 434-0730

Tazewell County Deferred Prosecution
10th Circuit (Tazewell)
Tazewell County Courthouse
414 Court St.
Pekin, IL 61455
Tel. (309) 477-2294
GHZ

Institute for Human Resource
(Divorce Mediation)
11th Circuit (Livingston)
Torrance Ave.
Pontiac, IL 61764
Tel. (815) 844-6109

Divorce Mediation
11th Circuit (Livingston)
Livingston County Courthouse
Pontiac, IL 61664
Tel. (815) 844-5166

(Divorce Mediation) Center for
Mastery Living
13th Circuit (Bureau)
530 Park Ave. E.
Princeton, IL 61356
Tel. (815) 872-0816
A

Quad-County Counseling Center
(Divorce/Custody Mediation)
13th Circuit (Bureau)
530 Park Ave. E.
Princeton, IL 61356
Tel. (815) 875-4458

Family Service Agency
8th Circuit (Adams)
915 Vermont
Quincy, IL 62301
Tel. (217) 222-8254

Great River Recover Resources, Inc.
8th Circuit (Adams)
537 Broadway
Quincy, IL 62301
Tel. (217) 224-6300

Catholic Social Services, Inc.
8th Circuit (Adams)
926 State St.
Quincy, IL 62301
Tel. (217) 222-0958

Newman Clinic
8th Circuit (Adams)
1225 Broadway
Quincy, IL 62301

Domestic Violence Project Learning
Center
8th Circuit (Adams)
2028 Broadway
Quincy, IL 62301

Domestic Violence Intervention
Program
8th Circuit (Adams)
521 Vermont
Quincy, IL 62301
Tel. (217) 228-6300 Ext. 480

Court-Annexed Mandatory Arbitration
17th Circuit (Winnebago)
Winnebago County Courthouse
400 W. State St., Room 345
Rockford, IL 61101
Tel. (815) 987-2568
Z

Champaign County Referred
Mediation Program
6th Circuit (Champaign)
Courtroom F, Champaign County
Courthouse
101 E. Main
Urbana, IL 61801
Tel. (217) 384-3868

Lake County Conciliation Program
19th Judicial Circuit (Lake County)
Lake County Courthouse
18 N. County St.
Waukegan, IL 60085
Tel. (312) 360-6480
AE

Mandatory Court-Annexed Arbitration
Program
19th Judicial Circuit Court, Lake
County
415 Washington St., Suite 106
Waukegan, IL 60085
Tel. (708) 360-5747
IJ

Dupage County Divorce/
Conciliation—Custody Disputes
18th Circuit (DuPage)
421 N. County Farm Rd.
Wheaton, IL 60187
Tel. (312) 682-7879
A

Court-Annexed Mandatory Arbitration
Program
18th Judicial Circuit of Ill.
126 S. County Farm Rd., Suite 2A
Wheaton, IL 60187
Tel. (708) 653-5803
IJZ

Horizons, the Center for Counseling
  (Mediation)
19th Circuit (McHenry)
1216 Seminary Ave.
Woodstock, IL 60098
Tel. (815) 338-9199


B.J. Jones Custody Mediation Service
19th Circuit (McHenry)
443 W. South St.
Woodstock, IL 60098
Tel. (815) 338-6352


Turning Point (Domestic Violence)
19th Circuit (McHenry)
311 Washington St.
Woodstock, IL 60098
Tel. (815) 338-8080



## INDIANA

Domestic Relations Counseling
  Bureau
T-742 City-County Bldg.
Indianapolis, IN 46204
Tel. (317) 236-3858



## KANSAS

Domestic Department—Court
  Services Dept.
29th Judicial District of Kans.
Wyandotte County Courthouse
710 N. 7th
Kansas City, KS 66101
Tel. (913) 573-2833
AEZ


Court Services Mediation
9th Judicial District Court
P.O. Box 543
McPherson, KS 67460
Tel. (316) 241-3510
ABD


Domestic Court Services
Johnson County District Court
905 W. Spruce, Box 787
Olathe, KS 66061
Tel. (913) 782-7252
AE

Dispute Resolution Services
Johnson County District Court & City
  Municipal Courts
Kansas Legal Services, Inc.
465 S. Parker, Suite 103
Olathe, KS 66061
Tel. (913) 764-8585
ABCDIKLZ


Domestic Relations
Crawford County District Court
P.O. Box 11348
Pittsburg, KS 66762
Tel. (316) 232-2460


Domestic Mediation Program
Sedgwick County District Court
525 N. Main St.
Wichita, KS 67203
Tel. (316) 268-7302
A


Victim-Offenders Mediation Services
Sedgwick County District Court
2020 E. Central
Wichita, KS 67214
Tel. (316) 264-5445
Z


Neighborhood Justice Center
Sedgwick County District Court
301 N. Main, Suite 700
Wichita, KS 67202
Tel. (316) 263-2251
KL



## LOUISIANA

Small Claims Arbitration
Baton Rouge City Court
P.O. Box 3438
Baton Rouge, LA 70821
Tel. (504) 389-5279
K


Winnsboro City Court
P.O. Box 689
Winnsboro, LA 71295
Tel. (318) 425-4508
HKL

MAINE

Medical Malpractice Screening Panels
Maine Superior Court
Penobscot County Courthouse
97 Hammond St.
Bangor, ME 04401
Tel. (207) 947-0751
Z

ADR Pilot Project (Superior Court
  Administrator)
Maine Superior Court
P.O. Box 328-DTS
Portland, ME 04112
Tel. (207) 879-4701
IJZ

Court Mediation Service
State of Maine Judicial Dept.
P.O. Box 328-DTS
Portland, ME 04112
Tel. (207) 879-4301
ABCDEIJKL

MARYLAND

Anne Arundel County Child Custody
  Mediation
Circuit Court of Anne Arundel
  County
Circuit Courthouse
P.O. Box 2395
Annapolis, MD 21404
A

Child Care Mediation Services
Circuit Court for Baltimore City
Courthouse East, Room 522
111 N. Calvert St.
Baltimore, MD 21202
Tel. (301) 396-1184
ABCDZ

Child Custody Mediation
Harford County Circuit Court
Bel Air, MD 21014
A

Child Custody Mediation
Montgomery County Circuit Court
50 Courthouse Sq.
Rockville, MD 20850
A

Law Settlement
Circuit Court for Baltimore County
County Courts Bldg.
401 Bosley Ave.
Towson, MD 21204
Tel. (301) 887-2920
IJ

Support & Custody Division for the
  Circuit Court for Baltimore County
County Courts Bldg.
401 Bosley Ave.
Towson, MD 21204
Tel. (301) 887-6578
A

Equity Settlement
Circuit Court for Baltimore County
County Courts Bldg.
401 Bosley Ave.
Towson, MD 21204
Tel. (301) 887-2920
BCD

Custody Mediation Program
Circuit Court for Prince George's
  County
Office for Domestic Relations Causes,
  Room 406
Courthouse, 4th Fl.
Upper Marlboro, MD 20772
Tel. (301) 952-3953
A

Standing Master
Circuit Court for Carroll County
Courthouse
Westminster, MD 21157
Tel. (301) 857-2672
ABCD

Pre-Trial Settlement
Circuit Court for Carroll County
Courthouse
Westminster, MD 21157
Tel. (301) 857-2953
IJ

MASSACHUSETTS

Family Service Mediation
Probate and Family Court
649 High St.
Dedham, MA 02026
Tel. (617) 326-7200
ABCDI

Mediation Project
University of Mass.
425 Amity St.
Amherst, MA 01002
Tel. (413) 545-2462
ABHDKLZ

Cape Cod Mediation Program
P.O. Box 930
Barnstable, MA 02111
Tel. (508) 362-5850

Suffolk Superior Court Pilot
    Mediation Project
Superior Court Dept.
2 Center Plaza, 5th Fl.
Boston, MA 02108
Tel. (617) 742-8575
IJ

Face-to-Face Mediation Program
Mayor's Office of Consumer Affairs &
    Licenses
Boston City Hall, Room 613
Boston, MA 02201
Tel. (617) 725-3320

Crime & Justice Foundation
    Mediation Program
Boston Municipal Court
20 West St.
Boston, MA 02111
Tel. (617) 426-9800
ABDHIJKL

Crime & Justice Foundation
    Mediation Program
Boston Municipal Court
95 Berkeley St.
Boston, MA 02116
Tel. (617) 426-9800
ADHIJKL

University of Mass. Graduate Program
    in Dispute Resolution
Downtown Campus, 8th Fl.
University of Mass. — Boston
Boston, MA 02125
Tel. (617) 956-1080
K

Brockton Mediation Program
Brockton Consumer Advisory
    Commission
50 Maple Ave., City Hall Annex
Brockton, MA 02401
Tel. (508) 580-7184

Brockton District Court Mediation
    Project
District Court of Brockton
155 W. Elm St.
Brockton, MA 02401
Tel. (508) 587-8000
GHL

Brookline Mediation Collaborative
43 Garrison Rd.
Brookline, MA 02146
Tel. (617) 277-8107

Harvard Mediation Program
Mass. District Courts
Harvard Law School, Pound 418
Cambridge, MA 02138
Tel. (617) 495-1854
HK

Cambridge Dispute Settlement Center
One West St.
Cambridge, MA 02139
Tel. (617) 876-5376

Family Service Clinic
Middlesex Probate Court
40 Thorndike St.
Cambridge, MA 02141
Tel. (617) 494-4557
AE

The Children's Hearing Project
Cambridge District Court
99 Bishop Allen Dr.
Cambridge, MA 02139
Tel. (617) 661-4700
Z

Urban Mediation Project
Dorchester District Court/Roxbury
    District Court
Dorchester Youth Collaborative
1514-A Dorchester Ave.
Dorchester, MA 02122
Tel. (617) 288-7148
ABEGHIJKL

Mediation Services
Dudley District Court
W. Main St.
Dudley, MA 01570
Tel. (508) 949-2973

Martha's Vineyard Mediation
   Program, Inc.
Edgartown District Court
P.O. Box 1284
Edgartown, MA 02539
Tel. (508) 627-3751
AHIKLZ

Fitchburg Mediation Project
Central Court Service, Inc.
c/o Fitchburg District Court
100 Elm St.
Fitchburg, MA 01420
Tel. (508) 345-2111

Framingham Court Mediation
   Services, Inc.
Framingham District Court
600 Concord St.
Framingham, MA 01701
Tel. (508) 872-9495

Franklin Mediation Services
Franklin County District, Probate
   Court
10 Osgood St.
Greenfield, MA 01301
Tel. (413) 774-7469
ABCDHIKLZ

North Essex Mediators
Community Action, Inc.
25 Locust St.
Haverhill, MA 01830
Tel. (508) 373-1971

Housing Services Program
Housing Assistance Corporation
460 W. Main St.
Hyannis, MA 02601
Tel. (508) 771-5400

Cape Cod Dispute Resolution Center,
   Inc.
Barnstable District Court/Orleans 2nd
   District Court
76 Enterprise Rd.
Hyannis, MA 02601
Tel. (508) 775-8788
DHIKL

Community Mediation, Inc.
Plymouth District Court
A Project of S. Shore Housing
   Development Corporation
169 Summer St.
Kingston, MA 02364
Tel. (617) 585-3885
LZ

Alternative Dispute Resolution
   Program
167 Dutton St.
Lowell, MA 01852
Tel. (508) 459-0551 Ext. 138

Family Mediation Program
Bristol County, 3rd District County
   Juvenile Court
261 Union St., Room 102
New Bedford, MA 02740
Tel. (508) 991-4912
AFZ

Bristol County Probate & Family
   Court
505 Pleasant St.
New Bedford, MA 02740
Tel. (508) 999-5249

Hampshire Probate Court
33 King St.
Northampton, MA 01060
Tel. (413) 586-8503

Family Mediation Program
Center for Individual & Family
   Services
81 Old Colony Way
Orleans, MA 02633
Tel. (508) 255-2981

Victim-Offender Service
Quincy District Court Mediation
   Services
One Dennis F. Ryan Pkwy.
Quincy, MA 02169
Tel. (617) 471-1650

Salem Mediation Program
Salem District Court
65 Washington St.
Salem, MA 01970
Tel. (508) 745-4165

District Court Department Mediation
   Program
Administration Office of the District
   Court Dept.
Holyoke Square
Salem, MA 01970
Tel. (508) 745-9010

Essex Probate & Family Court
Probation Dept.
32 Federal St.
P.O. Box 555
Salem, MA 01970

Somerville Mediation Program
One Summer St.
Somerville, MA 02143
Tel. (617) 776-5931

Dispute Resolution Services, Inc.
Springfield, Westfield, Chicopee,
  Holyoke Districts
9 Stockbridge St.
Springfield, MA 01103
Tel. (413) 787-6480
ABDHIKLZ

Neighborhood Youth Mediation Project
New North Citizen's Council
2383 Main St.
Springfield, MA 01107
Tel. (413) 737-2632

Hampden County Superior Court
  Mediation Project
Hall of Justice
Springfield, MA 01102
Tel. (413) 781-8100
IJ

Family Mediation Service
Springfield Juvenile Court
Center for Human Development
332 Birnie Ave.
Springfield, MA 01107
Tel. (413) 733-6624
FGZ

Mediation Services
81 Plantation St.
Worcester, MA 01608
Tel. (508) 755-7660

Community Mediation Center
Dudley, Clinton, Spencer District
  Courts
WCAC 340 Main St., Room 555
Worcester, MA 01608
Tel. (508) 754-5322
HIJKLZ


MICHIGAN

Lenawee County Circuit Court
  Mediation
Lenawee County Probate & Juvenile
  Court
Lenawee County Clerk
425 N. Main St.
Adrian, MI 49221
Tel. (517) 263-8831 or 2180
DIJ

Mediation
Circuit Court, Lenawee County
425 N. Main
Adrian, MI 49221
Tel. (517) 263-8831
DJ

Domestic Relations Mediation/Friend
  of the Court
39th Circuit Court, Lenawee County
P.O. Box 577
Adrian, MI 49221
Tel. (517) 263-8831
ABE

Referee/Friend of the Court
39th Circuit Court, Lenawee County
P.O. Box 577
Adrian, MI 49221
Tel. (517) 263-8831
ABEZ

Washtenaw County Consumer
  Affairs—Dispute Resolution
15th District Court
Washtenaw County Service Center
Ann Arbor, MI 48107
Tel. (313) 971-6054
H

Washtenaw County Consumer
  Services—Citizen Dispute
14A District
P.O. Box 8645
Ann Arbor, MI 48107
Tel. (313) 971-6054

Citizen Dispute Resolution Division
22nd Judicial Circuit
Consumers Services Dept.
4133 Washtenaw, P.O. Box 8645
Ann Arbor, MI 48107-8645
Tel. (313) 971-6054
KL

Mediation
52nd Judicial Circuit
Huron County Circuit Court
250 E. Huron Ave.
Bad Axe, MI 48413
Tel. (517) 269-7112
IJ

Circuit Court Mediation Program
18th Judicial Circuit Court
515 Center Ave., 8th Fl.
Bay City, MI 48708
Tel. (517) 893-5513
CDIJZ

SODA
Gogebic County Probate Court
Courthouse
Bessemer, MI 49911
Tel. (906) 663-4147
H

Friends of the Court—Referee
   Program (Benzie County)
19th Judicial Circuit
P.O. Box 70
Beulah, MI 49617
Tel. (616) 882-9671
AB

Mediation (Domestic)
49th Judicial Circuit
400 Elm St.
P.O. Box 822
Big Rapids, MI 49307
Tel. (616) 592-0780
ABCD

Mediation (Civil)
49th Judicial Circuit Court
P.O. Box 822
Big Rapids, MI 49307
Tel. (616) 592-0780
IJ

Friend of Court
49th Judicial Circuit
400 Elm St.
Big Rapids, MI 49307
Tel. (616) 592-0115
ABC

Civil Mediation
77th District Court
Gary M. Lough, Mediation Clerk
400 Elm St., Room 118
Big Rapids, MI 49307
Tel. (616) 592-0796
IJKL

Alternative Dispute Resolution
   Program
48th District Court
4280 Telegraph Rd.
Bloomfield Hills, MI 48013
Tel. (313) 674-1141
HIJKL

Dispute Resolution Clearinghouse &
   Settlement Center
P.O. Box 7011
Bloomfield Hills, MI 48302-7011
Tel. (313) 338-4280
IJKLZ

Livingston County Catholic Social
   Services
44th Circuit Court
8599 W. Grand River Ave.
Brighton, MI 48116
Tel. (313) 227-2151
ABCDG

Mediation
67th District Court
2065 S. Center Rd.
Burton, MI 48519
Tel. (313) 257-3170
IJKL

City of Burton Diversion Program
67th District Court, Burton Division
2065 S. Center Rd.
Burton, MI 48519
Tel. (313) 742-1050
HZ

Mediation
28th Circuit Court
P.O. Box 226
Cadillac, MI 49601
Tel. (616) 779-9490
DIJ

Tuscola County Friend of the Court
   Referee Hearings
Circuit Court
440 N. State St.
Caro, MI 48723
Tel. (517) 673-4848
ABCDE

Cass County Circuit Court Mediation
43rd Judicial Circuit
Circuit Court Courthouse
Cassopolis, MI 49031
Tel. (616) 445-8621 Ext. 271
IJZ

Informal Divorce Mediation
33rd Judicial Circuit
Friend of the Court
County Bldg.
Charlevoix, MI 49720
Tel. (616) 547-7206
A

Mediation Friend of Court Referee
5th Circuit Court/Baton & Barry
   Counties
Baton County Courthouse
Charlotte, MI 48813
Tel. (517) 543-7500
ABCDIJ

Criminal Sexual Conduct Diversion
    Program
53rd Circuit Court
P.O. Box 70
Cheboygan, MI 49721
Tel. (616) 627-8818
Z

Mediation
53rd Circuit Court
P.O. Box 70
Cheboygan, MI 49721
Tel. (616) 627-8818
IJ

Friend of the Court Mediation
Branch County Circuit Court
Branch County Courthouse
31 Division St.
Coldwater, MI 49036
Tel. (517) 279-8411
AB

Mediation Tribunal Assoc.
28th District Court
340 E. Congress, Suite 700
Detroit, MI 48226
Tel. (313) 224-5606
IJ

3rd Judicial Circuit of Michigan
    Mediation Panel
24th Judicial District Court of
    Michigan
3rd Judicial Circuit of Michigan
1207 City-County Bldg.
Detroit, MI 48226
Tel. (313) 224-5439
Z

Mediation Tribunal Assoc.
36th District Court
340 E. Congress, Suite 600
Millender Center
Detroit, MI 48226
Tel. (313) 224-5606
IJL

Mediation Tribunal Assoc., Inc.
3rd Circuit
340 E. Congress, Suite 700
Detroit, MI 48226
Tel. (313) 224-5606
DJKL

Visiting Judge Settlement Conferences
3rd Circuit
711 City-County Bldg.
Detroit, MI 48226
Tel. (313) 224-5363
ABCDIJ

Wayne County Circuit Court
    Arbitration Commission
31st District Court
City-County Bldg.
2 Woodward Ave.
Detroit, MI 48226
Tel. (313) 876-7710
IJ

Wayne County Mediation
33rd Judicial District Court
City-County Bldg.
2 Woodward Ave.
Detroit, MI 48226
Tel. (313) 224-5260
IJZ

Mediation Tribunal Assoc.
26th District Court, Division 1
3rd Judicial Circuit of Michigan
City-County Bldg., Room 1207
Detroit, MI 48226
Tel. (313) 224-5439

Detroit Neighborhood Reconciliation
8605 W. Vernor
Detroit, MI 48209
Tel. (313) 841-0120

Community Conciliation Center
16349 E. Warren
Detroit, MI 48224
Tel. (313) 885-9040

Housing Dispute Center
2900 Cadillac Tower
Detroit, MI 48226
Tel. (313) 962-0466

Neighborhood Mediation Service
City of East Lansing
410 Abbott Rd.
East Lansing, MI 48823
Tel. (517) 337-1731

Professional Consultant
23rd Judicial Circuit of Mich.
1430 N. Huron Rd.
East Tawas, MI 48730
Tel. (517) 362-4855
A

Small Claims Mediation
47th District Court
32795 W. 10 Mile Rd.
Farmington, MI 48024
Tel. (517) 477-5630
K

Circuit Court Mediation, Civil Cases
7th Judicial Circuit Court of Genesee
    County
Courthouse, Room 408
900 S. Saginaw St.
Flint, MI 48502
Tel. (313) 257-3252
IJ

Circuit Court Mediation, Divorce
    Cases
7th Judicial Circuit Court of Genesee
    County
Courthouse, Room 408
900 S. Saginaw St.
Flint, MI 48502
Tel. (313) 257-3252
BCD

Referee-Friend of the Court Hearings
7th Judicial Circuit Court of Genesee
    County
Courthouse, Room 508
900 S. Saginaw St.
Flint, MI 48502
Tel. (313) 257-3087
ABCD

Genesee Community Mental Health
    Child & Adolescent Services
1102 Mackin Rd.
Flint, MI 48503
Tel. (313) 257-3706

Mediation
46th Circuit
225 W. Main St.
Gaylord, MI 49735
Tel. (517) 732-6484 Ext. 242
DIJ

Settlement Conference
46th Circuit
225 W. Main St.
Gaylord, MI 49735
Tel. (517) 732-6484
DIJ

Mediation
55th Judicial Circuit Court
401 W. Cedar Ave.
Gladwin, MI 48624
Tel. (517) 426-9237
J

Circuit Court Mediation
20th Judicial Circuit Court
303 County Bldg.
Grand Haven, MI 49417
Tel. (616) 846-8320
IJZ

Circuit Court Referee
20th Judicial Circuit Court
303 County Bldg.
Grand Haven, MI 49417
Tel. (616) 846-8320
AB

Grand/Kent Community
    Reconciliation Center, Inc.
61st District Court
701 4th St. N.W.
Grand Rapids, MI 49504
Tel. (616) 774-0121
AGHIJKL

Kent Community Reconciliation
    Center
701 4th St., N.W.
Grand Rapids, MI 49504
Tel. (616) 774-0121

Wayne County Mediation Tribunal
32A District Court
19617 Harper Ave.
Harper Woods, MI 48225
IJ

Small Claims Mediation
43rd District Court/HP Division
43 E. 9 Mile Rd.
Hazel Park, MI 48030
Tel. (313) 547-3034
K

Small Claims Mediation
2nd District Court, 2nd Division
49 N. Howell St.
Hillsdale, MI 49242
Tel. (517) 437-7329
K

Civil Infraction Informal Hearings
2nd District Court, 2nd Division
49 N. Howell St.
Hillsdale, MI 49242
Tel. (517) 437-7329
Z

Friend of the Court
12th Judicial Circuit Court
County Courthouse
Houghton, MI 49931
Tel. (906) 482-2101
AB

Friend of the Court
12th Judicial Circuit
County Courthouse
Houghton, MI 49931
Tel. (906) 482-2102
ABCE

Domestic Mediation
44th Circuit Court
210 Highlander Way
Howell, MI 48843
Tel. (517) 546-8079
ABCD

Child & Family Services
44th Circuit Court
3075 E. Grand River
Howell, MI 48843
Tel. (517) 546-7530
ABCDG

Mediation
Ionia County Probate Court
Courthouse
Ionia, MI 48846
Tel. (616) 527-5315
IZ

Mediation
95B District Court
Courthouse
P.O. Box 609
Iron Mountain, MI 49801
Tel. (906) 774-0506
Z

41st Circuit Court
Dickinson County Courthouse
Iron Mountain, MI 49801
Tel. (906) 774-2266
IJZ

Western Upper Peninsula Assessment
  Services
Gogebic County Probate Court
200 E. Ayer St.
Ironwood, MI 49938
Tel. (906) 932-2350
Z

Jackson County Clerk's Office Court
  Services
4th Judicial Circuit Court
312 S. Jackson St.
Jackson, MI 49201
Tel. (517) 788-4267
ABCDGIZ

Mediation Clerk (Jackson County
  Mediation)
4th Judicial Circuit
312 S. Jackson St.
Jackson, MI 49201
Tel. (517) 788-4382
IJ

Domestic Relations Mediation
4th Judicial Circuit
312 S. Jackson St.
Jackson, MI 49201
Tel. (517) 788-4470
ABCDE

Circuit Court Civil Mediation
9th Circuit Court
Kalamazoo County Bar Assoc.
227 W. Michigan
Kalamazoo, MI 49007
Tel. (616) 384-8257
IJ

Circuit Court Domestic Relations
  Mediation
9th Circuit Court
227 W. Michigan
Kalamazoo, MI 49007
Tel. (616) 383-8950
CD

Community Dispute Resolution
  Center
303 N. Rose St., Suite 226
Kalamazoo, MI 49007
Tel. (616) 385-2090

Civil Mediation—Commercial
30th Judicial Circuit Court
Town Center Bldg.
333 S. Capitol, Suite C
Lansing, MI 48933
Tel. (517) 482-0650
I

Domestic Relations Mediation
Town Center Bldg.
333 S. Capitol, Suite C
Lansing, MI 48933
Tel. (517) 482-0650
BCD

Domestic Relations Conciliation
30th Judicial Circuit Court
303 W. Kalamazoo St.
Lansing, MI 48933
Tel. (517) 374-7330
ABCDG

Mediation, Tort Panel
30th Judicial Circuit, Ingham County
333 S. Capitol Ave., Suite C
Lansing, MI 48933
Tel. (517) 482-0650
J

Christian Conciliation Service
1441½ E. Michigan Ave.
Lansing, MI 48912
Tel. (517) 485-2270

Domestic Relations Referee
40th Judicial Circuit Court
Office of Friend of the Court
255 Clay St.
Lapeer, MI 48446
Tel. (313) 667-0377
AB

Mediation (Civil Cases)
40th Judicial Circuit Court
Lapeer County Circuit Court
255 Clay St.
Lapeer, MI 48446
Tel. (313) 667-0320
IJ

Mediation
19th Judicial Circuit
P.O. Box 484
Manistee, MI 49660
Tel. (616) 723-6664
DIJ

Friend of the Court/Referee
19th Judicial Circuit Court
P.O. Box 37
Manistee, MI 49660
Tel. (615) 723-8412
ABCE

Mediation
11th Judicial Circuit
Courthouse
P.O. Box 186
Manistique, MI 49854
Tel. (906) 341-5913
J

Mediation
Marquette County Circuit Court
County Courthouse
Marquette, MI 49855
Tel. (906) 228-1530
ABIJ

Mediation
9th and 96th District Courts
234 W. Baraga Ave.
Marquette, MI 49855
Tel. (906) 228-1555
IJ

Pre-Trial Conference
Calhoun County Juvenile Court
315 W. Green St.
Marshall, MI 49068
Tel. (616) 781-0830
Z

Mediation
95A District
Menominee County Courthouse
Menominee, MI 49858
Tel. (906) 863-9408
IJ

Mediation
Oscoda County Probate Court
Box 399, Courthouse
Mio, MI 48647
Tel. (517) 826-3241 Ext. 42
Z

Macomb County Probate Court
    Mediation
21850 Dunham Rd.
Mt. Clemens, MI 48043-1075
Tel. (313) 469-5290
IJZ

Macomb County Circuit Court
  Mediation Program
39th District Court
16th Judicial District
Macomb County Circuit Court Bldg.
Mt. Clemens, MI 48043
Tel. (313) 469-6479
IJL

Macomb County Mediation Panel
42-1 District Court
Macomb County Circuit Court
Macomb County Court Bldg.
Mt. Clemens, MI 48043
Tel. (313) 469-6039
IJ

Mediation Civil Cases
21st Circuit Court
200 N. Main
Mt. Pleasant, MI 48858
Tel. (517) 772-0911 Ext. 288
IJ

Friend of the Court
21st Circuit Court
200 N. Main
Mt. Pleasant, MI 48858
Tel. (517) 772-0911 Ext. 288
ABG

Summary Jury Trial
21st Circuit Court
200 N. Main
Mt. Pleasant, MI 48858
Tel. (517) 772-0911 Ext. 288
IJ

76th District Court A.D.R.
200 N. Main St.
Mt. Pleasant, MI 48858
Tel. (517) 772-0911
K

Divorce Mediation
21st Circuit Court
200 N. Main
Mt. Pleasant, MI 48858
Tel. (517) 772-0911 Ext. 288
CD

Settlement Conference
21st Circuit Court
200 N. Main
Mt. Pleasant, MI 48858
Tel. (517) 772-0911 Ext. 288
IJ

Pre-Mediation of Small Claims
76th District Court
200 N. Main
Mt. Pleasant, MI 48858
Tel. (517) 772-0911
K

Catholic Family Services
106 N. Main St.
Mt. Pleasant, MI 48848
Tel. (517) 773-9328

Civil Mediation
14th Judicial Circuit
Mediation Clerk, Courtroom A, B, C,
  or D
990 Terrace
Muskegon, MI 49442
Tel. (616) 724-6291
IJ

Alternative Small Claims Dispute
  Resolution
42-2 District Court
30500 23 Mile Rd.
New Baltimore, MI 48047
Tel. (313) 949-2400
K

Soda/Ontonagon County
Ontonagon County Probate Court
725 Greenland Rd.
Ontonagon, MI 49953
Tel. (906) 884-4539
HZ

Mediation/Youth Division
Shirley K. Jackson, Clerk
Van Buren Probate Court
212 Paw Paw St.
Paw Paw, MI 49079
Tel. (616) 657-6854
Z

Final Pretrial/Settlement Conference
33rd Judicial Circuit Courts
200 Division St.
Petoskey, MI 49770
Tel. (616) 348-1748
CDIJZ

Informal Mediation
33rd Circuit Court
c/o Friend of the Court
200 Division St.
Petoskey, MI 49770
Tel. (616) 348-1717
AE

Mediation
33rd Circuit Court
200 Division St.
Petoskey, MI 49770
Tel. (616) 348-1748
IJZ

Civil Case Status Conference
35th District Court
660 Plymouth Rd.
Plymouth, MI 48170
Tel. (313) 459-4740
IZ

District Court Mediation Service
52-4 District Court
1200 N. Telegraph Rd.
Pontiac, MI 48053
Tel. (313) 338-2100
IJ

Paralegal Dept. Support Mediation
Oakland County Circuit Court
Friend of the Court
1200 N. Telegraph
Pontiac, MI 48053
Tel. (313) 858-0592
B

Mediation
6th Circuit Court
1200 N. Telegraph Rd.
Pontiac, MI 48053
Tel. (313) 858-0350
IJZ

Oakland County Friend of the Court,
    Family Counseling
6th Judicial Circuit Court
1200 N. Telegraph Rd.
Pontiac, MI 48053
Tel. (313) 858-0441
AE

Oakland County Bar Assoc.
43rd District Court/Hazel Park
    Division
District Court Mediation
1200 N. Telegraph Rd.
Pontiac, MI 48053
Tel. (313) 338-2100
Z

District Court Mediation Services
Oakland County District Courts
1200 N. Telegraph Rd., Suite 532
Pontiac, MI 48053-1057
Tel. (313) 338-2100
IJLZ

Christian Conciliation Service
35th District Court
27350 W. Chicago Blvd.
Redford, MI 48239
Tel. (313) 937-3939
ACDGKLZ

Small Claims
89th District Court
Courthouse
P.O. Box 110
Rogers City, MI 49779
K

Small Claims Mediation
34th District Court/Civil Dept.
11131 S. Wayne Rd.
Romulus, MI 48174
Tel. (313) 941-4462 Ext. 210
IJK

General Civil Mediation
34th District Court
11131 S. Wayne Rd.
Romulus, MI 48174
Tel. (313) 941-4446 Ext. 210
IJL

Mediation
10th Circuit Court
111 S. Michigan Ave.
Saginaw, MI 48602
Tel. (517) 790-5472
IJ

Community Dispute Resolution
    Center
120 N. Michigan Ave., Suite 314
Saginaw, MI 48607
Tel. (517) 790-5944

Friend of Court
24th Judicial Circuit Court
Courthouse
60 W. Sanilac Ave.
Sandusky, MI 48471
Tel. (313) 648-2120

Mediation for the Courts of Sanilac
    County
24th Judicial Circuit Court
Courthouse
60 W. Sanilac Ave.
Sandusky, MI 48471
Tel. (313) 648-2120
IJZ

Referee
50th Judicial Circuit Court—
 Chippewa & Mackinac Counties
Chippewa County Courthouse
Court St.
Sault Ste. Marie, MI 49783
Tel. (906) 635-6338
ABCD

Mediation
50th Judicial Circuit Court—
 Chippewa & Mackinac Counties
Chippewa County Courthouse
Court St.
Sault Ste. Marie, MI 49783
Tel. (906) 635-6338
Z

46th District Court Small Claims
 Mediation
26000 Evergreen
Southfield, MI 48076
Tel. (313) 354-9506
K

46th District Court General Civil
 Mediation
46th District Court
26000 Evergreen
Southfield, MI 48076
Tel. (313) 354-9506
IJ

Circuit Court Mediation
34th Judicial Circuit
P.O. Box 749
Standish, MI 48658
Tel. (517) 846-6200
Z

34th & 23rd Circuit Mediation
 Program
Roscommon County Probate Court
P.O. Box 745
Standish, MI 48658
Tel. (517) 846-6131
Z

Spousal Maintenance, Contract &
 Tort Mediation
23rd Judicial Circuit
P.O. Box 658
Tawas City, MI 48764-0658
Tel. (517) 362-3485
CDIJ

Complaint Hearings
23rd District Court
23511 Goddard
Taylor, MI 48180
Tel. (313) 374-1334
GHZ

13th Circuit Court
328 Washington St.
Travers City, MI 49684
Tel. (616) 922-4707
ABIJ

Grand Traverse–Leelanau–Antrim Bar
 Assoc.
Box 1958
Traverse City, MI 49685
Tel. (616) 922-4490

Small Claims Mediation
52nd 1st District Court
1010 E. West Maple Rd.
Walled Lake, MI 48088
Tel. (313) 624-6580
J

Friend of the Court/Mediation
34th Judicial Circuit Court
P.O. Box 427
West Branch, MI 48661
Tel. (517) 345-5520
AB

Out County Services & Family
 Counseling
3100 Henry Ruff Rd.
Westland, MI 48185

Newaygo County Circuit Court
 Mediation
27th Circuit Court
1084 Wilcox Ave.
P.O. Box 608
White Cloud, MI 49349
Tel. (616) 689-7269
ABCDEIJ

27th Circuit Friend of the Court
27th Circuit Court
1084 Wilcox Ave.
White Cloud, MI 49349
Tel. (616) 689-7260
ABCD

MISSOURI

Community Mediation Service
University of Mo.
Columbia School of Law, 104 Law
   Bldg.
Columbia, MO 65211
Tel. (314) 882-2052
GHIJKL

Appellate Settlement Conferences
Western District Mo. Court of
   Appeals
1300 Oak
Kansas City, MO 64106
Tel. (816) 474-5511
ABCDGIJKLZ

Dispute Resolution Section/Kansas
   City Human Resources
Kansas City Municipal Court
City Hall, Human Relations Dept.
414 E. 12th St., 4th Fl.
Kansas City, MO 64106
Tel. (816) 274-1031
ABCDGHIJKLZ

Appellate Settlement Conferences
Eastern District Mo. Court of Appeals
Wainwright State Office Bldg.
111 N. 7th
St. Louis, MO 63101
Tel. (314) 444-9697
ABCDGIJKLZ

Housing Law & Homelessness Clinic:
   Mediation Project
Missouri Circuit Court, St. Louis
   City
St. Louis University School of Law
3700 Lindell Blvd.
St. Louis, MO 63108
Tel. (314) 658-2778
L

Dispute Resolution Program
University of Mo. at St. Louis
7952 Natural Bridge Rd.
St. Louis, MO 63121-4499
Tel. (314) 553-6040
IJKL

Opportunity Clearing House
Circuit Courts in St. Louis City
400 Laclede Ave.
St. Louis, MO 63103
Tel. (314) 652-0360
Z

Dispute Resolution Program
University of Mo. at St. Louis
8001 Natural Bridge Rd.
St. Louis, MO 63121
Tel. (314) 553-6040
IJKLZ

Pre-Argument Conference Program
8th Circuit Court of Appeals
1114 Market
St. Louis, MO 63101
Tel. (314) 539-3669
IJKL

MONTANA

Family Court Services
11th Judicial District Court
723 5th Ave., E.
Kalispell, MT 59901
Tel. (406) 752-5300

Family Court Services
11th Judicial District Court
723 5th Ave., E.
Kalispell, MT 59901
Tel. (406) 752-5300 Ext. 349
AEFG

NEVADA

Mediation
Second Judicial District Court
75 Court St.
Reno, NV 89501
Tel. (702) 328-3119
ABCDG

NEW JERSEY

Community Dispute Program
Waterford Township Municipal Court
Municipal Bldg., 125 Auburn Ave.
Atco, NJ 08004
Tel. (609) 767-2147

Atlantic County Early Settlement
   Panel
c/o Atlantic County Bar Assoc.
1201 Bacharach Blvd.
Atlantic City, NJ 08401
Tel. (609) 344-0333

Superior Court Arbitration Program
Superior Court, Atlantic County
Atlantic County Civil Courts Bldg.
1201 Bacharach Blvd.
Atlantic City, NJ 08401
Tel. (609) 345-6700 Ext. 3209

Superior Court/Special Civil Part
  Mediation Project
1201 Bacharach Blvd.
Atlantic City, NJ 08401
Tel. (609) 345-6700 Ext. 3324

Special Civil Part ESP (Early
  Settlement Panel)
Superior Court of N.J., Atlantic
  County
1201 Bacharach Blvd.
Atlantic City, NJ 08401
Tel. (609) 345-6700 Ext. 3329
IJZ

Landlord-Tenant/Mediation
Superior Court of N.J., Atlantic
  County
1201 Bacharach Blvd.
Atlantic City, NJ 08401
Tel. (609) 345-6700
L

Personal Injury Arbitration
Atlantic County Superior Court
1201 Bacharach Blvd.
Atlantic City, NJ 08401
Tel. (609) 345-6700 Ext. 332
Z

Community Justice Institute
Atlantic County Superior Court of
  N.J.
1201 Bacharach Blvd.
Atlantic City, NJ 08401
Tel. (609) 345-7267
AKZ

Small Claims Mediation
Superior Court of N.J., Atlantic
  County
1201 Bacharach Blvd.
Atlantic City, NJ 08401
Tel. (609) 345-6700
K

Law ESP (Early Settlement Panel)
Atlantic County Superior Court
1201 Bacharach Blvd.
Atlantic City, NJ 08401
Tel. (609) 345-6700 Ext. 3326
IJZ

Automobile Arbitration
Atlantic County Superior Court
1201 Bacharach Blvd.
Atlantic City, NJ 08401
Tel. (609) 345-6700 Ext. 3596
Z

Audubon Neighborhood Dispute
  Committee.
Community Center Bldg.
Oak St. & Oakland Ave.
Audubon, NJ 08106
Tel. (609) 547-0712

Community Dispute Program
Bellmawr Borough Municipal Court
21 East Browing Rd.
Bellmawr, NJ 08031
Tel. (609) 931-1081

Community Dispute Program
Gloucester Township Municipal Court
P.O. Box 8
Blackwood, NJ 08012
Tel. (609) 228-4000
H

Blackwood Community Dispute Panel
P.O. Box 8
Blackwood, NJ 08012
Tel. (609) 228-4000

Community Dispute Resolution
  Committee
Montville Township Municipal Court
26 Hill St.
Boontown, NJ 07005
Tel. (201) 227-1839
DEGHKL

Community Dispute Program
Bordentown City Municipal Court
324 Farnsworth Ave.
Bordentown City, NJ 08505
Tel. (609) 298-2448

Community Dispute Program
Bordentown Township
Municipal Dr.
Bordentown Township, NJ
  08505-2193
Tel. (609) 298-2802

Winslow Township Community
  Dispute Resolution Committee
Rt. 73
Braddock, NJ 08037
Tel. (609) 567-0700

Community Dispute Program
Logan Township Municipal Court
73 Main St.
Bridgeport, NJ 08014-0314
Tel. (609) 467-3425

Cumberland County Matrimonial
    Early Settlement Program
Cumberland County Courthouse
Broad & Fayette Sts.
Bridgeton, NJ 08302
Tel. (609) 451-8000

Cumberland County Custody/
    Visitation Mediation Program
Cumberland County Courthouse
Broad & Fayette Sts.
Bridgeton, NJ 08302
Tel. (609) 451-8000

Auto & Personal Injury Arbitration
Superior Court of N.J.
Cumberland County Courthouse
P.O. Box 716
Bridgeton, NJ 08302
Tel. (609) 451-8000 Ext. 331
IJ

Community Dispute Program
Mendham Borough Municipal Court
Cherry Lane
Brookside, NJ 07926
Tel. (201) 543-7526

Mt. Olive Township Community
    Dispute Resolution Program
Municipal Bldg., Rt. 46
Budd Lake, NJ 07828
Tel. (201) 691-0263

Consent Conferences
Superior Court of Camden County
Superior Court, Family Part
Camden County Hall of Justice
5th St. & Mickle Blvd.
Camden, NJ 08103
Tel. (609) 757-8281

Family Court, Mediation Program
Hall of Justice
5th St. & Mickle Blvd., 2nd Fl.
Camden, NJ 08103
Tel. (609) 757-1798

Family Specialists of Supreme Court
    of N.J., Family Part
Hall of Justice
5th St. & Mickle Blvd., 2nd Fl.
Camden, NJ 08103
Tel. (609) 757-1728 or 1750

Camden County Conference Program
Probation Dept.
P.O. Box 1928
Camden, NJ 08101
Tel. (609) 757-8963

Superior Court Arbitration Program
Superior Court of Camden County
Camden County Hall of Justice
5th St. & Mickle Blvd.
Camden, NJ 08103
Tel. (609) 757-8180

Early Settlement Panel Program
Superior Court of N.J., Camden
    Vicinage
Hall of Justice, Suite 330
5th St. & Mickle Blvd.
Camden, NJ 08103
Tel. (609) 757-8164
J

Community Disputes Resolution
    Committee
Municipal Courts of Camden County
Camden County Hall of Justice, Suite
    660
5th St. & Mickle Blvd.
Camden, NJ 08103
Tel. (609) 757-8188
H

Family Part, Superior Court
Superior Court
Hall of Justice
5th St. & Mickle Blvd.
Camden, NJ 08103
Tel. (609) 757-1788
ABCDEGZ

Mental Health Services of Cape May
    County, Inc.
Drawer Number 632
Cape May Courthouse
Cape May, NJ 08210
Tel. (609) 465-4100

Small Claims/Landlord Tenant
  Mediation
Cape May County Superior Court
DN-203 Central Mail Room
Cape May Courthouse
Cape May, NJ 08210
Tel. (609) 889-6504
KL

Law Division/Early Settlement Panel
Cape May County Superior Court
DN-209 Central Mail Room
Cape May Courthouse
Cape May, NJ 08210
Tel. (609) 889-6504
IJZ

Community Dispute Program
Carneys Point Municipal Court
303 Harding Hwy.
Carneys Point, NJ 08069
Tel. (609) 299-1013

Cherry Hill Township Community
  Resolution Committee
820 Mercer St.
Cherry Hill, NJ 08002
Tel. (609) 488-7850

Community Dispute Program
Cherry Hill Township Municipal
  Court
820 Mercer St.
Cherry Hill, NJ 08002
Tel. (609) 665-6500

Community Dispute Program
Chester Township Municipal Court
Municipal Bldg.
Parker Rd.,
P.O. Box 428
Chester, NJ 07930
Tel. (201) 879-5541

Community Dispute Program
Chester Borough Municipal Court
Municipal Bldg.
300 Main St., P.O. Box 487
Chester, NJ 07930-0487
Tel. (201) 879-5361

Community Dispute Program
Cinnaminson Municipal Court
1621 Riverton Rd.
Cinnaminson, NJ 08077
Tel. (609) 829-4027

Clarksboro Community Dispute
  Resolution Committee
P.O. Box 317
Clarksboro, NJ 08020
Tel. (609) 423-3010

Community Dispute Program
Clayton Municipal Court
125 N. Delsea Dr.
Clayton, NJ 08312
Tel. (609) 881-8964

Gloucester City Community Dispute
  Program
313 Monmouth St.
Gloucester City, NJ 08030
Tel. (609) 456-3958 Ext. 408

Collingswood Community Dispute
  Resolution Committee
28 West Collings Ave.
Collingswood, NJ 08108
Tel. (609) 854-7535

Community Dispute Program
Delran Municipal Court
1050 Chester Ave.
Delran, NJ 08075
Tel. (609) 461-3888

Community Dispute Program
Deptford Municipal Court
1011 Cooper St.
Deptford, NJ 08096
Tel. (609) 845-5300

Community Dispute Program
Denville Municipal Court
Municipal Bldg.
Denville, NJ 07834
Tel. (201) 625-8320

Community Dispute Program
East Hanover Municipal Court
411 Ridgedale Ave.
East Hanover, NJ 07936
Tel. (201) 887-1860

Family and Neighborhood Counseling
  Unit
East Orange Municipal Court
221 Freeway Dr., E. & Munn Ave.
East Orange, NJ 07018
Tel. (201) 266-5009

Superior Court/Special Civil Part
  Mediation Project
Superior Court of Union County
Union County Courthouse
2 Broad St.
Elizabeth, NJ 07207
Tel. (201) 527-4395

Union County Arbitration Program
Superior Court of Union County
Union County Courthouse
2 Broad St.
Elizabeth, NJ 07207
Tel. (201) 527-4329
J

Pro-Se Assistance
Special Civil Part
Union County Courthouse
Elizabeth, NJ 07207
Tel. (201) 527-4414
IJKL

Fair Lawn Community Dispute
  Resolution Committee
8-01 Fair Lawn Ave.
Fair Lawn, NJ 07410
Tel. (201) 794-5349

Community Dispute Program
Florence Township Municipal Court
Municipal Complex, Broad St.
Florence, NJ 08518
Tel. (609) 499-2222

Franklin Township Municipal Court
  Community Dispute
Resolution Committee
Delsea Dr., Municipal Bldg.
Franklinville, NJ 08322-0300
Tel. (609) 694-1661

Custody/Visitation Mediation
Superior Court, Family Division
P.O. Box 1259
Freehold, NJ 07728-1066
Tel. (201) 308-3709
AE

Slip & Fall Arbitration
Superior Court of N.J.
Arbitration Dept.
Monmouth County Courthouse
Freehold, NJ 07728
Tel. (201) 431-6530
J

Statewide Automobile Arbitration
Superior Court of N.J.
Arbitration Dept.
Monmouth County Courthouse
Freehold, NJ 07728
Tel. (201) 431-6530
J

Personal Injury Arbitration
Superior Court of N.J.
Arbitration Dept.
Monmouth County Courthouse
Freehold, NJ 07728
Tel. (201) 431-6530
J

Civil Arbitration
Special Civil Part
Monmouth County Special Part
Monmouth County Courthouse
Freehold, NJ 07728
Tel. (201) 577-6741
IJ

Small Claims Mediation
Special Civil Part
Monmouth County Special Civil Part
Monmouth County Courthouse
Freehold, NJ 07728
Tel. (201) 577-6741
K

Community Dispute Program
Borough of Gibbsboro Municipal
  Court
Boro Hall, Kirkwood Rd.
Gibbsboro, NJ 08026
Tel. (609) 783-6655

Community Dispute Program
Greenwich Municipal Court
Municipal Bldg., Broad & Walnut Sts.
Gibbstown, NJ 08027
Tel. (609) 423-0113

Elk Township Community Disputes
  Resolution Committee
RD 1, Box 316
Glassboro, NJ 08028
Tel. (609) 881-6631

Community Dispute Program
Glassboro Municipal Court
Main & High Sts.
Glassboro, NJ 08028
Tel. (609) 881-0383

Superior Court Arbitration Program
Bergen County Courthouse
10 Main St.
Hackensack, NJ 07601
Tel. (201) 646-2354 Ext. 2888

Bergen County Neighborhood Dispute
   Program
133 River St.
Hackensack, NJ 07026
Tel. (201) 676-2542

Early Settlement Program
Bergen County Courthouse, Room
   222
Hackensack, NJ 07601
Tel. (201) 646-3553

Custody/Visitation Mediation
Bergen County Courthouse, Room
   222
Hackensack, NJ 07601
Tel. (201) 646-3373

Victim/Offender Reconciliation
   Mediation Program
Superior Court of N.J., Chancery
   Division, Family Part
133 River St.
Hackensack, NJ 07601
Tel. (201) 646-2521
HZ

Blue Ribbon Preliminary Hearing
   Panel
Bergen County Courthouse, Room
   148A
Hackensack, NJ 07601
Tel. (201) 646-2120

Automobile Arbitration: Personal
   Injury Arbitration: Mandatory
Superior Court of N.J.
Conference Panels
Civil Courts Management Office
Courthouse, Room 415
Hackensack, NJ 07601
Tel. (201) 646-2064
IJ

Special Civil Part Mandatory
   Settlement Conference Panel
Special Civil Part
Courthouse, Room 430
Hackensack, NJ 07601
Tel. (201) 646-3606
Z

Family Intake
Superior Court of N.J.
Courthouse, Room 102A
Hackensack, NJ 07601
Tel. (201) 646-3356
ABCZ

Haddon Heights Community Dispute
   Resolution Committee
Municipal Court of Haddon Heights
625 Station Ave.
Haddon Heights, NJ 08035
Tel. (609) 547-2920

Hopatcong Boro Community Dispute
   Resolution Committee
Hopatcong Municipal Court
Municipal Bldg.
River Styx Rd.
Hopatcong, NJ 07843
Tel. (201) 398-7553
HIKL

Hudson County Family Court
   Custody Mediation Project
Administration Bldg.
595 Newark Ave.
Jersey City, NJ 07306
Tel. (201) 795-6834

Automobile Arbitration, Civil Division
Superior Court of N.J., Hudson
   Vicinage
583 Newark Ave.
Jersey City, NJ 07306
Tel. (201) 795-6372
J

Contract Arbitration, Civil Division
Superior Court of N.J., Hudson
   Vicinage
583 Newark Ave.
Jersey City, NJ 07306
Tel. (201) 795-6372
I

Small Claims Mediation
Superior Court of N.J., Hudson
   Vicinage
595 Newark Ave.
Jersey City, NJ 07306
Tel. (201) 795-6142
K

Neighborhood Dispute Settlement
Municipal Courts
Probation Dept.
595 Newark Ave.
Jersey City, NJ 07306
Tel. (201) 915-1201
HZ

Personal Injury Arbitration, Civil
 Division
Superior Court of N.J., Hudson
 Vicinage
583 Newark Ave.
Jersey City, NJ 07306
Tel. (201) 795-6372
J

Special Civil Arbitration
Superior Court of N.J., Hudson
 Vicinage
595 Newark Ave.
Jersey City, NJ 07306
Tel. (201) 795-5142
IJ

Early Settlement Panels, Family
Superior Court of N.J., Hudson
 Vicinage
595 Newark Ave.
Jersey City, NJ 07306
Tel. (201) 795-6632
D

Community Dispute Program
Jefferson Township Municipal Court
Weldon Rd.
Lake Hopatcong, NJ 07849
Tel. (201) 697-1500

Community Dispute Program
Lawnside Municipal Court
Boro Hall, 4 Douglas Venue
Lawnside, NJ 08045
Tel. (609) 573-6209

Lawrence Township Community
 Dispute Resolution Committee
Lawrence Township Municipal Court
2207 Lawrence Rd.
Lawrenceville, NJ 08648
Tel. (609) 896-9407
HZ

Lindenwold Community Disputes
 Committee
Lindenwold Municipal Bldg.
2001 Egg Harbor Rd.
Lindenwold, NJ 08021
Tel. (609) 783-2121

Community Dispute Program
Mantua Municipal Court
Police Administration Bldg.
S. Main St.
Mantua, NJ 08051-1096
Tel. (609) 468-3078

Community Dispute Program
Medford Municipal Court
Cranberry Hall, Charles St.
Medford, NJ 08055
Tel. (609) 654-8813

Morris County Family Mediation &
 Conciliation Services
86 River Rd.
Montville, NJ 07045
Tel. (201) 335-1022

Community Dispute Program
Moorestown Municipal Court
Municipal Complex
111 W. 2nd St.
Moorestown, NJ 08057
Tel. (609) 235-0922
H

Superior Court Arbitration Program
Superior Court of N.J.
Morris County Courthouse
Court St.
Morristown, NJ 07960
Tel. (201) 285-6406
IJZ

Morris County Family Mediation &
 Conciliation Services
Superior Court of N.J., Morris
 County, Family Part
Courthouse, Box X
Morristown, NJ 07960
Tel. (201) 285-6560
AG

Early Settlement Program
Superior Court of N.J.
Court St.
Morris County Courthouse
Morristown, NJ 07960
Tel. (201) 285-6406
IJZ

Mount Ephraim Municipal Court,
 Community Disputes Resolution
 Committee
121 S. Black Horse Pike
Mount Ephraim, NJ 08059
Tel. (609) 931-0994

Burlington County Comprehensive
Justice Center
County Courts Facility
Mount Holly, NJ 08060
Tel. (609) 261-5160

Custody Mediation Program
Superior Court of Burlington County
Courts Facility, 3rd Fl.
Mount Holly, NJ 08060
Tel. (609) 265-5146
A

Burlington County Mediation Program
Superior Court of Burlington County
Family Case Management, 3rd Fl.
New Court Facility, 49 Rancocas Rd.
Mount Holly, NJ 08060
Tel. (609) 265-5468
A

Comprehensive Justice
Maple Shade Municipal Court
County Courts Facility
Mount Holly, NJ 08060
Tel. (609) 256-5160
HLZ

Matrimonial Early Settlement Panel
Family Division, Superior Court
Courts Facility, 3rd Fl.
Mount Holly, NJ 08060
Tel. (609) 265-5146
BCD

Custody Mediation Program
Superior Court of Burlington County
Courts Facility, 3rd Fl.
Mount Holly, NJ 08060
Tel. (609) 265-5144
A

Superior Court Arbitration Program
Burlington County Superior Court
Burlington County Courts Facility
49 Rancocas Rd.
Mount Holly, NJ 08060
Tel. (609) 265-5310

Community Dispute Program
Mount Holly Municipal Court
23 Washington St.
Mount Holly, NJ 08060
Tel. (609) 267-0170

Matrimonial Early Settlement Panel
Superior Court of Burlington County,
Family Division
Courts Facility, 3rd Fl.
Mount Holly, NJ 08060
Tel. (609) 265-5146
BCD

Community Dispute Resolution
Committee
Harrison Township Municipal Court
110 S. Main St.
Mullica Hill, NJ 08062
Tel. (609) 478-4049
HLZ

National Park Community Disputes
Resolution Committee
7 S. Grove Ave.
National Park, NJ 08063
Tel. (609) 845-1197

Superior Court Arbitration Program
Superior Court of Middlesex County
Middlesex County Courthouse
1 JFK Sq.
New Brunswick, NJ 08903
Tel. (201) 745-4313

Middlesex County Juvenile
Conference Committee
Superior Court of N.J.
Middlesex County Family Court
1 JFK Sq.
New Brunswick, NJ 08901
Tel. (201) 745-4193
Z

Middlesex County Family Part,
Custody Mediation
1 JFK Sq.
New Brunswick, NJ 08901
Tel. (201) 745-5810

Middlesex County Family Court Pre-
Screening Unit
P.O. Box 789
New Brunswick, NJ 08903
Tel. (201) 745-4216

Middlesex County Special Civil Part,
Small Claims Mediation
P.O. Box 1146
New Brunswick, NJ 08903
Tel. (201) 745-4415

Citizens Dispute Settlement Program
P.O. Box 789
New Brunswick, NJ 08903
Tel. (201) 745-3886


Special Masters Asbestos Litigation
Superior Court of N.J.
Middlesex County Courthouse
New Brunswick, NJ 08903
Tel. (201) 745-3070
J


Child Custody/Visitation Mediation
    Program
Superior Court of N.J.
Middlesex County Courthouse
New Brunswick, NJ 08903
Tel. (201) 745-3810
A


Neighborhood Dispute Panel/
    Domestic Dispute Panel
Pemberton Township Municipal Bldg.
New Lisbon, NJ 08064
Tel. (609) 894-8206


Alternate Dispute Resolution
Superior Court, Special Civil Part
470 Martin Luther King Blvd.
Newark, NJ 07102
Tel. (201) 621-5373
IJKL


Essex County Auto Arbitration
Superior Courts Bldg.
50 W. Market St.
Newark, NJ 07102
Tel. (201) 621-5415


Essex County Special Civil Part,
    Mediation
Essex County Courts Bldg.
Newark, NJ 07102
Tel. (201) 621-5373


Superior Court Arbitration Program
Superior Court of Essex County
Essex County Courts Bldg., Room
    712
Newark, NJ 07102
Tel. (201) 621-5415

Essex County Family Mediation
    Program
New Courts Bldg., Room 122/123
Newark, NJ 07102
Tel. (201) 621-4223/4224/4225


PIE (Prevention, Intervention &
    Education)
Superior Court of N.J., Family
    Division
Lincoln Park
P.O. Box 1806
Newark, NJ 07101
Tel. (201) 623-0600
HZ


Family Mediation Program
Superior Court of N.J., Essex
    Vicinage, Family Part
Essex County Courts Bldg., Room
    123
Newark, NJ 07102
Tel. (201) 621-4226
A


Juvenile Conference Committees
Superior Court of N.J., Chancery
    Division, Family Part
Old County Courts Bldg., Room B-10
Newark, NJ 07102
Tel. (201) 621-6330
HZ


Shoplifting Awareness & Prevention
    Program
Superior Court of N.J., Chancery
    Division, Family Part
New County Courts Bldg., Room 710
Newark, NJ 07102
Tel. (201) 621-4225
HZ


Arbitration & Mediation Program/
    Superior Court Law Division
465 Dr. Martin Luther King Jr. Blvd.
Newark, NJ 07102
Tel. (201) 621-5686
IJ


Intake Conferences
Superior Court of N.J., Chancery
    Division, Family Part
New County Courts Bldg., Room 714
Newark, NJ 07102
Tel. (201) 621-4239
HZ

Essex County Probation Violation
    Mediation
Superior Court, Criminal Part, Essex
    County
County Court Bldg., Room 111
Newark, NJ 07102
Tel. (201) 621-4207
Z

Community Dispute Program
Newfield Municipal Court
West Blvd. & Salem Ave.
Newfield, NJ 08344
Tel. (609) 697-1100

Cape May County Early Settlement
    Program
Professional Plaza, Angelsea Dr.
N. Wildwood, NJ 08260
Tel. (609) 729-1919

Early Settlement Program
Superior Court of N.J., Chancery
    Division, Family Part
c/o Piro, Zinna, Cifelli & Paris
360 Passaic Ave.
Nutley, NJ 07110
Tel. (201) 661-0710
BCDZ

Parsippany Community Dispute
    Resolution Committee
3333 Rt. 46
Parsippany, NJ 07054-1287
Tel. (201) 263-4372

Juvenile Intake Service (Juvenile
    Conference Committee)
Courthouse Annex
63–65 Hamilton St.
Paterson, NJ 07505
Tel. (201) 881-4048

Juvenile Intake Service (Pre-Judicial
    Conferences)
Passaic County Superior Court/Family
    Part
Courthouse Annex
63–65 Hamilton St.
Paterson, NJ 07505
Tel. (201) 881-4048
H

Small Claims Settlement
Superior Court of N.J., Special Civil
    Part
71 Hamilton St.
Paterson, NJ 07505
Tel. (201) 881-4105 Ext. 4198
K

Early Settlement Panels
Superior Court of N.J., Family Part
Courthouse Annex
63–65 Hamilton St.
Paterson, NJ 07505
Tel. (201) 881-4280

Superior Court Arbitration Program
Superior Court of Passaic County
Passaic County Courthouse
77 Hamilton St.
Paterson, NJ 07505
Tel. (201) 881-4116

Landlord & Tenant Settlement
Superior Court, Special Civil Part
71 Hamilton St.
Paterson, NJ 07505
Tel. (201) 881-4108
L

Tenancy Settlement Mediation
    Program
Superior Court, Special Civil Part
Passaic County Board of Social
    Services
80 Hamilton St.
Paterson, NJ 07505
Tel. (201) 470-5032
L

Family Court Intake Service
Passaic County Family Court
63–65 Hamilton & Ward Sts.
Paterson, NJ 07505
Tel. (201) 881-4044
ABCE

Juvenile Intake Service (Juvenile
    Conference Committees)
Passaic County Superior Court,
    Family Part
Courthouse Annex
63–65 Hamilton St.
Paterson, NJ 07505
Tel. (201) 881-4048
H

Paulsboro Community Dispute
Program
1211 N. Delaware St.
Paulsboro, NJ 08066
Tel. (609) 423-3888

Community Dispute Program
Penns Grove Municipal Court
W. Main & State Sts.
Penns Grove, NJ 08069
Tel. (609) 299-0911

Community Dispute Program
Pennsauken Municipal Court
2400 Bethel Ave.
Pennsauken, NJ 08109
Tel. (609) 663-1403
H

Community Dispute Program
Phillipsburg Municipal Court
675 Corliss Ave.
Phillipsburg, NJ 08865
Tel. (201) 454-3211

Pitman CDRC
Pitman Municipal Court
110 S. Broadway
Pitman, NJ 08071
Tel. (609) 589-3144
HLZ

West Windsor Community Dispute
Resolution Coordinator
Municipal Bldg.
271 Clarksville Rd., Box 38
Princeton Junction, NJ 08550
Tel. (609) 799-0915

Essex County Bar Assoc.
Essex County Municipal Courts
Community Dispute Resolution
Project
5 Becker Farm Rd.
Roseland, NJ 07068-1776
Tel. (201) 533-1779
HKLZ

Community Dispute Program
Somerdale Municipal Court
105 Kennedy Blvd.
Somerdale, NJ 08083
Tel. (609) 783-0958

Superior Court Arbitration Program
Superior Court of Somerset County
Somerset County Courthouse
P.O. Box 3000
Somerville, NJ 08876
Tel. (201) 231-7000 Ext. 7285

Custody/Visitation Dispute Resolution
Program
Superior Court of N.J., Family Part
Family Case Management
P.O. Box 3000
Somerville, NJ 08876
Tel. (201) 231-7111
A

Somerset County Dissolution Early
Settlement
Family Court Services
P.O. Box 3000
Somerville, NJ 08876
Tel. (201) 231-7111

Custody/Visitation Mediation Program
Superior Court of N.J., Family Part
Family Case Management Office
P.O. Box 3000
Somerville, NJ 08876
Tel. (201) 231-7600
A

Community Dispute Program
Woolwich Municipal Court
P.O. Box 204
Swedesboro, NJ 08085
Tel. (609) 467-1555
HKLZ

Swedesboro Community Disputes
Resolution Committee
Boro Hall
Kings Hwy.
Swedesboro, NJ 08085
Tel. (609) 467-2424

Community Dispute Program
West Deptford Municipal Court
Crown Point Rd. & Grove Ave.
Thorofare, NJ 08086
Tel. (609) 848-4587

Community Dispute Resolution
Program
Hopewell Township Municipal Court
Hopewell Township Municipal Bldg.
Rt. 546
Titusville, NJ 08560
Tel. (609) 737-1035
HKZ

Preventative Dispute Resolution
    Program
Superior Court of N.J., Family Part
Ocean County Justice Complex
CN 2191, Room 209
Toms River, NJ 08754
Tel. (201) 929-2072
AGKL

Automobile Arbitration
Ocean County Court
Ocean County Courthouse
CN 2191
Toms River, NJ 08753
Tel. (201) 929-4701
J

Mercer County Automobile
    Arbitration Program
Superior Court of Mercer County
Mercer County Courthouse
Assignment Clerk's Office
P.O. Box 8068
Trenton, NJ 08650
Tel. (609) 989-6174
JZ

Mercer County Mediation Unit
Mercer County Family Court
650 S. Broad St.
Trenton, NJ 08611
Tel. (609) 989-6850
AGZ

Mercer County Mediation Unit
Superior Court of Mercer County
650 S. Broad St., 3rd Fl.
Trenton, NJ 08611
Tel. (609) 989-6744
AGHZ

Small Claims Mediation
Superior Court of N.J., Special Civil
    Part
Mercer County Courthouse
P.O. Box 8068
Trenton, NJ
Tel. (609) 989-6206
K

Community Dispute Program
Washington Township Municipal
    Court
Municipal Bldg., Box 1106, Greentree
    Rd.
Turnersville, NJ 08012
Tel. (609) 589-0546
DGHKLZ

Community Dispute Program
Southampton Municipal Court
Town Hall, U.S. 206 & Retreat Rd.
P.O. Box 2417
Vincentown, NJ 08088
Tel. (609) 859-2747

Community Dispute Program
Voorhees Municipal Court
620 Berlin Rd.
Voorhees, NJ 08043
Tel. (609) 429-0770

Community Dispute Program
Wenonah Municipal Court
Railroad Station & Mantua Ave.
Wenonah, NJ 08090
Tel. (609) 468-0242

Community Dispute Program
Haddon Township Municipal Court
Haddon & Reeves Ave.
Westmont, NJ 08108
Tel. (609) 854-0880

Community Dispute Program
Westville Municipal Court
114 Crown Point Rd.
Westville, NJ 08093
Tel. (609) 456-0666
KLZ

Community Dispute Program
Monroe Municipal Court
125 Virginia Ave.
Williamstown, NJ 08094-9411
Tel. (609) 728-2144
H

Neighborhood Mediation Panel
Willingboro Municipal Court
Municipal Complex
Salem Road
Willingboro, NJ 08046
Tel. (609) 877-2200 Ext. 216
Z

Family Court Intake—Gloucester
    County Probation
P.O. Box 638
Woodbury, NJ 08096
Tel. (609) 853-3660

Gloucester County Community
  Dispute Resolution Program
24 Municipal Courts of Gloucester
  County
Gloucester County Probation
  Department
P.O. Box 638
Woodbury, NJ 08096
Tel. (609) 853-3455
H


Woodbury Citizens Resolution
  Dispute Committee
Woodbury Municipal Court
200 N. Broad St.
Woodbury, NJ 08096-1759
Tel. (609) 845-0691
GHKL


Statutory Automobile Arbitration
Superior Court/Civil Division
Civil Case Management
Old Courthouse
Woodbury, NJ 08096
Tel. (609) 853-3295
JZ


Vicinage 15-Summary Jury Trial
  Program
Superior Court of N.J., Civil Part
Civil Case Management Office
Old Courthouse
Woodbury, NJ 08096
Tel. (609) 853-3294
IJZ


Expanded Arbitration Pilot Project
Gloucester County Superior Court,
  Civil Part
Civil Case Management
Old Courthouse
Woodbury
Woodbury, NJ 08096
Tel. (609) 853-3295
I


Community Disputes & Resolution
  Committee, Woodbury Heights
Municipal Court of Woodbury
  Heights
220 Ivy Dr.
Woodbury Heights, NJ 08097
Tel. (609) 848-6553
AEFGKLZ


NEW YORK

Albany Dispute Mediation Program,
  Inc.
Albany County
West Mall Office Plaza
845 Central Ave., Suite 106
Albany, NY 12206
Tel. (518) 438-3951
ABCDEHIKL


Community Dispute Resolution
  Centers Program
Unified Court System, State of New
  York
Alfred E. Smith Office Bldg., 1st Fl.
Box 7039
Albany, NY 12225-0039
Tel. (518) 473-4160
AHIJKLZ


Arbitration
3rd Judicial District, Albany County
Courthouse
Albany, NY 12207
Tel. (518) 445-7714
IJ


Tri-County Mediation Center
1 Kimball St.
Amsterdam, NY 12010
Tel. (518) 842-4245
ABDHIKL


Arbitration
7th Judicial District, Cayuga County
Courthouse
Auburn, NY 13021
Tel. (315) 253-1400
IJ


Dispute Settlement Center of Genesee
  County
Main St.
Batavia, NY 14020
Tel. (716) 343-8180 Ext. 250


Dispute Resolution Center of
  Wyoming County
Batavia City Hall
Main St.
Batavia, NY 14020
Tel. (800) 828-5000

Arbitration
7th Judicial District, Steuben County
Supreme Court, 3 Pulteney Sq.
Bath, NY 14810
Tel. (607) 776-7879
IJ

ACCORD
Broome County Family Court
The Cutler House
834 Front St.
Binghamton, NY 13905
Tel. (607) 724-5153
ABDHIKLZ

Arbitration
6th Judicial District, Broome County
Courthouse, Room 201
Binghamton, NY 13902
Tel. (607) 772-2448
IJ

Arbitration
12th Judicial District, Bronx
Bronx County Courthouse
851 Grand Concourse
Bronx, NY 10451
Tel. (212) 590-3646
IJ

Brooklyn Mediation Center
210 Joralemon St., Room 618
Brooklyn, NY 11201
Tel. (718) 834-6671

Brooklyn Mediation Center
Kings County Criminal Court; N.Y.
  Summons
210 Joralemon St., Room 618
Brooklyn, NY 11201
Tel. (718) 834-6675
H

Arbitration
2nd Judicial District, Kings County
Civic Center–Montague St.
Brooklyn, NY 11201
Tel. (718) 643-5268
IJ

BBB Dispute Settlement Center
City, Town, Village, Family Courts
Regional Office
346 Delaware Ave.
Buffalo, NY 14202
Tel. (716) 856-7180
AEGHIJKLZ

Arbitration
8th Judicial District, Erie County
Supreme Court, 92 Franklin St.
Buffalo, NY 14202
Tel. (716) 852-1291
IJ

Arbitration
7th Judicial District, Ontario County
Courthouse
Canandaigua, NY 14424
Tel. (716) 394-4100
IJ

New Justice Conflict Resolution
  Services
120 East Center St.
Canastota, NY 13032
ABDHIKL

Northern N.Y. Center for Conflict
  Resolution
Village & Town Justice Courts (No.
  N.Y.)
East Main St.
P.O. Box 70
Canton, NY 13617
Tel. (315) 386-4677
ABCDEHIKLZ

Putnam County Mediation Program
P.O. Box 776
Carmel, NY 10512
Tel. (914) 225-9555

Arbitration
9th Judicial District, Putnam County
Courthouse
Carmel, NY 10512
Tel. (914) 225-3641
IJ

Common Ground
P.O. Box 329
1 Bridge St.
Catskill, NY 12414
Tel. (518) 943-9205

Community Mediation Center, Inc.
District Court
356 Middle Country Rd.
Coram, NY 11727
Tel. (516) 736-2626
HKZ

The Neighborhood Justice Project of
the Southern Tier
Family Court County Court Corning/
Hornell County Court
147 E. 2nd St.
Corning, NY 14830
Tel. (607) 936-8807
ABCDHIJKLZ


New Justice Mediation
Services
Charles M. Drumm Center
111 Port Watson St.
Cortland, NY 13045
Tel. (607) 753-6952


Delaware County Dispute Resolution
Center
72 Main St.
Delhi, NY 13753
Tel. (607) 746-6392 Ext. 7345


Northern N.Y. Center for Conflict
Resolution, Inc.
Unified Court System of N.Y.
Essex County Center
North County Community College
Elizabethtown, NY 12932
Tel. (518) 873-9910
ABCDEHIKLZ


Neighborhood Justice Project of the
Southern Tier, Inc.
Family & Criminal Courts
451 E. Market St.
Elmira, NY 14901
Tel. (607) 734-3338
ABCDEHIJKLZ


Arbitration
6th Judicial District, Chemung
County
Supreme Court
203–205 Lake St.
Elmira, NY 14902
Tel. (607) 737-2847
IJ


Nassau County Community Dispute
Center
American Arbitration Assoc.
585 Stewart Ave.
Garden City, NY 11530
Tel. (615) 222-1660

Arbitration
7th Judicial District, Livingston
County
Courthouse
Geneseo, NY 14454
Tel. (716) 243-2500
IJZ


Center for Dispute Settlement, Inc.
Livingston County Satellite Office
4241 Lakeville Rd.
Geneseo, NY 14454
Tel. (716) 243-4410


Center for Dispute Settlement, Inc.
One Franklin Sq.
Geneva, NY 14456
Tel. (315) 789-0364


Arbitration
9th Judicial District, Orange
Orange County Government Center
255–275 Main St.
Goshen, NY 10924
Tel. (912) 294-5151
IJ


Washington County Mediation
Services
5 North St.
Granville, NY 12832
Tel. (518) 642-1237


EAC, Inc.–Mediation Alternative
Project
Nassau County Family Court
50 Clinton St.
Hempstead, NY 11550
Tel. (516) 489-7733
ADHIL


Arbitration Program
10th Judicial District, Nassau County
District Court
99 Main St.
Hempstead, NY 11550
Tel. (516) 566-2247
IJ


Herkimer Mediation Project
216 Henry St.
Herkimer, NY 13350
Tel. (315) 866-4268
AHIKLZ

Common Ground Dispute Mediation
    Center
Hudson City Small Claims, Col
    County Family Court, Local
Box 1
Green & State Sts.
Hudson, NY 12534
Tel. (518) 828-8461
ABCDEHIJKLZ

Community Dispute Resolution
    Center
124 The Commons
Ithaca, NY 14850
Tel. (607) 273-9347

Arbitration
6th Judicial District, Tompkins
    County
Courthouse
Ithaca, NY 14850
Tel. (607) 272-0466
IJ

Arbitration
11th Judicial District, Queens County
Courthouse
88-11 Sutphin Blvd.
Jamaica, NY 11435
Tel. (718) 520-3136
IJ

Dispute Settlement Center of
    Chautauqua County
Jamestown Municipal Bldg.
300 E. 3rd St.
Jamestown, NY 14701
Tel. (716) 664-4223

Queens Mediation Center
119-45 Union Tpk.
Kew Gardens, NY 11375
Tel. (718) 793-1900

Arbitration
3rd Judicial District, Ulster County
Courthouse
Kingston, NY 12401
Tel. (914) 339-5680
IJ

Adirondack Mediation Services
Warren County Family Court
Warren County Municipal Center
Lake George, NY 12845
Tel. (518) 793-3587

Dispute Settlement Center of Niagara
    County
1 Locks Plaza
Lockport, NY 14094
Tel. (716) 439-6684

Community Dispute Resolution
    Center of Jefferson & Lewis
    Counties
5402 Dayan St.
Lowville, NY 13637
Tel. (315) 376-7991

Center for Dispute Settlement, Inc.
Wayne County Satellite Office
26 Church St.
Lyons, NY 14489
Tel. (315) 946-9300

Arbitration
7th Judicial District, Wayne County
Courthouse
Lyons, NY 14489
Tel. (315) 946-4895
IJ

Orange County Mediation Project,
    Inc.
57 North St.
P.O. Box 520
Middletown, NY 10940
Tel. (914) 342-6807

Arbitration
1st Judicial District, New York
N.Y. County Courthouse
60 Centre St.
New York, NY 10007
Tel. (212) 374-8510
IJ

Rockland Mediation Center
    Volunteer Counseling Service
151 S. Main St.
New City, NY 10956
Tel. (914) 634-5729

Ulster-Sullivan Mediation, Inc.
P.O. Box 726
New Paltz, NY 12561
Tel. (914) 691-6944
ABCDHKL

Center for Public Resources
366 Madison Ave.
New York, NY 10017

Summons Part of Criminal Court
346 Broadway
New York, NY 10007
Tel. (212) 766-4230

Bronx Criminal Court
215 E. 161st St.
New York, NY 10451
Tel. (212) 590-2380

Washington Heights–Inwood Coalition
652 W. 187th St.
New York, NY 10033
Tel. (212) 781-6722

IMCR Dispute Resolution Center
425 W. 144th St.
New York, NY 10021
Tel. (212) 690-5700

Alternative Dispute Resolution by
    Arbitration Program
Unified Court System, State of N.Y.
80 Centre St., Room 598
New York, NY 10013
Tel. (212) 587-4571
IJ

Small Claims Assessment Review
Supreme Court
Office of Court Administrator
80 Centre St.
New York, NY 10013
Tel. (212) 587-4781
Z

Arbitration
9th Judicial District, Rockland County
Courthouse
New City, NY 10956
Tel. (914) 638-5387
IJ

Arbitration
8th Judicial District, Niagara County
Supreme Court, 775 3rd St.
Niagara Falls, NY 14302
Tel. (716) 284-3147
IJ

Dispute Resolution Center for
    Chenango County
Norwich Center Office Plaza
27 W. Main St.
Norwich, NY 13815
Tel. (607) 336-5442

Dispute Settlement Center of
    Cattaraugus County
110 W. State St.
P.O. Box 68
Olean, NY 14760
Tel. (716) 373-5133

Agree-a-Center for Dispute Settlement
9 S. Main St.
Oneonta, NY 13820
Tel. (607) 432-5484
ABCDHIJKL

Resolve—A Center for Dispute
    Settlement, Inc.
198 W. 1st St.
Oswego, NY 13126
Tel. (315) 342-3092

ACCORD, A Center for Dispute
    Resolution
77 North Ave.
Oswego, NY 13127
Tel. (607) 687-4864
ABDHKLZ

Arbitration
7th Judicial District, Yates County
Courthouse
226 Main St.
Penn Yan, NY 14527
Tel. (315) 536-2854
IJ

Northern N.Y. Center for Conflict
    Resolution, Inc.
Clinton County Center, Hawkins
    Hall, Room 031F
SUNY at Plattsburg
Plattsburg, NY 12901
Tel. (518) 564-2327

Mediation Center of Dutchess County
327 Mill St.
Poughkeepsie, NY 12601
Tel. (914) 471-7213
AHIKLZ

Arbitration
9th Judicial District, Dutchess County
Courthouse
Poughkeepsie, NY 12601
Tel. (914) 294-5151
IJ

Arbitration
10th Judicial District, Suffolk County
Courthouse, 235 Griffing Ave.
Riverhead, NY 11901
Tel. (516) 548-3785
IJ

Center for Dispute Settlement, Inc.
87 N. Clinton Ave., Suite 510
Rochester, NY 14604
Tel. (716) 546-5110

Arbitration
7th Judicial District, Monroe County
Hall of Justice
Rochester, NY 14614-2189
Tel. (716) 428-2020
IJ

Center for Dispute Settlement, Inc.
Supreme Court of N.Y.
87 N. Clinton Ave.
Rochester, NY 14604
Tel. (716) 546-5110
ABCDEHIJLKZ

Saratoga Mediation Services
238 Church St.
Saratoga Springs, NY 12803
Tel. (518) 793-7015
ABHIKL

Community Dispute Settlement
  Program
Law, Order & Justice Center
144 Barrett St.
Schenectady, NY 12305
Tel. (518) 346-1281

Arbitration
4th Judicial District, Schenectady
  County, Supreme Court
620 State St.
Schenectady, NY 12305
Tel. (518) 382-3322
IJ

The Village Hall
Elm Lake Rd., P.O. Box 471
Speculator, NY 12164
Tel. (518) 548-8213

Staten Island Community Dispute
  Resolution Center
Richmond County, Criminal Courts
42 Richmond Terr., 4th Fl.
Staten Island, NY 10301
Tel. (718) 720-9410
HIJKL

Arbitration
5th Judicial District, Onondaga
  County
Courthouse
Syracuse, NY 13202
Tel. (315) 425-2030
IJ

Volunteer Center's Dispute Resolution
  Program
City Court
Civic Center
Syracuse, NY 13202
Tel. (315) 425-3935
AHILZ

New Justice Service, Inc.
5th Judicial District
210 E. Fayette St.
Syracuse, NY 13202
Tel. (315) 471-4676
ABCDEHIKLZ

Community Dispute Settlement
  Program
12 King St.
Troy, NY 12180
Tel. (518) 274-5920

Arbitration
3rd Judicial District, Rensselaer
  County
Courthouse
Troy, NY 12180
Tel. (518) 270-3709
IJ

Oneida County Justice Center
N.Y. State Unified Court System
214 Rutger St.
Utica, NY 13501
Tel. (315) 797-6473
CDGHIJKLZ

Arbitration
5th Judicial District, Oneida County
Courthouse
Utica, NY 13501
Tel. (315) 798-5889
IJ

Arbitration
7th Judicial District, Seneca County
Courthouse
Waterloo, NY 13165
Tel. (315) 539-9227
IJ

Community Dispute Resolution
Center
Community Action Planning Council
of Jefferson County, Box 899
Watertown, NY 13601
Tel. (315) 782-4900

Arbitration
6th Judicial District, Schuyler
Supreme Court of Schuyler County
100 N. Franklin St., P.O. Box 9
Watkins, NY 14891
Tel. (607) 535-7760
IJ

Neighborhood Justice Project
111 9th St.
P.O. Box 366
Watkins Glen, NY 14891
Tel. (607) 535-4757

Cayuga County Dispute Resolution
Center, Inc.
9021 N. Seneca St.
Weedsport, NY 13166
Tel. (315) 834-6881

Arbitration
9th Judicial District, Westchester
County
Courthouse, 111 Grove St.
White Plains, NY 10601
Tel. (914) 285-3800
IJ

Westchester Mediation Center Cluster,
Inc.
P.O. Box 281
Yonkers, NY 10703
Tel. (914) 963-6500
HIKL


NORTH CAROLINA

Arbitration
19B Judicial District
173 Worth St.
Asheboro, NC 27203
Tel. (919) 629-2131
IJZ

Summary Jury Trial, 28th Judicial
District
Superior Court, 28th Judicial District
Buncombe County Courthouse
Asheville, NC 28801
Tel. (704) 251-6037
IJ

Orange County Dispute Settlement
Center
15-B District Court
302 Weaver St.
Carrboro, NC 27510
Tel. (919) 929-8800
ABDHKL

Community Relations Council/
Dispute Settlement Program
817 E. Trade St.
Charlotte, NC 28202
Tel. (704) 336-2424
AHIKL

Summary Jury Trial, 26th Judicial
District
Superior Court, 26th Judicial District
Mecklenburg County Courthouse
Charlotte, NC 28202
Tel. (704) 342-6827
IJ

Custody Mediation, 26th Judicial
District
District Court
Mecklenburg County Courthouse
Charlotte, NC 28202
Tel. (704) 342-6735
A

Dispute Settlement Center of Durham
14th Judicial District, State of N.C.
P.O. Box 2321
Durham, NC 27702
Tel. (919) 683-1978
ABCDEHIJKLZ

Arbitration, 14th Judicial District
District Court
P.O. Box 1772
Durham, NC 27702
Tel. (919) 560-6830
IJZ

Cumberland County Dispute
Resolution Center
12th Judicial District, State of N.C.
310 Green St., Room 204
Fayetteville, NC 28301
Tel. (919) 486-9465 or 0114
HIKLZ

Custody Mediation
12th Judicial District, District Court
P.O. Box 363
Fayetteville, NC 28302
Tel. (919) 486-1754
A

Custody Mediation, 27A Judicial
District
District Court
Gaston County Courthouse
Gastonia, NC 28052
Tel. (704) 868-5822
A

Arbitration
27A Judicial District
Gaston County Courthouse
Gastonia, NC 28052
Tel. (704) 868-5822
IJZ

Goldsboro-Wayne Dispute Settlement
Center
1309 E. Walnut St.
Goldsboro, NC 27530
Tel. (919) 735-6121
AHIKL

Alamance County Dispute Settlement
Center
Alamance County District Court
P.O. Box 982
Graham, NC 27253
Tel. (919) 228-7394
H

Arbitration
15A Judicial District
Alamance County Courthouse
Graham, NC 27253
Tel. (919) 228-0210
IJZ

Mediation Services of Guilford
County
1105 E. Wendover Ave.
Greensboro, NC 27405
Tel. (919) 273-5667
AHIKL

Arbitration, 3rd Judicial District
Superior Court/District Court
P.O. Box 1465
Greenville, NC 27835
Tel. (919) 830-6465
IJZ

Henderson County Dispute Settlement
Center
The Federal Bldg.
140 4th Ave.
Hendersonville, NC 28734
AHIKL

Arbitration
25th Judicial District
111 Main Ave., N.E.
Hickory, NC 28601
Tel. (704) 322-5508
IJZ

Arbitration
15B Judicial District
Orange County Courthouse
Hillsborough, NC 27278
Tel. (919) 732-8181
IJZ

Chatham County Dispute Settlement
Program
Chatham County District Court
P.O. Box 1151
Pittsboro, NC 27312
Tel. (919) 542-4075
ABDHIKL

Mediation Services of Wake County
Box 1462
Raleigh, NC 27602
Tel. (919) 821-1296
AHIKL

Summary Jury Trial, 10th Judicial
District
Superior Court, 10th Judicial District
P.O. Box 1916
Raleigh, NC 27602
Tel. (919) 733-6600
IJ

Arbitration, 29th Judicial District
District Court
Rutherford County Courthouse
Rutherfordton, NC 28139
Tel. (704) 287-2604
IJZ

Piedmont Mediation Center
P.O. Box 169
Statesville, NC 28677
Tel. (704) 873-7624
AHIKL

Arbitration
30th Judicial District
437 N. Main St.
Waynesville, NC 28786
Tel. (704) 456-3796
IJZ

NORTH DAKOTA

North Dakota Supreme Court
State Capitol Bldg.
Bismarck, ND 58505


OHIO

Honorable John E. Olsen
Ashtabula Municipal Court
4400 Main Ave.
Ashtabula, OH 44004-6990

POSITRACT (Positive Treatment
    Alternatives for Athens County
    Teens)
Athens County Juvenile Court
Courthouse, 4th Fl.
Athens, OH 45701
Tel. (614) 592-3260
HZ

Judge Michael J. Voris
Court of Common Pleas
48 N. Market St.
Batavia, OH 45103

Clermont County Common Pleas
    Court Arbitration
270 Main St.
Batavia, OH 45103
Tel. (513) 732-7108
IJZ

Hon. Ronald E. Hadley
Logan County Common Pleas Court
Courthouse
Bellefontaine, OH 43311

Arbitration
Court of Common Pleas of Stark
    County
Stark County Courthouse
115 Central Plaza N.
Canton, OH 44702
Tel. (216) 438-0707
IJ

Mediation
Court of Common Pleas of Stark
    County
Stark County Courthouse
115 Central Plaza N.
Canton, OH 44702
Tel. (216) 438-0707
IJ

Private Complaint Program
Hamilton County Municipal Court
Hamilton County Justice Center,
    Room 111
PCP 314 9th St. Pkwy.
Cincinnati, OH 45202
Tel. (513) 763-5130
HZ


AMEND
YWCA
9th & Walnut Sts.
Cincinnati, OH 45202


Center for Mediation of Disputes,
    Common Pleas Demonstration
Hamilton County Court of Common
    Pleas
325 Hamilton County Courthouse
1000 Main St.
Cincinnati, OH 45202
Tel. (513) 632-8963
ABCDEIJZ


Compulsory Arbitration
Hamilton County Court of Common
    Pleas
355 Hamilton County Courthouse
1000 Main St.
Cincinnati, OH 45202
Tel. (513) 632-8751
IJKLZ


Center for Mediation of Disputes, Inc.
Hamilton County Court of Common
    Pleas
Common Pleas Project
8 W. 9th St.
Cincinnati, OH 45202
Tel. (513) 721-4466
ABCDEIJZ


John Henn
430 N. Court St.
Circleville, OH 43113


Mediation Division
City of Cleveland Municipal Court
City of Cleveland Prosecutor's Office
1200 Ontario St., 8th Fl.
Cleveland, OH 44113
Tel. (216) 664-4800
GHZ

Community Youth Mediation Program
Cuyahoga County
3000 Bridge Ave.
Cleveland, OH 44113
Tel. (216) 771-7297
Z

Intake Department
Franklin County Court of Common
  Pleas
50 E. Mound St.
Columbus, OH 43215
Tel. (616) 462-4470
HKZ

Duane E. Hays, Administrative
  Director
Franklin County Court of Common
  Pleas
369 S. High St.
Columbus, OH 43215

Franklin County Court of Common
  Pleas Compulsory Arbitration
369 S. High St.
Columbus, OH 43215
Tel. (614) 462-5326
IJLZ

Settlement Week
Franklin County Court of Common
  Pleas
Harold Paddock Hall of Justice, 10th
  Floor
369 S. High St.
Columbus, OH 43215
Tel. (614) 462-3152
IJZ

Franklin County Municipal Court
  Small Claims Division
375 S. High St.
Columbus, OH 43215
Tel. (614) 645-7381
IJKL

Monte Crockett
50 E. Mound St.
Columbus, OH 43215

Custody and Visitation Services
Franklin County Court of Common
  Pleas, Domestic Division
375 S. High St., 15th Fl.
Columbus, OH 43215
Tel. (614) 462-4462
A

Local Rule 67 Mediation
Franklin County Court of Common
  Pleas, General Division
Hall of Justice, 10th Fl.
369 S. High St.
Columbus, OH 43215
Tel. (614) 462-3152
IJZ

Settlement Week
Franklin County Municipal Court
375 S. High St., 10th Fl.
Columbus, OH 43215
Tel. (614) 645-8214
IJKL

Steve Schwartz, Referee
2310 2nd St.
Cuyahoga Falls, OH 44221

Ted Fields, Conciliation Court Officer
Conciliation Court, Domestic
  Relations Court
303 W. 2nd St.
Dayton, OH 45422

Juvenile Diversion
Defiance County Common Pleas
Juvenile Court
Courthouse
Defiance, OH 43512
Tel. (419) 782-0226
Z

Small Claims Division
Defiance Municipal Court
324 Perry St.
Defiance, OH 43512
Tel. (419) 782-5756
K

Small Claims Conciliation Program
Delaware Municipal Court
Delaware, OH 43015
Tel. (614) 353-1285
K

Divorce Mediation Program
Hancock County Court of Common
  Pleas
Hancock County Mental Health
  Clinic
2515 N. Main St.
Findlay, OH 45840
Tel. (419) 422-3711
ABCDE

Stephen Powell, Referee
Butler County Juvenile Court
Butler County Courthouse
Hamilton, OH 45011

Arbitration and Mediation
Butler County Court of Common
    Pleas
Butler County Courthouse
2nd & High Sts.
Hamilton, OH 45011
Tel. (513) 887-3288
IJ

David Cheney, Referee
1000 Wardhill
Lima, OH 45804

Fact Finding
Court of Common Pleas
1 N. Main St.
London, OH 43140

Domestic Referee
Court of Common Pleas, Madison
    County
London, OH 43140

Probation Officer
Court of Common Pleas, Madison
    County
London, OH 43140

Small Claims Court
Mansfield Municipal Court
30 N. Diamond St.
Mansfield, OH 44902
Tel. (419) 755-9603
K

Soni Tron
Marysville Municipal Court
Marysville, OH 43040

Sandra Phillips
93 Public Sq.
Medina, OH 44256

Thomas E. Walser, Referee
Courthouse
Newark, OH 43055

Licking County Small Claims Court
Licking County Municipal Court
Newark City Bldg.
40 W. Main St.
Newark, OH 43055
Tel. (614) 439-6640
K

Hon. Ross Avellone, Presiding Judge
Lake County Court of Common Pleas
47 N. Park Pl.
Painesville, OH 44077

Compulsory Arbitration
Lake County Court of Common Pleas
Lake County Courthouse
P.O. Box 490
Painesville, OH 44077
Tel. (216) 357-2723
Z

James Koerner
47 N. Park Pl.
Painesville, OH 44077

Citizens Dispute Settlement Program
Toledo Municipal Court
555 N. Erie St.
Toledo, OH 43624
Tel. (419) 245-1951
GHLZ

Domestic Relations Mediation
    Program
Lucas County Court
429 Michigan St.
Toledo, OH 43624
Tel. (419) 245-4878
A

Lesley Sekella, Court Administrator
Warren Municipal Court
141 South St., S.E.
Warren, OH 44483

Wayne County Municipal Court
Doug Lenhart
538 N. Market St.
Wooster, OH 44691
K

Rebecca L. Rubin, Family Services
    Coordinator
Domestic Relations Court
45 N. Detroit St.
Xenia, OH 45385

## OKLAHOMA

Community Mediation Services
Canadian County Courthouse
201 N. Choctaw
El Reno, OK 73036
HIJKLZ

Northwest Conflict Resolution
   Services
Major County Courthouse
P.O. Box 130
Fairview, OK 73737
Tel. (405) 227-2711
HIJKLZ

Panhandle Dispute Mediation
   Program
Texas County Courthouse, 2nd Fl.
319 N. Main
Guymon, OK 73942
Tel. (405) 338-3220
HIJKLZ

Southwest Dispute Mediation Program
Greer County Courthouse
Mangum, OK 73554
Tel. (405) 782-3127
HIJKLZ

Sooner Settlement
City of Norman
201 W. Gray, P.O. Box 370
Norman, OK 73070
Tel. (405) 366-5423
HIJKLZ

Dispute Mediation Program for
   Northeastern Okla.
Nowata County Courthouse, 2nd Fl.
229 N. Maple
Nowata, OK 74048
Tel. (918) 273-1092
HIJKLZ

Okla. Victim Restitution/Juvenile
   Offender Responsibility Program
Dept. of Human Services
P.O. Box 25352
Oklahoma City, OK 73125
Tel. (405) 521-2276
Z

Post Conviction Program
Dept. of Corrections
3400 N. Martin Luther King
Box 1140
Oklahoma City, OK 73136
Tel. (405) 425-2608
Z

Oklahoma Merit Protection Commission
310 Northeast 28th, Suite 201
Oklahoma City, OK 73105
Tel. (405) 525-9144
Z

Oklahoma City Dispute Mediation
   Program
Municipal Court Bldg.
700 Couch Dr.
Oklahoma City, OK 73102
Tel. (405) 231-3844
GHIJKLZ

Dept. of Human Services Employee
   Mediation Program
Personnel Resources Division
Employee Relations Unit
P.O. Box 25352
Oklahoma City, OK 73125
Tel. (405) 521-4245
Z

Agriculture Mediation Program
P.O. Box 60288
Oklahoma City, OK 73146
Tel. (405) 525-2055
Z

First Step Mediation Program
Pawnee County Courthouse, 1st Fl.
Pawnee, OK 74058
Tel. (918) 762-3464
HIJKLZ

Dispute Resolution Center
P.O. Box 1953
Stillwater, OK 74076
Tel. (405) 743-4909
HIJKLZ

Southeast Dispute Mediation Program
Murray County Courthouse
Box 240
Sulphur, OK 73086
Tel. (405) 226-2132
HIJKLZ

Early Settlement, A Precourt Hearing
Program
Police Courts Bldg.
600 Civic Center, Room 234
Tulsa, OK 74103
Tel. (918) 596-7786
HIJKLZ

The Peoples' Dispute Intervention
Center
Latimer County Courthouse
109 N. Central St.
Wilburton, OK 74578
Tel. (918) 465-3902
HIJKLZ

OREGON

Clackamas County Family Court
Service
Clackamas County Circuit Court
704 Main St., Suite 200
Oregon City, OR 97045
Tel. (503) 655-8415
ABCDZ

PENNSYLVANIA

Hickory Ridge Chemical Dependency
Program
Washington County Magisterial
Districts
337 Hickory Grade Rd.
Bridgeville, PA 15017
Tel. (412) 221-3444
Z

Custody Conciliator of Butler County
Court of Common Pleas
305 Morgan Center
Butler, PA 16001
Tel. (412) 284-5180
A

Compulsory Arbitration
Bedford County Court of Common
Pleas
Office of Court Administrator
9th Judicial District, P.O. Box 189
Carlisle, PA 17013
Tel. (717) 249-1133
IJL

Compulsory Arbitration
Cumberland County Court of
Common Pleas
Office of Court Administrator
9th Judicial District, P.O. Box 189
Carlisle, PA 17013
Tel. (717) 249-1133
IJL

Divorce Master
Court of Common Pleas, 46th Judicial
District
1 N. 2nd St.
Clearfield, PA 16830
Tel. (814) 765-2641
Z

Child Custody Mediation
Court of Common Pleas, 46th Judicial
District
1 N. 2nd St.
Clearfield, PA 16830
Tel. (814) 765-2641
A

Protection for Abuse Mediation
Court of Common Pleas, 46th Judicial
District
1 N. 2nd St.
Clearfield, PA 16830
Tel. (814) 765-2641
G

Domestic Relations Hearing Officer
Court of Common Pleas, 46th Judicial
District
107½ E. Market St.
Clearfield, PA 16830
Tel. (814) 765-5339
B

Special Appointments
Bucks County Court of Common
Pleas
Court Administrator, Courthouse
Doylestown, PA 18901
Tel. (215) 348-6040
I

Court Conciliation & Evaluation
Service
Bucks County Court of Common
Pleas
16 N. Franklin St., Suite 100A
Doylestown, PA 18901
Tel. (215) 348-3808
A

Arbitration
Bucks County Court of Common
  Pleas
Courthouse
Doylestown, PA 18901
Tel. (215) 348-6040
IJKL


Bucks County Domestic Relations
  Section
Bucks County Court of Common
  Pleas
30 E. Court St.
Doylestown, PA 18901
Tel. (215) 348-6791
BC


Board of Viewers
Bucks County Court of Common
  Pleas
Court Administrator, Courthouse
Doylestown, PA 18901
Tel. (215) 348-6040
Z


Youth Aid Panels of Bucks County
Bucks County Court of Common
  Pleas
Bucks County Juvenile Court
Broad & Court Sts.
Doylestown, PA 18901
Tel. (215) 348-6514
HZ


Officer of the Master in Divorce
Bucks County Court of Common
  Pleas
30 E. Court St.
Doylestown, PA 18901
Tel. (215) 348-6844
CDZ


Masters in Divorce
Cambria County Court of Common
  Pleas
Court Administrator's Office
Courthouse
Ebensburg, PA 15931
Tel. (814) 472-5440
DZ

Domestic Relations Hearing &
  Permanent Hearing Office
Cambria County Court of Common
  Pleas
First United Federal Bldg.
Ebensburg, PA 15931
Tel. (814) 472-5433
BD


Custody and Visitation Masters
Cambria County Court of Common
  Pleas
Court Administrator's Office,
  Courthouse
Ebensburg, PA 15931
Tel. (814) 472-5440
A


Custody Counselor
Erie County Court of Common Pleas
Erie County Courthouse
Erie, PA 16510
Tel. (814) 451-6235
A


Erie County Juvenile Diversion
  Committee Program
Court of Common Pleas, Juvenile
  Division
c/o Juvenile Probation Dept.
Erie County Courthouse
Erie, PA 16501
Tel. (814) 451-6318
HZ


Peer Jury Program
Court of Common Pleas, Juvenile
  Division
c/o Juvenile Probation Dept.
Room 1, Basement, Erie County
  Courthouse
Erie, PA 16501
Tel. (814) 451-6220
HIZ


Bucks County Mediation Service
9300 New Falls Rd.
Fallsington, PA 19054
Tel. (215) 295-8154
LZ


Compulsory Arbitration
Court of Common Pleas
111–117 Baltimore St.
Adams County Courthouse
Gettysburg, PA 17325
Tel. (717) 334-6781 Ext. 291
IKL

Health Care Conciliation Program
Washington County Court of
  Common Pleas
3 Governor's Plaza N., Suite 304
2101 N. Front St.
Harrisburg, PA 17110
Tel. (717) 783-3110

Health Care Conciliation Program
Court of Common Pleas, 32nd
  Judicial District
3 Governor's Plaza N., Suite 304
2101 N. Front St.
Harrisburg, PA 17110
Tel. (717) 783-3110
BG

Custody Conciliation
Dauphin County Court of Common
  Pleas
108–112 Walnut St.
Harrisburg, PA 17101
Tel. (717) 238-4776
A

Protection from Abuse
Central Pennsylvania Legal Services
213 A N. Front St.
Harrisburg, PA 17101
Tel. (717) 232-0581
E

Domestic Relations Section
Dauphin County Court of Common
  Pleas
P.O. Box 67
Harrisburg, PA 17108
Tel. (717) 255-2690
B

Divorce Masters
Dauphin County Court of Common
  Pleas
125 Locust St.
Harrisburg, PA 17101
Tel. (717) 234-3289
CD

Health Care Conciliation Program
3 Governor's Plaza N.
2101 N. Front St.
Harrisburg, PA 17110
Tel. (717) 783-3110
Z

Compulsory Arbitration
Dauphin County Court of Common
  Pleas
P.O. Box 1295
Harrisburg, PA 17108
Tel. (717) 255-2668
K

Accelerated Rehabilitative Disposition
Dauphin County Court of Common
  Pleas
P.O. Box 1295
Harrisburg, PA 17108
Tel. (717) 255-2770
H

Compulsory Arbitration
Wayne County Court of Common
  Pleas
c/o Wayne County Court
  Administrator
Judges Chambers, Wayne County
  Courthouse
Honesdale, PA 18431
Tel. (717) 253-5970 Ext. 106
IJK

Domestic Relations
Court of Common Pleas, 22nd
  Judicial District
Wayne County Courthouse
Honesdale, PA 18431
Tel. (717) 253-5970 Ext. 152
BCD

District Justice Courts
c/o Wayne County Court
  Administrator
Judges Chambers, Wayne County
  Courthouse
Honesdale, PA 18431
Tel. (717) 253-5970 Ext. 106
GHIJKL

Masters System for Divorce &
  Custody
Wayne County Court of Common
  Pleas
c/o Wayne County Court
  Administrator
Judges Chambers, Wayne County
  Courthouse
Honesdale, PA 18431
Tel. (717) 253-5970 Ext. 106
ACD

Compulsory Arbitration
Court of Common Pleas
Carbon County Courthouse
Jim Thorpe, PA 18229
Tel. (717) 325-8556
IJ

Family Service Assoc. of Bucks
  County
Bucks County Court of Common
  Pleas
One Oxford Valley 717
Langhorne, PA 19047
Tel. (215) 757-6916
AZ

Youth Services of Bucks County, Inc.
Bucks County Court of Common
  Pleas
517 E. Lincoln Hwy.
Langhorne, PA 19047
Tel. (215) 752-7050
AGHZ

Crawford County Domestic Relations
  Support Program
Crawford County Court of Common
  Pleas
Courthouse
Meadville, PA 16335
Tel. (814) 336-1151
AB

District Justice Court
Snyder County Courthouse
P.O. Box 217
Middleburg, PA 17842
Tel. (717) 837-4213
GHKL

Domestic Relations
Snyder County Court of Common
  Pleas
Snyder County Courthouse
P.O. Box 217
Middleburg, PA 17842
Tel. (717) 837-4230
BCD

Board of Arbitration
Snyder County Courthouse
P.O. Box 217
Middleburg, PA 17842
Tel. (717) 837-4230
IKLZ

Judicate, Inc.
1608 Walnut St., Suite 1200
Philadelphia, PA 19103
Tel. (215) 546-6200
DIJKL

Dispute Resolution Program
Philadelphia Municipal Court
City Hall Annex, 10th Fl.
Philadelphia, PA 19107
Tel. (215) 686-2973
HKL

Allegheny Service Institute (ASI)
Washington County Magisterial
  Districts
P.O. Box 90026
Pittsburgh, PA 15224
Tel. (412) 621-2276
Z

Civil Court Arbitration
Allegheny County Court of Common
  Pleas
621 City-County Bldg.
Pittsburgh, PA 15219
Tel. (412) 355-5625
K

Alternative Dispute Resolution
Schuylkill County Court of Common
  Pleas
Schuylkill County Courthouse
2nd & Laurel Blvd.
Pottsville, PA 17901
Tel. (717) 628-1333
H

ARD
Berks County Court of Common Pleas
Berks County Courthouse
33 N. 6th St.
Reading, PA 19601
Tel. (215) 378-8283
ABCDZ

ADR Program for Disposition of
  Criminal Cases
Lackawanna County Court of
  Common Pleas
20 N. Washington Ave.
Scranton, PA 18503
Tel. (717) 963-6773
G

Masters for Custody & Visitation
Lackawanna County Court of
  Common Pleas
Court Administrator's Office
200 N. Washington Ave.
Scranton, PA 18503
Tel. (717) 963-6773
A

District Justice
District Justice Court
RD #1, Box 51T
Rt. 522
Selinsgrove, PA 17870
Tel. (717) 374-0111
GHKL

Custody Conferencing
Bucks County Court
773 2nd St. Pike
Southampton, PA 18966
Tel. (215) 322-1908
A

Northumberland County Alternative
  Dispute Program
Northumberland County Court
2nd & Market Sts., 2nd Fl.
Sunbury, PA 17801
Tel. (717) 988-4167
ABCD

Custody Mediation
Bradford County Court of Common
  Pleas
Towanda, PA 18848
Tel. (717) 265-1708
A

Mental Health
Mental Health Review Officer
One Neshaminy Interplex, Suite 205
Trevose, PA 19047
Tel. (215) 638-3388
Z

Office of Child Custody Mediation
Fayette County Court of Common
  Pleas
County Courthouse
Uniontown, PA 15401
Tel. (412) 430-1230
A

Underage Drinking Offender Program
Washington County Magisterial
  Districts
87 E. Maiden St.
Washington, PA 15301
Tel. (412) 228-0810
Z

Family Court Master
Tioga County Court of Common
  Pleas
Tioga County Courthouse
Wellsboro, PA 16901
Tel. (717) 724-1906 Ext. 384
ABCD

Chester County Court of Common
  Pleas
High & Market Sts.
West Chester, PA 19380
Tel. (215) 344-6170
ABCDZ

PUERTO RICO

Dispute Resolution Center
General Court of Justice/San Juan
  Judicial Center
P.O. Box 887, Hato Rey Station
San Juan, PR 00919
Tel. (809) 763-4813
ABCDGHIKLZ

RHODE ISLAND

Court-Annexed Arbitration
Superior Court
Garrahy Judicial Complex, Room 309
One Dorrance Plaza
Providence, RI 02903
Tel. (401) 277-6147
IJZ

SOUTH CAROLINA

2nd Circuit Community Juvenile
  Arbitration Program
P.O. Box 2327
Aiken, SC 29802
Tel. (803) 242-1569
Z

Juvenile Arbitration Program
2nd Circuit Court, Family
P.O. Box 2327
Aiken, SC 29802
Tel. (803) 642-1569
Z

Pre-Trial Intervention
10th Circuit Court
P.O. Box 4046
Anderson, SC 29622
Tel. (803) 260-4042
HZ

Mediation Services for Farm
    Borrowers
Circuit Court of Common Pleas
P.O. Box 61974
Charleston, SC 29418
Tel. (803) 552-6120
Z

Alternative Dispute Resolution Pilot
    Program
171 Ashley Ave.
Charleston, SC 29425
Tel. (803) 792-3627
HZ

Pretrial Intervention
General Sessions Court
P.O. Box 728
Chester, SC 29706
Tel. (803) 377-1141
Z

Appeals Arbitration
Supreme Court or Court of Appeals
P.O. Box 11330
Columbia, SC 29211
Tel. (803) 734-1080
Z

VICTOR of the Midlands, Inc.
Magistrate and Municipal Courts
P.O. Box 5755
Columbia, SC 29250
Tel. (803) 256-2351
HIJKLZ

13th Circuit Pre-Trial Intervention
    Program
County Courthouse Annex
Greenville, SC 29601
Tel. (803) 298-8717
HZ

Lexington County Community
    Juvenile Arbitration Program
Lexington County Family Court
114-A N. Lake Dr.
Lexington, SC 29072
Tel. (803) 359-8355
H

Charleston County Ad Hoc Mediation
    Program
Family Court of the 9th Judicial Circuit
960 Cliffwood Dr.
Mt. Pleasant, SC 29464
Tel. (803) 884-6473
ABCDE

Fairfield County Substance Abuse
    Committee
Fairfield County District Court
P.O. Box 388
Winnsboro, SC 29180
Tel. (803) 635-2335
H

SOUTH DAKOTA

Settlement Conference
Supreme Court, State Capitol
Pierre, SD 57501
Tel. (605) 773-4897
BCDIJ

Child Support Referees
Circuit Court, State Capitol
Pierre, SD 57501
Tel. (605) 773-4869
B

TENNESSEE

Judicial District 23
111 Sycamore St.
Ashland City, TN 37015
Tel. (615) 792-3075
B

Child Support Referee for the 3rd
    Judicial District
Civil Court, Judicial District 3
128 S. Main, Suite 206
P.O. Box 145
Greeneville, TN 37743
Tel. (615) 639-0049
BCZ

Child Support Referees
Judicial District 8
P.O. Box 101
Jacksboro, TN 37757
Tel. (615) 562-5174
B

Child Support Referees
Judicial District 9
100 Court St.
Kingston, TN 37763
Tel. (615) 376-1985
BC

Child Support Referees
Judicial District 6
422 Supreme Court Bldg.
Nashville, TN 37219
Tel. (615) 741-2687
AB

Child Support Referees
Judicial District 4, Circuit &
    Chancery Courts
420 Supreme Court Bldg.
Nashville, TN 37219
Tel. (615) 741-3194
B

Child Support Referees
Judicial District 10
422 Supreme Court Bldg.
Nashville, TN 37219
Tel. (615) 741-2687
AB

Rent-a-Judge
Civil Court
422 Supreme Court Bldg.
Nashville, TN 37219
Tel. (615) 741-4416
Z

Child Support Enforcement, 12th
    Judicial District of Tenn.
Child Support Referee
126 1st Ave., N.W.
Winchester, TN 37398
Tel. (615) 967-4043
B

TEXAS

The Dispute Resolution Center
P.O. Box 9257
Amarillo, TX 79105-9257
Tel. (806) 372-3381
ABDEHIJKLZ

The Dispute Resolution Center
512 E. Riverside, Suite 202
Austin, TX 78704
Tel. (512) 443-5981
ABCDGHIJKLZ

Jefferson County Mediation Center
Small Claims, County Court, District
    Court
Old Building, 3rd Fl.
1149 Pearl St.
Beaumont, TX 77701
Tel. (409) 835-8747
ABDHIKLZ

Nueces County Dispute Resolution
    Services
901 Leopard St., Suite 110
Corpus Christi, TX 78401
Tel. (512) 888-0650
ADEHIJKLZ

Dispute Mediation Service
Civil, District, Juvenile, Family,
    County, Justice of the Peace, Dallas
3310 Live Oak, Suite 202 LB9
Dallas, TX 75204-6133
Tel. (214) 821-4380
ABDEIJKLZ

Dallas County Family Court Services
Family District Courts
Old Red Courthouse
100 S. Houston, 3rd Fl.
Dallas, TX 75202
Tel. (214) 653-7674
A

Dallas Bar Assoc./ADR Community
    Mediator Training Program
c/o Steve Brutsche
15303 Dallas Pkwy., Suite 700, LB17
Dallas, TX 75248
Tel. (214) 701-7040
IJLZ

Rio Grande Dispute Resolution Center
123 Pioneer Plaza, Suite 210
El Paso, TX 79901
Tel. (915) 533-4800
AIJKLZ

Tarrant County Dispute Resolution
    Center
1300 Summit St., Suite 222
Fort Worth, TX 76102
Tel. (817) 877-4554
ABCDGHIJKLZ

Dispute Resolution Center
1302 Preston St., Room 100
Houston, TX 77002
Tel. (713) 221-8274
ADGHIJKLZ

Center for Dispute Resolution
P.O. Box 1282
Lewisville, TX 76067
Tel. (214) 221-9333
ABCDGHIJKLZ

South Plains Dispute Resolution
    Center
P.O. Box 3730
Lubbock, TX 79452
Tel. (806) 762-8721
ABDEGHIJKLZ

Dispute Mediated Settlements
199th District Court
1919 Independence Pkwy.
Plano, TX 75075
Tel. (214) 867-0460
ABDLZ

Bexar County Mediation Center
436 S. Main, Heritage Plaza
San Antonio, TX 78204
Tel. (512) 220-2128
ABCDGHIJKLZ


UTAH

Vernon Barrett
12717 S. 1480 East
Draper, UT 84020

B.J. Dobbins
489 E. 6325 South
Murray, UT 84107

Timothy W. Healy
Juvenile Court Committee
444 26th St.
Ogden, UT 84401

Howard H. Maetani
District Court Committee
County Bldg.
Provo, UT 84601

Michael Eardley/Sharyn Shappart
3rd Circuit Court
451 S. 200 East
Salt Lake City, UT 84111

Richard W. Birrell
Juvenile Court Committee
3522 S. 700 West
Salt Lake City, UT 84119

Commissioner Program
3rd District Court
District Court Committee
240 E. 400 South
Salt Lake City, UT 84111
Tel. (801) 535-5210
ABCDE

Beckie Rock
5153 S. 2870 East
Salt Lake City, UT 84124

Shirlee Pennington
1824 Severn Dr.
Salt Lake City, UT 84124

Gwen Rowley
2741 Juniper Way
Salt Lake City, UT 84117

Prelitigation Medical Malpractice
Utah State Prelitigation
Heber W. Wells Bldg.
Salt Lake City, UT 84145
Tel. (801) 530-6990
Z

Bonnie Posselli
8275 So. Main
Sandy, UT 84092


VERMONT

Burlington Mediation Center
Vermont District Court, Chittenden
    Circuit
431 Pine St.
Burlington, VT 05401
Tel. (802) 860-1029
K

Lamoille Small Claims Mediation
    Program
Vermont District Court Lamoille Cty
Quest RD 1 #1440-10
Johnson, VT 05656
Tel. (802) 635-7349
K

Rutland Superior Court Mediation
  Services
83 Center St.
Middlebury, VT 05753
Tel. (802) 775-1727
ABCDE

Washington County Mediation Project
Vermont District Court, Washington
  Circuit
Woodbury College
659 Elm St.
Montpelier, VT 05602
Tel. (802) 229-0517
ABCDKLZ

Family Mediation Program
Vermont District Court, Lamoille
  Circuit
Lamoille Family Center
P.O. Box 274
Morrisville, VT 05661
Tel. (802) 888-5229
AGZ

Orleans County Mediation Project
Orleans County District Court
10 Clark St.
Newport, VT 05855
DIKL

Vermont Family Mediation Program
P.O. Box 328
Worcester, VT 05682
Tel. (802) 223-3408
ABCD

VIRGINIA

2A Judicial District Mediation
  Program
2A Judicial District Court
P.O. Box 446
Accomack, VA 23301
Tel. (804) 787-1822
ABCD

18th Judicial District Court Service
  Unit
Juvenile & Domestic Relations
520 King St.
Alexandria, VA 22314
Tel. (703) 838-4144
ABCD

9th Judicial District Mediation
  Program
P.O. Box 62
Appomattox, VA 24522
Tel. (804) 966-2603
ABCD

10th Judicial District Court Service
  Unit
Court Service Officer
P.O. Box 26
Appomattox, VA 24522
Tel. (804) 352-8224
AB

Arlington JDR Court Mediation
  Service
P.O. Box 925
Arlington, VA 22216
Tel. (703) 358-4499
ABCE

16th District Juvenile & Domestic
  Relations Court Service
411 E. High St.
Charlottesville, VA 22901
Tel. (804) 979-7191
AB

12th Judicial District Mediation
  Program
P.O. Box 20
Chesterfield, VA 23832
Tel. (804) 788-1372
ABCD

Southampton Dept. of Social Services
Southampton County Juvenile
  Domestic Relations Court
Welfare Bldg.
State Rt. 35 N.
P.O. Box 405
Courtland, VA 23827
Tel. (804) 653-2764
A

19th Judicial District Court Service
  Unit
Juvenile & Domestic Relations
4000 Chain Bridge Rd.
Fairfax, VA 22030
Tel. (703) 691-3241
ABCD

Juvenile and Domestic Relations
Fairfax Juvenile & Domestic Relations
  District Court
Colleague, Court Service Officer
4000 Chain Bridge Rd.
Fairfax, VA 22030
Tel. (703) 246-3040
ABCE

Rappahannock Mediation Coalition
15th District Juvenile & Domestic
  Relations Court
601 Caroline St., 4th Fl.
Fredericksburg, VA 22401
Tel. (703) 372-1068
ABCE

Social Services Child Welfare Unit
2177 George Washington Pkwy.
P.O. Box 1917
Grafton, VA 23692
Tel. (804) 898-7284
ABCD

Hampton Department of Social
  Services
8th District Juvenile & Domestic
  Relations & Circuit Court 1, 2, 3
1320 LaSalle Ave.
Hampton, VA 23669
Tel. (804) 722-7931
AE

Isle of Wright Dept. of Social Services
Isle of Wright County Courthouse
Isle of Wright, VA 23430
Tel. (804) 357-3191
ABCD

20th Judicial District Court Service
  Unit
Leesburg, VA 22075
ABCD

Loudoun Court Service Mediation
  Center
20th Judicial District Court
1 E. Market St., 3rd Fl.
Leesburg, VA 22075
Tel. (703) 777-0303
ABEGZ

24th Judicial District Court Service
  Unit
1101 Court St., P.O. Box 60
Lynchburg, VA 24504
ABCD

Lynchburg Dept. of Human Service
  Mediation Program
Division of Social Services
701 Hollins St., Box 955
Lynchburg, VA 24504
Tel. (804) 847-1551
ABCD

Mediation
Lynchburg Juvenile & Domestic
  Court
Lynchburg Social Services
701 Hollins St.
Lynchburg, VA 24504
Tel. (804) 847-1354
A

31st Judicial District Mediation
  Program
9311 Lee Ave.
Manassas, VA 22110
Tel. (703) 335-6200
ABCE

21st Judicial District Mediation
  Program
21st Judicial District Juvenile &
  Domestic Relations Court
P.O. Drawer 751
Martinsville, VA 24114
Tel. (703) 632-3424
ABEH

Newport News Court Service Unit
  Mediation
Newport News Juvenile & Domestic
  Relations District Court
230 25th St.
Newport News, VA 23607
Tel. (804) 247-8781
ABCDEFGHZ

Newport News Dept. of Social
  Services
2410 Wickham Ave.
Newport News, VA 23607
Tel. (804) 247-2300
ABCD

4th District Court Service Unit
  Mediation Program
Norfolk Juvenile & Domestic
  Relations District Court
P.O. Box 809
Norfolk, VA 23501
Tel. (804) 683-8311
ABCE

Norfolk Dept. of Social Services
220 W. Brambleton Ave.
Norfolk, VA 23510
Tel. (804) 627-4861
ABCD

Probation Administrator
29th Judicial District Court Service
    Unit
Pearisburg, VA 24134
ABCD

Colleague, Court Service Officer
27th Judicial District Court Service
    Unit
143 3rd St., N.W.
Pulaski, VA 24301
Tel. (703) 980-8888
ABCD

14th District Court Service Unit
    Program
Henrico County Juvenile & Domestic
    Relations District Court
P.O. Box 27032
Richmond, VA 23273
Tel. (804) 672-4420
ABE

13th Judicial District Mediation
    Program
Richmond Juvenile & Domestic
    Relations District Court
2000 Mecklenburg St.
Richmond, VA 23223
Tel. (804) 780-4477
ABE

23rd Judicial District Mediation
    Program
P.O. Box 1374
Salem, VA 24153
Tel. (703) 387-6016
ABCD

Roanoke County Dept. of Social
    Services
220 E. Main St.
P.O. Box 31
Salem, VA 24153
Tel. (804) 347-6087
ABCD

Roanoke County Custody/Visitation
    Mediation Program
Roanoke County and City of Salem
P.O. Box 1127
Salem, VA 24153
Tel. (703) 387-6187
A

Juvenile & Domestic Relations Court
    Service Unit
25th District Juvenile & Domestic
    Relations Court
P.O. Box 1336
Staunton, VA 24401
Tel. (703) 885-0848
ABEG

Virginia Beach Family Mediation
    Program
Virginia Beach Circuit; Virginia Beach
    Juvenile & Domestic Relations
    Court
3432 Virginia Beach Ave.
Virginia Beach, VA 23452
Tel. (804) 431-3265
ABEZ

Juvenile & Domestic Relations Court
    Mediation Program
Family Counseling Unit, Bldg. 3300
397 Little Neck Rd., Suite 200
Virginia Beach, VA 23452
Tel. (804) 427-4361
ABCD

James City County DSS Mediation
    Counseling Program
Juvenile & Domestic Relations Court
5249 Olde Towne Rd.
Williamsburg, VA 23185
Tel. (804) 565-6855
A

26th Judicial District Mediation
    Program
26th Judicial District Court
5 N. Kent St., Judicial Center
Winchester, VA 22601
Tel. (703) 667-5770
ABCD

Court Services
Winchester/Frederick County Juvenile
    & Domestic Relations Court
5 N. Kent St., 2nd Fl.
Winchester, VA 22601
Tel. (703) 667-5770
A

WASHINGTON

Whatcom County Mandatory
   Arbitration Program
Whatcom County Superior Court
311 Grand Ave.
Bellingham, WA 98225
Tel. (206) 676-6803
IJ

Snohomish County Mandatory
   Arbitration Program
Snohomish County Superior Court
Courthouse Complex
3000 Rockefeller Ave.
Everett, WA 98201
Tel. (206) 328-3421
BCIJZ

Dispute Resolution Center,
   Snohomish County
Snohomish County Courts
P.O. Box 839
Everett, WA 98206
Tel. (206) 339-1335
ABCDHIJKLZ

Dispute Resolution Center
South District Court/Snohomish
   County
20520 68th Ave., W.
Linwood, WA 98201
Tel. (206) 339-1335
KL

Thurston County Mandatory
   Mediation Program
Thurston County Superior Court
2000 Lakeridge Dr., S.W., Bldg. 2
Mail Stop FQ-11
Olympia, WA 98502
Tel. (206) 786-5557
AB

Thurston County Mandatory
   Arbitration Program
Thurston County Superior Court
2000 Lakeridge Dr., S.W., Bldg. 2
Mail Stop FQ-11
Olympia, WA 98502
Tel. (206) 786-5557
BIJZ

Kitsap County Mandatory Arbitration
   Program
Kitsap County Superior Court
614 Division St.
Port Orchard, WA 98366
Tel. (206) 876-7140
DIJL

Victim Offender Reconciliation
   Program
King County Superior Court
1305 4th Ave., Suite 606
Seattle, WA 98101
Tel. (206) 621-8871
H

King County Family Court Services
King County Superior Court
King County Courthouse
516 3rd Ave., Room W364
Seattle, WA 98104
Tel. (206) 296-9390
A

King County Superior Court
   Mandatory Arbitration
King County Superior Court
King County Courthouse
516 3rd Ave., Room W855
Seattle, WA 98104
Tel. (206) 296-9365
IJ

Spokane County Mandatory
   Arbitration Program
Spokane County Superior Court
W. 1116 Broadway
Spokane, WA 99260
Tel. (509) 456-5790
IJKL

Mandatory Arbitration for Pierce
   County Superior Court
County-City Bldg., Room 110
Tacoma, WA 98402
Tel. (206) 591-7464
IJL

Clark County Mandatory Arbitration
   Program
Clark County Superior Court
P.O. Box 5000
Vancouver, WA 98668
Tel. (206) 525-2049
IJ

Douglas County Mandatory
  Arbitration Program
Douglas County Superior Court
203 S. Rainier
Waterville, WA 98858
Tel. (509) 745-8529
IJ

Chelan County Mandatory Arbitration
  Program
Chelan County Superior Court
P.O. Box 880
Wenatchee, WA 98807
Tel. (509) 664-5212
IJZ

Yakima County Mandatory Arbitration
  Program
Yakima County Superior Court
N. 2nd and E. B Sts.
Yakima, WA 98901
Tel. (509) 575-4120
IJ


WISCONSIN

TRY Mediation, Inc.
Eau Claire County Circuit Court
Eau Claire County Courthouse
721 Oxford Ave., Room A276
Eau Claire, WI 54703
Tel. (715) 839-6295
AKL

Dane County Case Mediation
  Program
Dane County Circuit Court
City-County Bldg., Room 243
210 Martin Luther King Blvd.
Madison, WI 53709
Tel. (608) 267-2523
CDIJLZ

Medical Mediation Panels
Wisconsin Supreme Court
110 E. Main St., Suite 210
Madison, WI 53703
Tel. (608) 266-7711
Z

Milwaukee Mediation Center
Milwaukee County Circuit Court
Wisconsin Correctional Service
436 W. Wisconsin Ave.
Milwaukee, WI 53203
Tel. (414) 271-2512
AFGIKLZ

Racine County Family Court
  Commissioner
Racine County Courthouse
730 Wisconsin Ave.
Racine, WI 53403

Dispute Settlement Center of Racine
  County, Inc.
Racine County Circuit Court
730 Wisconsin Ave., 4th Fl.
Racine, WI 53403
Tel. (414) 636-3279
GHIJKLZ

Mediation Center of Waukesha
  County
414 W. Moreland Blvd., Room 200
Waukesha, WI 53188
Tel. (414) 544-5431
ABDHIKLZ

Family Mediation of Marathon
  County
Marathon County Circuit Court
Marathon County Health and Social
  Services
300 E. Thomas St.
Wausau, WI 54401
Tel. (715) 847-5700
AZ

## INDUSTRY GROUPS

Following is a Federal Trade Commission compilation of industry groups that offer alternative dispute resolution programs. Publication of this list does not constitute an endorsement of any of these programs. Citizens should always look for a better alternative before agreeing to dispute resolution by an industry-connected group.

Still, it is often helpful to know of an industry-connected ADR program, especially if no other alternative seems to make sense. Most industry programs bind the company but not the consumer, who, even after an adverse decision, can still go elsewhere—even to court. If you use this list, call the appropriate industry group to be sure that the information you need remains up-to-date.

*Manufacturers, Trade Associations, and Other In-House Dispute Resolution Programs*

(**) indicates free programs

### ADVERTISING

National Advertising (NAD)/Council
  of Better Business Bureaus
845 Third Ave.
New York, NY 10022
(212) 754-1320
(written complaints only)

Direct Marketing Association (DMA)
Mail Order Action Line
6 E. 43rd St.
New York, NY 10017
(written complaints only)

### AIRLINES

International Airline Passengers
Consumer Affairs Department
P.O. Box 870188
Dallas, TX 75287
1 (800) 527-5888
(complaint handling for members
  only)

### APPLIANCES

Major Appliance Consumer Action
  Panel (MACAP)
20 N. Wacker Dr.
Chicago, IL 60606
(312) 984-5858
1 (800) 621-0477 (outside Illinois)
(written complaints only)

### AUTOMOBILES

**American Automobile Association
  (AAA)
1000 AAA Dr.
Heathrow, FL 32746-5064
1 (800) 477-6583
(free arbitration to members only)
(AUTOSOLVE participants include:
  Hyundai and Toyota)

**Automotive Consumer Action
  Program (AUTOCAP)
National Administrator
National Automobile Dealers
  Association
8400 Westpart Dr.
McLean, VA 22102
1 (800) 252-6232

(AUTOCAP participants include: Alfa
Romeo, Austin Rover Cars
[Sterling], BMW, Fiat, Honda
[including Acura], Isuzu, Jaguar,
Mazda, Mitsubishi, Nissan
[Datsun], Peugeot, Rolls-Royce,
Saab-Scania, Volvo, and Yugo)

\*\*BBB Auto Line
Council of Better Business Bureaus
4200 Wilson Blvd., Suite 800
Arlington, VA 22203
(703) 276-0100
(Arbitration Programs for: AMC,
Audi, General Motors and its six
divisions, Honda, Jeep, Nissan,
Peugeot, Porsche, Renault, Saab,
and Volkswagen)

Chrysler Customer Service
P.O. Box 1086
Detroit, MI 48288
1 (800) 992-1997

\*\*Ford Consumer Appeals Board
P.O. Box 43360
Detroit, MI 48243
1 (800) 392-FORD

## CARPETS AND RUGS

Carpet and Rug Institute
Director of Governmental Affairs
Suite 500
1155 Connecticut Ave., N.W.
Washington, D.C. 20036
(202) 429-6629
(written inquiries only)

## CLOTHING

American Collectors Association
Director of Public Relations
P.O. Box 39106
Minneapolis, MN 55439-0106
(612) 926-6547

American Apparel Manufacturers
Association
Director of Public Relations
2500 Wilson Blvd., Suite 301
Arlington, VA 22201
(703) 524-1864
(written complaints only)

## DEBT COLLECTION

American Collectors Association
Director of Public Relations
4040 W. 70th St.
P.O. Box 35106
Minneapolis, MN 55435
(complaint handling for members
only; referral/information to non-
members)

## DOOR-TO-DOOR SALES

Direct Selling Association
Code Administrator
1776 K Street, N.W., Suite 600
Washington, DC 20006
(202) 293-5760
(complaint handling for consumers of
member companies)

## ELECTRONICS

\*\*Electronic Industries Association
Consumer Affairs Department
2001 Pennsylvania Ave., N.W. 10th
Floor
(202) 457-4977
Washington, DC 20006
(informal arbitration for consumers;
written and telephone complaints)

## EMPLOYMENT AGENCIES

National Association of Personnel
Consultants
3133 Mt. Vernon Ave.
Alexandria, VA 22305
(703) 684-0180
(complaint handling and arbitration
for members only)

## FINANCIAL PLANNING

International Association for Financial
Planning
National Headquarters
2 Concourse Pkwy., Suite 800
Atlanta, GA 30328
(404) 395-1605
(complaint handling for members)

## FUNERAL AND CEMETERY SERVICES

**Funeral Service Consumer
  Assistance Program
1614 Central St.
Evanston, IL 60201
1 (800) 662-7666
(arbitration and consumer
  information)

Cemetery Consumer Service Council
  Assistant Secretary
P.O. Box 3574
Washington, DC 20007
(703) 379-6426

## FURNITURE

Furniture Industry Consumer Advisory
  Panel (FICAP)
Executive Director
P.O. Box 951
High Point, NC 27261
(written inquiries only)

## HEALTH CARE

American Health Care Association
1201 L Street, N.W.
Washington, DC 20005
(202) 842-4444

Blue Cross and Blue Shield
  Association Consumer Affairs
Subscribers should contact local Blue
  Cross and Blue Shield office.
(complaint handling and information)

## HEARING AIDS

National Hearing Aid Society
20361 Middlebelt Rd.
Livonia, MI 48152
1 (800) 521-5247
(complaints about members)

## HOME BUILDERS

National Association of Home Builders
Director of Consumer Affairs/Public
  Liaison
15th and M Streets, N.W.
Washington, DC 20005
(202) 822-0409
1 (800) 368-5242 (outside District of
  Columbia)
(information & referrals only)

## HOME OWNERS WARRANTIES

Home Owners Warranty Program
  (HOW)
P.O. Box 152087
Irving, TX 75015-2087
(214) 402-7600
(dispute resolution against member
  builders)

## HOME STUDY AND VOCATIONAL SCHOOLS

National Association of Trade &
  Technical Schools
Accrediting Commission
251 Wisconsin Ave., N.W.
Washington, DC 20007
(202) 333-1021
(written inquiries only)

National Home Study Council
Assistant to Executive Director
1601 18th St., N.W.
Washington, DC 20009
(202) 234-5100
(written inquiries only)

## HOUSEHOLD GOODS

**American Movers Conference
  Household Goods Dispute
  Settlement Program
2200 Mill Rd.
Alexandria, VA 22314
(703) 838-1930
(administered by the American
  Arbitration Association)

## MAGAZINE SUBSCRIPTIONS

**Magazine Publishers Association
Customer Service Manager
575 Lexington Ave., 5th floor
New York, NY 10022
(212) 752-0055
(written complaints only)

## MAIL ORDER

**Direct Marketing Association
Consumer Relations Department
6 E. 43rd St.
New York, NY 10017
(212) 689-4977
(written complaints only)

## MOBILE HOMES

Manufactured Housing Institute
1745 Jefferson Davis Hwy., Suite 511
Arlington, VA 22202
(703) 979-6620

## MORTGAGES

Mortgage Bankers Association of
    America
Public Affairs Coordinator
1125 15th St., N.W., 7th Fl.
Washington, D.C. 20005
(202) 861-6565
(complaints about members)

## PROFESSIONAL SERVICES

National Association of Securities
    Dealers, Inc.
33 Whitehall St.
New York, NY 10004
Attn: Ruth Brooks
(212) 858-4483
(consumer complaints & arbitration)

National Futures Association
Attn: Arbitration Administrator
200 W. Madison St.
Chicago, IL 60606
(312) 781-1410
(arbitration program for members and
    non-members)

## TRAVEL SERVICES

**American Society of Travel Agents,
    Inc. (ASTA)
Attn: Consumer Affairs
P.O. Box 23992
Washington, D.C. 20026-3992
(703) 739-2782
(written complaints only & arbitration)

**U.S. Tour Operators Association
President
211 E. 51st St., Suite 12-B
New York, NY 10022
(212) 944-5727
(complaints about members)

# Appendix B
# Small Claims Court Jurisdictional Limits

The following list provides small claims court jurisdictional (dollar) limits for every state in the union. Because states from time to time increase dollar limits on small claims, check with local courts for up-to-the-minute advice on state limits and local rules. This list is reprinted from the national edition of *Everybody's Guide to Small Claims Court* by Ralph Warner, published by Nolo Press. That book includes rules for each state, including the court in which the plaintiff must sue, whether attorneys are permitted, and whether decisions may be appealed.

### ALABAMA

Small Claims Docket (District Court)
*Dollar Limit:* $1,000.

### ALASKA

Small Claims (District Court Judges and Magistrates)
*Dollar Limit:* $5,000.

### ARIZONA

Justice Court (Small Claims Division)
*Dollar Limit:* $1,000.

### ARKANSAS

Urban: Municipal Court (Small Claims Division)
Rural: Justice of the Peace
*Dollar Limit:* $3,000.

## CALIFORNIA

Small Claims Division (Municipal or
    Justice Court)
*Dollar Limit:* $5,000 (for no more
    than two cases brought by same
    plaintiff in same year), and $2,500
    (for cases after the second).

## COLORADO

County Court (Small Claims
    Division)
*Dollar Limit:* $2,000.

## CONNECTICUT

Small Claims (Superior Court)
*Dollar Limit:* $2,000.

## DELAWARE

Justice of the Peace (no small claims
    system)
*Dollar Limit:* $2,500.

## DISTRICT OF COLUMBIA

Superior Court (Small Claims and
    Conciliation Branch)
*Dollar Limit:* $2,000.

## FLORIDA

Summary Procedure (County Court)
*Dollar Limit:* $2,500.

## GEORGIA

(Magistrate Court)
*Dollar Limit:* $5,000.

## HAWAII

Small Claims Division (District Court)
*Dollar Limit:* $2,500; no limit in
    landlord-tenant residential deposit
    cases. For return of leased/rented
    personal property, the property must
    not be worth more than $1,500.
    Counterclaims up to $10,000.

## IDAHO

Small Claims Department of
    Magistrate's Division
(District Court)
*Dollar Limit:* $2,000.

## ILLINOIS

Small Claims (Circuit Court)
*Dollar Limit:* $2,500 (Small Claims);
    $1,000 (Cook County "Pro Se," a
    branch of the court in which parties
    represent themselves).

## INDIANA

Small Claims Court; Small Claims
    Docket (Circuit Court, Superior
    Court, and County Court)
*Dollar Limit:* $3,000; in landlord-
    tenant repossession cases, total rent
    due cannot exceed $3,000.

## IOWA

Small Claims Docket (District Court)
*Dollar Limit:* $2,000.

## KANSAS

Small Claims (District Court)
*Dollar Limit:* $1,000.

## KENTUCKY

Small Claims Division (District Court)
*Dollar Limit:* $1,500.

## LOUISIANA

Rural (Justice of the Peace); Urban
(City Court: Small Claims Division)
*Dollar Limit:* $2,000 generally, and
$1,500 for recovery of property
(Justice of the Peace).

## MAINE

Small Claims (District Court)
*Dollar Limit:* $1,400.

## MARYLAND

Small Claims Action (District Court)
*Dollar Limit:* $2,500.

## MASSACHUSETTS

Small Claims Division (Boston—
Municipal Court; Elsewhere—
District Court)
*Dollar Limit:* $1,500; no limit for
action for property damage caused
by a motor vehicle.

## MICHIGAN

Small Claims Division (District Court)
*Dollar Limit:* $1,500.

## MINNESOTA

Conciliation Court (County Court)
*Dollar Limit:* $3,500.

## MISSISSIPPI

Justice Court
*Dollar Limit:* $1,000.

## MISSOURI

Small Claims Court (Circuit Court)
*Dollar Limit:* $1,500.

## MONTANA

Small Claims Court (Justice Court
and District Court)
*Dollar Limit:* $2,500.

## NEBRASKA

Small Claims Court (County or
Municipal Court)
*Dollar Limit:* $1,500.

## NEVADA

Small Claims (Justice Court)
*Dollar Limit:* $2,500.

# NEW HAMPSHIRE

Small Claims Actions (District or
    Municipal Court)
*Dollar Limit*: $2,500.

# NEW JERSEY

Small Claims Section (Special Civil
    Part of Law Division of Superior
    Court)
*Dollar Limit*: $1,000.

# NEW MEXICO

Metropolitan Court (Urban);
    Magistrate's Court (Rural)
*Dollar Limit*: $5,000 (Magistrate's
    Court); $5,000 (Metropolitan
    Court).

# NEW YORK

Small Claims (New York City Civil
    Court, Civil Courts outside of New
    York City, District Court in Nassau
    and Suffolk Counties [except 1st
    District], Justice Courts in rural
    areas)
*Dollar Limit*: $2,000.

# NORTH CAROLINA

Small Claims Actions (District Court)
*Dollar Limit*: $2,000.

# NORTH DAKOTA

Small Claims Court
*Dollar Limit*: $2,000.

# OHIO

Small Claims (Municipal and County
    Courts)
*Dollar Limit*: $1,000 for claims;
    $1,500 for counterclaims.

# OKLAHOMA

Small Claims (District Court)
*Dollar Limit*: $2,500.

# OREGON

Small Claims Department (District or
    Justice Court)
*Dollar Limit*: $2,500.

# PENNSYLVANIA

Philadelphia—Philadelphia Municipal
    Court; Everywhere else—District or
    Justice Court
*Dollar Limit*: $5,000 (Municipal
    Court); $4,000 (District or Justice
    Court).

# PUERTO RICO

District Court
*Dollar Limit*: $500.

# RHODE ISLAND

Small Claims (District Court)
*Dollar Limit*: $1,500.

## SOUTH CAROLINA

Magistrate's Court (no small claims procedure)
*Dollar Limit:* $2,500.

## SOUTH DAKOTA

Small Claims Procedure (Circuit or Magistrate's Court)
*Dollar Limit:* $2,000.

## TENNESSEE

Justice of the Peace Court (no specific small claims procedure)
*Dollar Limit:* $10,000; $15,000 if county population is over 700,000.

## TEXAS

Small Claims Court (Justice Court)
*Dollar Limit:* $2,500.

## UTAH

Small Claims (Circuit or Justice Court)
*Dollar Limit:* $1,000.

## VERMONT

Small Claims Procedure (District Court)
*Dollar Limit:* $2,000.

## VIRGINIA

General District Court (No Specific Small Claims Procedure)
*Dollar Limit:* $1,000.

## WASHINGTON

Small Claims Department (District Court)
*Dollar Limit:* $2,000.

## WEST VIRGINIA

Magistrate's Court
*Dollar Limit:* $3,000.

## WISCONSIN

Small Claims (Circuit Court)
*Dollar Limit:* $2,000. No limit on eviction suits.

## WYOMING

County Court or Justice of the Peace Court Code
*Dollar Limit:* $2,000.

# Appendix C
# Organizations That Research, Fund, or Promote Alternative Dispute Resolution

Dozens of American organizations research, fund, or promote alternative dispute resolution. You may want to consult some of these organizations for materials on ADR, particularly studies, reports, and pamphlets. The National Institute for Dispute Resolution and the Standing Committee on Dispute Resolution of the American Bar Association also publish directories of dispute resolution centers. Here are the names and addresses of some of the best-known organizations. For names of more, check with these organizations, as well as in books and periodicals dealing with dispute resolution.

American Arbitration
   Association
(research, promotion)
140 W. 51st St.
New York, NY 10020

Center for Public Resources
   Legal Program
(research, promotion)
680 5th Ave.
New York, NY 10019

Conservation Foundation
(research)
1250 24th St., N.W.
Washington, DC 20037

Council of Better Business
   Bureaus, Inc.
(promotion)
1515 Wilson Blvd.
Arlington, VA 22209

Ford Foundation
(funding)
320 E. 43rd St.
New York, NY 10017

Institute for Civil Justice
Rand Corporation
(research)
1700 Main St.
Santa Monica, CA 90406

John D. and Catherine T.
  MacArthur Foundation
(funding)
140 S. Dearborn St.
Chicago, IL 60603

National Center for State
  Courts
(research)
300 Newport Ave.
Williamsburg, VA 23185

National Institute for Dispute
  Resolution (NIDR)
(research, funding, promotion)
1901 L St., N.W., Suite 600
Washington, DC 20036

Society for Professionals in
  Dispute Resolution (SPIDR)
(research, promotion)
1730 Rhode Island Ave., N.W.
Washington, DC 20036

Standing Committee on
  Dispute Resolution
(research, promotion)
American Bar Association
1800 M St., N.W.
Washington, DC 20036

William and Flora Hewlett
  Foundation
(funding)
525 Middlefield Rd.
Menlo Park, CA 94025

In addition to these organizations and others, many universities have centers that conduct and publish research on ADR. Perhaps the best known are the Harvard Law School Program on Negotiation (whose several entities include the Dispute Resolution Program and the Harvard Negotiation Project); 500 Pound Hall; Cambridge, MA 02138; and the Institute for Legal Studies; University of Wisconsin Law School; Madison, WI 53706. Other well-known university ADR research programs include those at George Mason University (Department of Sociology and Anthropology); Georgia Institute of Technology; Harvard University (Center for International Affairs); Northwestern University (Research Center for Dispute Resolution at the Kellogg Graduate School of Management); Rutgers University, Newark (Center for Negotiation and Conflict Resolution); Stanford University (both the Center for Advanced Study in the Behavioral Sciences and the Law School); Syracuse University (Maxwell School of Citizenship and Public Affairs); the University of Colorado (Department of Sociology); the University of Hawaii (Department of Urban and Regional Planning); the University of Michigan (Center for Research on Social Organizations); and the University of Minnesota (Conflict Resolution Project).

# Appendix D
# Resources

There are hundreds of books plus innumerable booklets, pamphlets, reports, journals, newsletters, articles, videotapes, audiotapes, and other materials on the topic of dispute resolution. Most of these materials are of little interest to a person who has a dispute but is not concerned with the theory, narrow subtopics, legal technicalities, and statistics of dispute resolution or with the characteristics of programs that are inappropriate for the conflict at hand.

This appendix lists materials of special value to the more general reader. The author referred to many of them in researching this book. You can obtain other publications on dispute resolution by contacting the organizations listed in Appendix C and by visiting bookstores and libraries. Larger libraries now offer computerized services that can be a big time-saver. Some provide a display of all the library's books on a given subject; others (such as *InfoTrac* and, in law libraries, *LegalTrac*) display all articles on a particular subject—going back several years and including a large group of periodicals. In libraries without computerized services, refer to the card catalog, the *Reader's Guide to Periodical Literature*, and (in law libraries) the *Index to Legal Periodicals*.

## MATERIALS ON DISPUTE RESOLUTION IN GENERAL

### Books

*Alternative Dispute Resolution,* by L. Kanowitz; West, 1985.

*Dispute Resolution,* by Stephen B. Goldberg, Eric D. Green, and Frank E. A. Sander; Little, Brown and Co., 1985 with latest supplement.

*Dispute Resolution in America: Processes in Evolution,* by J. M. Marks, E. Johnson, Jr., and P. L. Szanton, 1988. (Available from the National Institute for Dispute Resolution; see Appendix C.)

*Getting Disputes Resolved: Designing Systems to Cut the Costs of Conflict,* by William L. Ury, Jeanne M. Brett, and Stephen B. Goldberg; Jossey-Bass, 1988.

*National Conference on Dispute Resolution and the State Courts;* National Institute for Dispute Resolution, 1989. (Limited quantities may still be available from the National Institute for Dispute Resolution; see Appendix C.)

*No Access to Law: Alternatives to the American Judicial System,* by Laura Nader, Editor; Academic Press, 1980.

### Journal

The only journal that attempts to comprehensively report important developments in ADR is the *Alternative Dispute Resolution Reporter,* published by the Bureau of National Affairs (BNA). It is available to new subscribers at $296 for one year from BNA; 1231 25th Street, N.W.; Washington, DC 20037. It can also be found in many law libraries.

### Videotapes

Many videotapes on dispute resolution are available for loan or purchase. Many of these show particular dispute resolution processes in action; some feature actual hearings, sessions, and trials, while others present re-creations in which actors play some or all of the roles. Key sources of videotapes (and lists of videotapes) are the National Institute for Dispute Resolution and the Standing Committee on Dispute Resolution of the American Bar Association (see Appendix C).

## RESOURCES ON SPECIFIC AREAS COVERED IN THIS BOOK

### Arbitration

*The Car Book,* by Jack Gillis with Karen Fierst; Perennial Library (Harper and Row), 1991 and previous years.

*Center for Auto Safety Consumer Guide to Better Business Bureau Arbitration,* by the Center for Auto Safety; Center for Auto Safety, 1990 and previous years. (Contact the Center for Auto Safety; 2001 S Street, N.W., Suite 410; Washington, DC 20009; [202] 328-7700).

*Lemon Book: Auto Rights for New and Used Cars,* by Ralph Nader and Clarence Ditlow with Laura Polacheck and Tamar Rhode; Moyer and Bell, 1990.

### Mediation

*Before You Sue,* by Fletcher Knebel and Gerald S. Clay; William Morrow, 1987.

*Mediation Consumer Guide and Directory of Mediators,* Speaking for Mediation, 1988. (Contact Speaking for Mediation; P.O. Box 1045; Berkeley, CA 94701.)

*The Mediation Process,* by Christopher W. Moore; Jossey-Bass, 1986.

### Negotiation

*Getting to Yes: Negotiating Without Giving In,* by Roger Fischer and William Ury; Houghton Mifflin, 1981; Penguin, 1983.

*You Can Negotiate Anything,* by Herb Cohen; Lyle Stuart, 1980; Bantam, 1982.

### Representing Yourself

Nolo Press—950 Parker Street; Berkeley, CA 94710; (415) 549-1976—is by far the leader in self-help legal books. Its books may be found in most bookstores.

A great advantage of Nolo books is that each comes with a card or page you can send in for a free two-year subscription to the publisher's newsletter, *Nolo News.* This newsletter provides information that updates the books; it also includes Nolo's book catalog.

*Representing Yourself,* by Kenneth Lasson and the Public Citizen Litigation Group; Public Citizen, 1983. (Contact Public Citizen; 2000 P Street, N.W.; Washington, DC 20036; [202] 293-9142.)

### Hiring a Lawyer

*The Lawyer Book,* by Wesley J. Smith; Price Stern Sloan, 1986.

*Martindale-Hubbell Law Directory;* Martindale-Hubbell, 1991 and previous years. (This annual set of volumes can be found in most law libraries and in many general libraries.)

### Small Claims Court

*Collect Your Court Judgment,* by Gini Graham Scott, Stephen Elias, and Lisa Goldoftas; Nolo Press, 1988.

*Everybody's Guide to Small Claims Court,* by Ralph Warner; Nolo Press, 1990 and previous years.

### Joint Action

*Consumer Class Actions,* by Yvonne Rosmarin and Jonathan Sheldon; National Consumer Law Center, 1990. (Contact the National Consumer Law Center; 11 Beacon Street; Boston, MA 02108; [617] 523-8010.)

*Class Action Reports* is the only journal devoted to this area. It is available in major and some other law libraries as well as by subscription (4900 Massachusetts Avenue, N.W., Suite 205; Washington, DC 20016; [202] 364-1031).

*Consumers Union Advocacy Training Project Training Materials Packet,* by Consumers Union (West Coast Regional Office); Consumers Union, 1989. (Contact Consumers Union; 1535 Mission Street; San Francisco, CA 94103; [415] 431-6747.)

*Giant Killers* by Michael Pertschuk; W. W. Norton and Co., 1986.

*A Public Citizen's Action Manual,* by Donald K. Ross; Grossman Publishers, 1973. (Contact Public Citizen; 2000 P Street, N.W.; Washington, DC 20036; [202] 293-9142.)

### Strategy and Tactics for Defendants/Respondents

*Payment Refused,* by William M. Shernoff; Richardson & Steirman, 1988. (Especially for readers whose insurance companies may be acting in bad faith.)

# Glossary

This glossary provides short definitions for certain key terms likely to be encountered in dispute resolution, particularly alternative dispute resolution. For longer definitions of these and other legal terms, check a legal dictionary such as *Black's Law Dictionary* (West, 1979) and the briefer paperback *Law Dictionary,* by Professor Steven H. Gifis (Barron's Educational Series, 1984, available in paperback).

**Alternative dispute resolution (ADR).** Dispute resolution processes other than litigation. As used in this book, small claims litigation is also considered a form of ADR. This book also refers to joint action as a form of ADR, even though dispute resolution professionals do not typically include this option when referring to ADR alternatives.

**Arbitration.** A dispute resolution process in which the dispute is submitted to one or more neutral third parties (arbitrators) who hear arguments, review evidence, and make a decision, called an "award."

**Conciliation.** As used in this book, a dispute resolution process in which a neutral third party (conciliator) contacts the parties individually by telephone or in person and attempts to help them settle their dispute.

**Conflict.** A real disparity between two parties, confirmed by one party having responded negatively to a claim or request made by the other.

**Difference.** A real or perceived disparity between what a person believes would be satisfactory and what exists. For example, when a consumer believes a product does not work as it should or as it has been represented to work, the consumer has a "difference" with the seller or the manufacturer, or both.

**Dispute.** A conflict that one or both parties are pursuing.

**Equitable relief.** A remedy (a means to redress an injury) available "at equity," as opposed to "at law" (see *legal remedy,* below). Common equitable remedies include specific performance, rescission, and injunction.

**Jurisdiction.** The power to hear and decide a case. Whether a particular court has jurisdiction over a case depends on issues such as the location(s) of the residences and businesses of the parties, the location(s) at which any contract was to have been performed, the location(s) of any event that has allegedly caused an injury, and the type of legal or equitable remedy sought by one or both parties.

**Legal remedy.** A remedy (a means to redress an injury) available "at law" as opposed to "in equity" (see *equitable relief,* above). The most common legal remedy is damages: money payable to an injured party.

**Med-Arb (pronounced "meed-arb").** A dispute resolution process in which the parties first undergo mediation and then, if the mediation does not resolve the dispute, arbitration.

**Mediation.** A dispute resolution process in which a neutral third party (mediator) meets with the parties simultaneously and attempts to help them settle their dispute.

**Neutral.** A third party to a dispute who has no legal, economic, or other interest in the matter. For example, an arbitrator or a mediator.

**Small claims court.** A court presiding over informal litigation of disputes limited by dollar amount sought and by type of claim(s) made.

**Venue.** Among those places where jurisdiction could be established, the appropriate place(s) for trial. Whether a particular court is a proper venue depends chiefly on the convenience of the parties, with an emphasis on the convenience of the defendant.

# Index